Ready for
Anything
Dead to Everything

Sheila Stewart Doom

Revival Literature
P. O. Box 6068 • Asheville, NC 28816

The Publisher has sought to recognize all copyrighted works quoted herein. However, much of the material recorded by Ruth Stewart Fajfr in her personal diaries cited no author or book. If we have inadvertently used any copyrighted material without proper acknowledgement in the publication of this book, we will gladly make such acknowledgements in subsequent editions.

ISBN 1-56632-112-3

Printed in the United States of America.

Verily, verily, I say unto you, Except a corn of wheat fall into the ground and die, it abideth alone: but if it die, it bringeth forth much fruit. He that loveth his life shall lose it; and he that hateth his life in this world shall keep it unto life eternal. If any man serve me, let him follow me; and where I am, there shall also my servant be: if any man serve me, him will my Father honour.

— JOHN 12:24-26

Lovingly dedicated to the Grandchildren of Ruth Stewart Fajfr

Susan Heather Jerby
Robert McCheyne Doom
James Stewart Doom
Jana Ruth Doom
Nicola Anne Dallaway
David James Stewart
Daniel Mark Stewart
Chad Stewart Wilkerson
Noemi Ruth Wilkerson
Jesse Benjamin Wilkerson
Doris Fajfr
Olga Fajfr
Rachel Fajfr
Robert Fajfr
Katya Fajfr
Tomas Fajfr
Marek Fajfr
and to their children
and their children's children

We will not hide them from their children, shewing to the generation to come the praises of the LORD, and his strength, and his wonderful works that he hath done. . . . That the generation to come might know them, even the children which should be born; who should arise and declare them to their children: That they might set their hope in God, and not forget the works of God, but keep his commandments.

— PSALMS 78:4,6,7

Prologue

We each have a unique story to tell. For the Christian that uniqueness is magnified, for as Ruth Fajfr says, "It is not so much what we have done, but what God has done" in our lives.

Our birth, our parents, our individual pecularities, our conversion to Christ—each facet of our life from beginning to end reveals an intricate and well-designed Divine plan to bring glory to our Creator and Redeemer. With Paul we should joyfully exclaim, "O the depth of the riches both of the wisdom and knowledge of God!" (Romans 11:33).

Yet, few of us seriously ponder the practical outworking of that Divine plan in our lives. We are too occupied with normal day-to-day activities to keep a record.

But not Ruth Fajfr. From the time she was in training, she felt the need to record God's faithfulness to her. In diaries, in letters, in scrapbooks, in photo albums, and even in her exhortations to women, she constantly recounted with amazement and joy, mixed with a note of surprise, what the Lord had done and was yet doing in her life.

One day I asked her, "Mother, if you could sum up in a few words what your life has illustrated, what would you say?"

She didn't hesitate for a moment. "God is faithful. That's what I have proved, over and over again. He has been faithful. That's one of my verses—I Corinthians 1:9, 'God is faithful by whom ye were called. . . .'"

Later, when considering whether or not to allow me to tell her story, she said, "Yesterday I was inspired to write something about my past—not my accomplishments, but the Lord's faithfulness. I confess to you I got discouraged at first. Until I heard the *inner voice* saying, 'Get thee out,' nothing worth telling happened in my life except my conversion, and even that was connected with faulty ideas—join the church, get baptized, etc. But when I started to remember my call, my response, and

7

then God's supernatural guidance and provisions, I got so excited. I couldn't stop writing! Maybe there is a story after all!"

Parts of Ruth Mahan Stewart Fajfr's story are easy to tell because she recorded them herself. Others are not so easy. The struggles experienced in her adjustment to her first marriage and later in placement of her children on the altar cut Ruth too deeply for her to record in detail. Yet in those crucibles of life Ruth's character crystallized into the godly woman she became.

The reader will find periods of her life omitted altogether, or swiftly passed over. This story includes her physical journey only as it pertains to her spiritual journey. There is a double purpose in writing the story of my mother. First, I desire that God might get all the glory for a life totally surrendered to His Lordship. Second, I want to show the faithfulness of our God to Mom's generation and to mine.

In telling my mother's story, I am telling my own. I stand amazed that God in His providence placed me in this family and at this time. In these pages you will find the inheritance passed on to me, to my children, and to my children's children. The precious truths the Lord taught Mom in times of great distress, she passed on to others who were seeking and hurting and suffering. There is no way to know how many lives she touched over her 91-year journey. I know only how my life was touched, not just to have her as my mother, but as my teacher.

I want her grandchildren and her great-grandchildren and the grandchildren and great-grandchildren of this generation to find the same great satisfaction she found in the One she loved and served.

Sheila Stewart Doom
May, 2003

Contents

Thankful Memories

O look along the past, and gather themes
For praise to Thee, my ever-gracious God;
It is a past of mercy, and it teems
With goodness at each step along the road.
Not always gladness and prosperity,
But always goodness from Thy patient hand;
Always the love that, even in saddest day,
Traced its clear prints upon time's silent sand.
I thank God for a holy ancestry;
I bless Thee for the godly parentage;
For seeds of truth, and light, and purity,
Sown in this heart from childhood's earliest age.
I thank the love that kept my life from sin
Even when my heart was far from God and truth
That gave me, for a lifetime's heritage,
The purity of unpolluted youth;
That kept my eyes from gazing on the wrong,
And taught them all the sweetness of the right;
That made me in my quiet hours to long
To get beyond this darkness into light;
That made me feel, even amid scenes most bright,
At times a strange voice and vacancy,
A longing for the real and infinite,
For something that would fill and satisfy;
For suns that would not set; for stars and skies
O'er which no sorrow-laden cloud would sweep;
Beauty that lives, and love that never dies;
A deeper and diviner fellowship.

—HORATIUS BONAR

Chapter One
The Little Missionary

I think my story is so wonderful because it is something that has happened to me, not something I have done. If you believe in sovereign grace, then I am a recipient!

—Ruth Stewart Fajfr

The steady drone of voices rolling over the top of her curls reminded Ruth of the bees her father kept near the old sawmill. Tongue between her small white teeth, she pushed the smooth, hard corn kernels into the shape of Smutty, the neighbor's pet hound.

"Look, Gladys," she whispered to the eight-year-old sitting beside her on the desk spacious enough to seat the two of them. "Look at my dog."

Ruth's big sister put a forefinger over her mouth and went back to anxiously chewing her pencil as she spelled words five times each on her paper.

The four-year-old wiggled. Longingly she looked at the sun beams as they filtered through the chalk dust and the soot from the old stove. Soon it would be time for recess and she could play with Gladys and Una Belle in the pine stand bordering the school yard.

"Four times four is sixteen, five times four is twenty, six times four is twenty-four, seven times . . ." Ruth had heard it chanted every day she had been at school. Bet she could say it all by herself. "Eight times four is thirty-two, nine times . . ." She silently mouthed the words to herself, as she carefully positioned a kernel in exactly the right place for the dog's eye.

Wouldn't the teacher be surprised if she knew her little visitor could recite the Pledge of Allegiance and the Star Spangled Banner? And, what would she think if that visitor knew the state capital of Florida and how to spell Mississippi?

A student with downcast eyes and fidgeting feet would stand at the front of the class and announce his piece, "Four score and seven years . . ." or sometimes it would be more exciting like, "The highway man came riding, riding up to the . . ."

Ruthie would watch, bright eyes shining and ears tuned to the rhythm and the rhyme of each familiar recitation. Music, that's what it sounded like. She could do that. She had already memorized lots of important things like rivers and countries, and famous names like Patrick Henry and Jefferson Davis.

That night at home, Ruthie asked her mother, "The children at school get up and recite a piece. Will you teach me a piece so I can get up and say it?"

Her mother looked at her somewhat surprisedly. "Now, Ruthie, I hope you are not being a bother down there at the schoolhouse. You know the teacher said you could tag along with your big sister as long as you didn't cause any trouble. She's been mighty good to let you in. You have another two years before you are old enough to start."

"But, Mama, I want to recite a piece. You know, something pretty like."

"I'll tell you what, Ruthie. The preacher said last week he'd give a prize for the person who could say the most Bible verses. Why don't I teach you some verses and you can stand up in front of the church and say them next week. Would you like that?"

So it was settled. Every evening while Gladys was doing her homework, Mama would sit down with Ruthie and go over a couple of verses. To her mother's amazement, Ruthie could recite five verses perfectly after the end of the first week. At the end of the second week she could quote ten verses. That was only the beginning.

By the time Ruthie was five it was evident she had picked up a whole year's learning. She was allowed to officially begin school.

Most Sundays the preacher in the little Baptist church they attended would look out over the congregation and ask, "Is there a little girl here who would like to recite some verses for us?" Ruthie would slip out of her place beside her mom and dad, and walk down the aisle. After the preacher lifted her onto the platform, she would turn to face the congre-

12

gation. "Matthew chapter five, verses one through twenty, 'And seeing the multitudes, he went up into a mountain: and . . .'"

Soon visiting preachers would each invariably ask Mr. or Mrs. Mahan, "Can I take Ruth along with me next Sunday? We are having a protracted meeting just down the road and we would like your daughter to recite."

It was not long before people began to call Ruthie "the little missionary."

One day she asked, "Mama, what is a missionary?"

"A missionary . . . ," her mother paused, struggling to choose the right words to explain. "Uh, well, a missionary . . . is a person who goes to China to tell people about Jesus."

"Where is China?" Ruthie quizzed her mother. "And how do you get there from here?"

"It's like this. The earth is round like a ball." Mrs. Mahan rolled her hand into a fist to show her daughter the shape of the earth. "If you could dig a well all the way through the earth, you would come out in China."

After that conversation, every time someone called Ruthie "the little missionary," she would think long and hard about it. She never questioned the accuracy of her mother's explanation about China. But she was puzzled as to how she could dig a well all the way through the earth without getting wet. All the wells she had seen were full of water. After a while she would give up, thinking that maybe the reason she could not solve the problem was because she was so young. "One day when I grow up, it will all be plain," she thought.

One day she was walking along the country road near her home after a summer rain. Water had collected in a rut at the side of the road, and, instead of going around it, she leaned over and looked. To her amazement, a little girl looked back at her from the dark depth of the pool.

"You must be a little girl in China. And if you are, I want you to know that when I grow up, I shall come and tell you all about Jesus. And if ever I learn how to get to Heaven, I'll tell you that too!" The little girl seemed to smile back at her in acknowledgment, and Ruthie determined with her whole heart that she would have to learn all she could so that little girl would one day hear about Jesus.

* * *

But where did this child with such a God-consciousness come from? Her father, Zedikiah Robinson Mahan, was an Alabama boy, trained by his father in the sawmill trade. In his late teens he *hoboed* out to Texas to seek his fortune. And find it he did. Her name was Prudye Ford. They met at an ice cream social at a Baptist church in Scurry County, Texas. Prudye's family worked picking cotton. Her father was a highly-respected Christian in the community and a member of the little country Baptist church, whose land he had donated. Prudye often told her children that the first time she laid eyes on Zed Mahan, she declared to herself, "He's mine, even if I never get him!" But get him she did! They married, settled into a shack in the middle of a field of cotton, worked the field and started a family. Soon their first child, Gladys, came, and three years later, Ruth. The year was 1909; the day, June 24th.

> Mama used to tell of how she ran from a "Norther," a Texas wind-storm, three times on the day that I was born! She didn't trust the shack in which we lived and so three times she ran to the main house which was much more substantial. She had heard tales of such winds taking the roof off a house, lifting the feather-bed up through the roof and placing it down in the middle of a field with the occupant still in it! She was not going to have this happen to her on this day. That night I made my appearance!

Picking cotton was slow, back-breaking work. Zed stuck it out for a few more years, but then he got to hankering for the lumber work he did as a boy with his father, Henry, and his brothers Arky and Roy. Besides, it was embarrassing struggling through a row of cotton only to look up and discover your little wife halfway up her second row! So back to Alabama Zed moved his family where his brother and he decided to start a sawmill business in Mobile County near the Gulf.

The two families lived in one big house the brothers built, and it was while living there that Ruth started to the little one-room schoolhouse. It was also there that she started memorizing scripture and accepted the fact that the two most important things in a person's life were being part of a family and going down to the church house.

There was always so much to do both inside and outside the house—corn to shuck, peas to pick, the cow to milk, butter to churn, and chickens and pigs to feed. If it was an outdoor chore Ruth loved it! Her little wiry body browned by the Alabama sun and her feet calloused by the dirt and sawdust around the house and mill, Ruth lived outside as much as possible. Soon the chores just fell into place. Gladys helped mother cook, clean and take care of the boys. Ruth ran to the chicken house for the eggs, ran to the river for water, and ran to get the kindlin' for the fire.

Her daddy often teased her.

"Ruth, I think we named you wrong. We should have called you 'Ruth Run.' Now, wouldn't that be some name for you?"

As busy as they found themselves, the Mahans did not neglect church. Every Sunday, it was Sunday school and church. Even after her father gave up the sawmill and moved the family to Gorgas, near Birmingham, where he found a job in a plant, it was the same. No matter that Mother had worked hard and long all day, if there were protracted meetings within five miles, she would take the whole family along. She would arrange a pallet on the floor under the bench in front of her for the baby to lie on while the preaching was going on. Little wonder Ruth grew up with a sense of the importance of God, God's house, preaching, and the Word of God.

And it wasn't just at church. At home, many times her mother would take down the Bible and gather the children around her to listen. To Ruth it seemed like she was always finding chapters in the Bible on judgment and the *Last Days*, or as her mother called it, *the end of the world*. Mrs. Mahan didn't seem to know you were supposed to *invite* little children to come to the Savior. Somehow she never seemed to come to that part. But early in life, the fear of God was instilled in Ruth's heart. She knew she was a sinner. Many times her mother or father had to take a switch to her. And she knew that the punishment for sin was being cast into outer darkness where there was "weeping and wailing and gnashing of teeth."

Oh, how Ruth's sins weighed heavily on her heart. If only she knew how to stop being bad. If only she could be as good as Gladys. Gladys seemed to have been born good and she bad. "If you are born bad is there any hope?"

Saviour, while my heart is tender,
I would yield that heart to Thee,
All my powers to Thee surrender,
Thine and only Thine to be.

Take me now, Lord Jesus, take me;
Let my youthful heart be Thine;
Thy devoted servant make me,
Fill my soul with love divine.

Send me, Lord, where Thou wilt send me,
Only do Thou guide my way;
May Thy grace through life attend me,
Gladly then shall I obey.

Let me do Thy will, or bear it,
I would know no will but Thine;
Shouldst Thou take my life or spare it,
I that life to Thee resign.

Thine I am, O Lord, for ever,
To Thy service set apart;
Suffer me to leave Thee never,
Seal Thine image on my heart.[1]

Chapter Two
A Recipient of Grace

When Ruth was about to turn twelve, her family moved to Vida, near Prattville in Autauga County. There her father took a job with the Alabama Power Company. In between Gorgas and Vida, Zed Mahan had tried his hand at selling an invention he and his brother Arky had rigged up. They called it the *Mahan Wagon Brake*. They even went so far as to get a patent. But they were twenty years behind time. Much to their dismay, they discovered that the automobile, for all its jolts and jerks, was becoming the popular mode of transportation and wagons would soon become a thing of the past!

Zed's family had suffered during his detour to a dream, even to the point that Prudye threatened to pick up the children and cart them all back to her home in Texas! Usually quiet and obedient, his little wife told him it was time to get a real job so he could stay at home and take care of his growing family. Their sixth child was on the way and she needed him.

Alabama Power Company supplied the family with a house situated on a hillside out in the country. Looking back, Ruth always considered these the happiest years of her childhood. There was always plenty to eat—vegetables from their big garden at the side of the house, chickens, a hog to slaughter every year, and the milk cow that kept them in fresh milk and butter. The Mahans even grew peanuts and sugar cane. What they didn't eat, they canned and preserved for the short winter months.

But to Ruth, the best thing about Vida was Nellie, a gentle horse that she claimed for her own. Now, when mother asked her to run into town for the week's supply of flour and sugar, she straddled Nellie bareback and away she would go.

Years later, Ruth found those days vivid in her memory.

We had a well, but for some reason the water was unsatisfactory, or maybe there was not enough of it. Papa boxed in a lovely spring some quarter of a mile further up the hill and from there we got drinking water and put up a wash tub and benches. I can still see Mama on a Thursday place all the dirty clothes in a sheet, throw the bundle over her back and carry it up the hill to the spring where Papa had already built a fire under the wash pot. It was a pleasant place, especially in spring and summer. We children loved to play around Mama while she scrubbed, boiled, rinsed and wrung out the clothes. Then we helped hang the clothes on lines, fences, bushes—every place possible to dry under that hot Alabama sky. Later as the sun was going down, we'd traipse back down the hill, arms loaded with sweet-smelling stacks of Mom's hours of labor. Later that night, Pop would get out his fiddle and we'd all gather on the front porch. Mama would have her lap full of peas to shell or a baby to rock to sleep. Pop would let me beat the straw. As he played, I would sit beside him with a straw between my fingers and tap the strings to the rhythm of the tune. Or if the nights were getting cooler, we'd gather around the radio Dad had put together with bits and pieces and listen to the station coming out of Atlanta, a full 200 miles away! WSB, the Voice of the South!

We were bussed to school in a wagon drawn by two mules. The seats were placed on each side of the transfer facing each other so the children could get in and out easily. In good weather, we older children would jump out and walk awhile until we got tired and then hop back in since the transfer was just going at a mule's pace! Other times, Gladys and I would leave the transfer halfway and take a short cut home across the train viaduct. I have often wondered what would have happened if a train had come while we were on the trestle because there was nowhere to go if it had!

On Ruth's twelfth birthday, she and the other children were sent to the neighbors early in the morning with no explanation. Halfway through the day they were called home to find a new baby sister, the best birthday present a girl could ask for! Mildred Inez became Ruth's special responsibility and though there was exactly a twelve year difference in their ages, a special bond existed between them that the coming years only strengthened.

On Sundays, as always, Zed would harness up Nellie to the wagon and away the whole family would go to the Baptist church in town. There was a Methodist church even closer to home and that meant double attendance. Whether the protracted meetings were at the Baptist or the Methodist church, the Mahans delighted in attending every night for one, two or three weeks.

It was during this time that both Gladys and Ruth were converted. Little is recorded about what actually brought them to the place of salvation, or who was preaching or what was being preached. Ruth, however, never doubted that this was the time that God began a work of grace in her heart. Years later she described it.

It is funny how you don't think a thing is significant at the time, but it changes your whole life. When I was little, the preacher had offered prizes to the child who would memorize the most Scripture. Since memorizing always came easily to me, I memorized the whole Sermon on the Mount. Mostly I did it for the challenge and for the prize I would get. One day, though, when I had just turned twelve, I was sitting on our front porch and thinking about what I had learned. My mother always helped me and she had explained some of the verses to me. Sitting there on that porch step, it was like a light was turned on. Suddenly and instantaneously, I knew that Jesus Christ died for my sins, that I belonged to Him and that He had a plan for my life.

The next Sunday, Gladys and Ruth were baptized in the outdoor baptismal pool in front of the Baptist church. Soon one of the ladies of the church asked Ruth to help in a Sunday School class. By the time she was fourteen Ruth was teaching the Junior Class, both in Sunday School and in Baptist Youth Training Union. Though she was only a few years older than her pupils, Ruth took her task very seriously and spent hours studying the Bible lessons.

In an old scrapbook, there is a photograph of Ruth standing behind a group of thirteen lively juniors. An inscription on the photograph reads: "Suffer little children to come unto me." A second photo shows Ruth with another young teacher, and a note underneath reading, "Corine Stephens and me at work, planning, scheming and dreaming always for our juniors."

One day while preparing her lesson, Ruth was intent on showing her students that God had a plan for their lives, that they needed not only to have their sins forgiven, but to dedicate their lives to the Lord. The lesson was on missions, and as she studied, the Lord spoke to her again. Ruth remembered her promise to the little girl from China and how all her life she had known she had a destiny.

"But, oh, Lord," she prayed. "How do I get ready to be a missionary? I don't have any money to go away to college. I wouldn't even know where to start preparing." Despite all the questions that flooded her mind, she knew without a doubt that the Lord was calling her and that He would make a way.

Ever interested in his children's getting the best education and recognizing his daughter's unusual zest for learning, Ruth's father decided to give up his good job and move to Montgomery, Alabama. He had long thought that Montgomery had the best high school in the state. The Mahans found a home on Columbus Street, only a stone's throw from the Capitol.

Ruth threw herself into her school work, but soon discovered this was one school where she was going to be challenged. English had always been her favorite subject so it was with confidence she turned in her first writing assignment. The next day she was called up to the teacher's desk.

"Ruth Mahan is your name. Is that right?" Miss Gussie Harris asked.

"Why, yes, ma'am." Puzzled, Ruth waited for the teacher to continue.

"Young lady, I cannot accept this paper. You have made one spelling error after another." Ruth saw red circles marching down the whole first page of her assignment. "Mind you, I must admit you have a way with words, but we really must improve your mechanics." With this she handed back the paper with instructions for Ruth to correct it by the next day.

The wind taken out of her sails, Ruth obediently rewrote the paper and returned it the next day. Again, Miss Gussie called her to her desk.

"Ruth, that is some improvement, but now we need to work on the punctuation. You would think you have been using a salt shaker with these commas. Let's go over the rules."

So it was that over the coming months she seemed to spend a lot of time with Miss Gussie and began to wonder if she had any talent at all for writing. One day, Miss Gussie called her to the teachers' lounge for a private session. Ruth sat before her wondering what was coming next. Miss Gussie was the hardest, strictest teacher she had ever had! Most of her teachers in the country school had seemed impressed with her swiftness to grasp facts and her interest in doing well and had been full of praise. But Miss Gussie!

"Ruth, you probably wonder why I have been so hard on you. Harder on you than on the other students. The reason is that you have a great potential. I want to get you ready for whatever it is life holds for you. Now, I have one important question for you. Have you ever considered going to college?"

"Ma'am, I really don't know what to do after I graduate. I've puzzled a lot about it." She hesitated. "I guess I could go to business school at night and maybe become a secretary."

"No, no. That's not what I am talking about. My dear Ruth, don't you sell yourself short. You need to go to a four-year liberal arts college, and then you can go out in the world and do anything you want to do. Now, you think about that and we will talk more about it later."

Much to Ruth's surprise, over the next couple of years other teachers singled her out and told her the same thing. She simply could not understand why. No one in her family had ever been to college and her parents had not even finished high school. They were poor, too poor for her to put an extra burden on them. College was an impossible dream. Why should she get her hopes up?

BE STRONG!
We are not here to play, to dream, to drift;
We have hard work to do and loads to lift;
* Shun not the struggle—face it;*
* 'Tis God's gift.*
*   BE STRONG!*
Say not the days are evil—Who's to blame?
And fold the hands and acquiesce—O shame!
Stand up, speak out, and bravely,
* In God's Name.*
*   BE STRONG!*
It matters not how deep entrenched the wrong,
How hard the battle goes, the day how long;
* Faint not! fight on!*
Tomorrow comes the song.

MATTIE D. BABCOCK
(FOUND COPIED IN RUTH'S DIARY, FEBRUARY, 1931)

* * *

The more ordinary the vessel, the more glory given to the treasure within!

* * *

But we have this treasure in earthen vessels, that the excellency of the power may be of God, and not of us.

— 2 CORINTHIANS 4:7

Chapter Three
The First Step of Faith

We are building a college to help Christian young people who have a vision for serving the Lord, but don't have the money to get an education.
— Bob Jones, Sr.

Sitting across from Ruth this Saturday morning was a man her father introduced as Bob Jones, an evangelist he had met only the night before. The two had sat beside each other at a meeting. In their conversation Zed had discovered that Dr. Jones was starting a college to help Christian young people. Immediately Zed informed him about his daughter Ruth who wanted to become a missionary.

"She's a smart one," Zed told Dr. Jones proudly, but quickly adding, "I just don't have the money to send her to college."

Bob Jones asked for the Mahan's address and the very next morning, he visited their home and offered to help Ruth on her way.

"What can you do to get yourself through college?" Dr. Jones asked. Ruth could hardly believe her ears. She thought for a minute, trying to make sure she understood the question.

"I can work. Right now I work at a laundry, and I'm going to school at night to learn how to be a secretary. But I can do anything." Ruth was eager for this man to know her willingness to tackle whatever it took to attend college.

"Well then, all you'll need is a good pair of walking shoes, two gingham dresses, a Sunday best, and a Scofield Bible," Dr. Jones explained to Ruth's delight. "College will cost $85 for the year, but I will find something for you to do. The main thing is to get ready and be there the day school begins."

"But, Mr. Jones, you don't even know me. How do you know you want me to go to your college?"

"I've already checked up on you. Been down to see your pastor and over to your old high school just this morning. You'll do." Without any formal interviews or application, Dr. Jones worked out the whole thing for Ruth.

Almost a year after graduating from high school and after months of wondering what she was to do next, Ruth found herself awe-struck at how the Lord was putting everything together. She really was on her way to preparing to be a missionary. No one in her family had ever gone to college so she had never imagined that she could go. Money, as always, would be a problem. But here was a man who told her she could do it.

Suddenly Ruth's life was in a whirl. She could not afford to buy everything, but she did get a Sunday dress and a new pair of shoes. Pop agreed to drive her to college, so on the appointed day he, Ruth, Gladys, and another new student set out for Lynn Haven, Florida.

"The devil wasn't too interested in our getting there. Our T-Ford Coupe rolled down a hill and turned over a few times with us in it. I was banged in the head and pretty scratched up. Pop's shoulder blade was broken and the other student's arm was broken, but we made it to Bob Jones College just a few days late," Ruth wrote in her college scrapbook.

Located only seven miles from Panama City and two miles from Lynn Haven on the beautiful St. Andrews Bay, Bob Jones College sat on a choice piece of property. Nevertheless, those first students to set foot on campus discovered a lot of mud puddles separating the newly constructed buildings. The students could sense that they were part of a grand new scheme—a part of Dr. Bob Jones' dream. It was his goal to provide Christian young people with an education, "not along a particular denominational line, but simply based on the Bible and those fundamentals of the faith around which believers had rallied down through the centuries."

That first school year at Bob Jones College commenced with a week of evangelistic services. A local newspaper reported on the opening of the college and published an interview with Dr. Bob Jones.

"We will have at least 100 students by the time the enrollment is complete today," he said. "There are sixteen young preachers among them. The Lord is with us."

Describing the evangelistic services in which he was preaching to the boys and girls and faculty for the first five days of the school term, Dr. Jones said, "Last night the power of God came down on the first service. A fine-looking young fellow got up and said, 'I am not a Christian, and I want to be saved.' About 20 more boys and girls followed him to the front and made a definite decision. Every member of the faculty said they had never seen such a manifestation of God's power."

The reporter added, "Would to God we might have such meetings in all our great educational centers!"

Ruth explained those early days in the following way:

> So there we were, just over a hundred students and Dr. Bob. But we also had a very fine Bible teacher, Mrs. George Fellows, from Moody. For English, I had an older teacher, Dr. John Collins, who had reached a place where he was more concerned about the Lord and the Lord's plan for our lives than to teach us English! That was part of the whole plan. He was there to challenge us to find out what the Lord wanted us to do and to do it.

It was as if that first class had been chosen uniquely by the Lord, though from the beginning that was not so apparent. In many ways they were just an ordinary bunch, "mostly country hicks" as Ruth later called them, but in those first few months they caught hold of something that was never to leave them. They were set on fire to go out and win souls for Christ. That first enrollment at Bob Jones College included students who would become evangelists, pastors, writers, college presidents, and one missionary—Ruth!

Immediately, Ruth found herself at home in this new environment. In her mind she had spent all those years of childhood to prepare for this moment. She took to Bob Jones College like a duck takes to water, throwing herself into the whole campus scene with gusto. As a charter member of the Bob Jones College student body, she became an officer of nearly every college organization. From the very beginning, Ruth found herself thrust into a place of leadership. Her special interest was the Interdenominational Student Union, whose purpose "was to unify and coordinate all the Christian work on the campus in order that they might pull together for the one Great Cause, the Lord Jesus Christ." Ruth spent hours going out on extension to minister in local churches with the Baptist Young People's Union and the Student Volunteer Band.

In Ruth's mind, the best of all activities was the debate teams. She could hardly wait at the beginning of each year to discover the topic. In 1929, the question for the girls' Literary Society debates was, "Resolved: that youth reared in the country are more fortunate than youth reared in the city."

Much to Ruth's delight, her team, Sigma Lambda Delta, won. That meant Sigma Lambda Delta would debate the boys! The question considered was: "Resolved: that Greece contributed more to civilization than Rome."

The Lynn Haven newspaper reported on the outcome of the first girl-boy debate at Bob Jones College.

> The declamation contest participated in by the college students proved to be . . . outstanding . . . but for thrills, entertainment and real merit, the final debate between the two literary societies was unsurpassed. The question, "Resolved: that Greece contributed more to civilization than Rome," was masterfully handled by both sides, the decision going to the affirmative which was so ably handled by Miss Evelyn Howell of Hartford, Ala., Miss Dorothy Harris of Ramer, Ala., and Miss Ruth Mahan of Montgomery, Ala. The negative side of the question was discussed by Linwood Wilson of Crewe, Va., Cecil Ellisor of Andalusia, Ala., and Bob Jones of Montgomery, Ala.

How could so momentous an event be summed up in a short paragraph? In Ruth's scrapbook a full page commemorates the victory. A dried flower and ribbon adorn a note stating, "We won!! Those precious boys!!! This is a rose from a bouquet Bob, Jr. gave to me while waiting for the decision of the judges. I had the final rebuttal against him. Poor boy. We exchanged ribbons at the Mosley Cafe, Tuesday night about 11:00. Mr. Skinner and Miss Holmes chaperoned us to Panama City after the debate. Oh, those thrills!"

Fifty years later, in her granddaughter's dorm room at Bob Jones University in Greenville, SC, Ruth reminded Dr. Bob, Jr. in a telephone conversation that there was one time in her life she had gotten the better of him!

Ruth always felt this part of her college life was one of the most important of her training.

I was chosen as a debater. I was last on the affirmative and Bob, Jr. was always last on the negative. When we got on that debate floor, you'd have thought we were sworn enemies! But this debating was part of my training. I never worked so hard in my life as I worked on those speeches because somehow though the other girls on the debate team were good speakers, they didn't know anything about unity, coherence and emphasis, things I guess I learned from Miss Gussie in high school. I wrote out their speeches and then I had to encourage them (they had boyfriends and I didn't!) to get down to serious business to learn their speeches. I tell you this because it was one of the foundational parts of my training at Bob Jones College that prepared me for what I was to do afterwards.

Life at BJC was not all studies and debate. When Ruth arrived on campus, Dr. Jones had a promised job waiting for her—waiting tables in the dining hall, and since she had experience, helping sort clothes at the laundry. Though not exactly the most glamorous tasks, they helped pay Ruth's way through college.

During the summers she always found a job waiting for her at the laundry in Montgomery. Furthermore, Dr. Bob developed a way to help his students make money in the summer. They could sell yearly subscriptions to the Bob Jones College magazine. The job required door-to-door sales of subscriptions for one dollar each, with a twenty-five cent student commission. At every available opportunity, she would venture out into the hot Alabama sun and knock on doors. The job took a great deal of courage and determination, but Ruth took heart when she remembered her buddies were out doing the same thing. She wasn't about to let them beat her at it. Without realizing it, she learned some valuable lessons in character and in approaching people.

Then came *Black Thursday* and the Great Depression! The year was 1929. Though some analysts had predicted the financial calamities, most people paid no attention. "There is no danger, nothing is going to happen," was the general attitude. Suddenly, with the fury of a devastating tornado, Black Thursday struck, leaving behind a trail of financial ruin. The world seemed to stop. Businesses closed because banks closed. Men who did not have strong faith in God and who could see no way to escape the economic chaos, chose to "end it all." Daily the newspapers reported the numbers of suicides.

Students flocked to Dr. Bob with hard-luck stories. "My father lost his job. A letter from home says not to expect any more help because it is all he can do to put food on the table for the family. Shouldn't we leave and go home and see if we can do something?"

Every one was a son or daughter to Bob Jones in those days. In fact, students affectionately called him "Uncle Bob." Dr. Jones' heart ached for the students and for their plight. Unlike them, however, he looked ahead and thought clearly and wisely. Time and again as a student would come to him and say he was going to have to quit, Dr. Jones would look him square in the eyes and say, "Never sacrifice the permanent on the altar of the immediate." He would then remind them that "The test of your character is what it takes to stop you."

In Ruth's case, Dr. Jones argued, "Ruth, if you go home, what will you do? That laundry is laying off people, not taking them on. If your father can't get work, how do you think you will? Stay here, finish school, learn to trust the Lord, and I'll do all I can to help you."

A few students did go home. Ruth stayed. To the end of her life she was amazed at how the Lord provided. The summer after the *crash,* a Montgomery businessman contacted her. Apparently, he had heeded the warnings of impending financial doom and had invested wisely. Over the years he had helped promising students pay college expenses but with the understanding that upon graduation they would get a job and pay him back. Then he could help other students in need. Someone had recommended Ruth to this businessman, and his offer of help came at a time of great need. When Ruth paid back the loan, the man confided in her that she was one of the few who had done so.

The summer before Ruth's senior year, her roommate, Jet Crane, from New Jersey, invited her for a month-long visit. When Mr. and Mrs. Raymond T. Crane arrived in a fine motorcar to take the girls to New Jersey, Ruth recognized that she was entering a new world, far from 222 Columbus Street in Montgomery, Alabama. Her past life could in no way prepare her for the pleasures ahead. On the long ride to New Jersey, they stopped off to play golf in Roanoke, Virginia. Then they visited the Natural Bridge and Caverns of Luray. Finally arriving at the Crane's beautiful home in New Jersey, Ruth witnessed luxury of which she had never dreamed.

One can only imagine the excitement a couple of days later when Ruth visited New York City for the first time in her life. They toured Mr.

Crane's office on Wall Street in the morning, the Stock Exchange in the afternoon, and took in a theater in the evening. Mrs. Crane suggested they buy a swim suit for Ruth as they planned to go to the beach the next day at Asbury Park.

That first week was filled with so much excitement, Ruth could hardly sleep at nights, but the second week was even more fantastic. Admiral Byrd had just returned from his expedition to the South Pole, and the country made preparation to shower him with honors. On June 19, New York City gave him a ticker tape parade and presented him with keys to the city. Ruth and Jet, with a bird's-eye view of the whole celebration from Mr. Crane's office, watched the parade.

Later, Mrs. Crane informed Ruth that she wanted to buy her a new dress. Oh, my! This small town girl felt she was dreaming. She walked out of the expensive department store with a beautiful navy dress, finer than any she had ever owned!

Those three weeks culminated with a party celebrating Ruth's twenty-first birthday! Throughout Ruth's life, the Lord graciously gave her little surprises along the way. It was as though He were telling her that the rewards for following Him were not all eternal rewards.

During those days in New Jersey, Ruth discovered the Cranes to be good Christian people with a real heart for the Lord and for the success of Bob Jones College. Soon after Ruth returned to college in the fall, the Lord moved on Mr. Crane's heart to send her enough money to pay for her first semester. She was learning that what the Lord purposes for His children, He provides—a valuable lesson for the years to come!

And the boys? Did she not have a boyfriend all this time? Ruth was a favorite with boys and girls alike. But the boys? They loved her! She was funny. She was dedicated. She was smart. She was easy to talk to and to confide in. But did she date? Who dates his sister? Unruly dark curls, a pug nose sprinkled with freckles—Ruth even looked like somebody's kid sister. Yet some of her best friends in college were preacher boys—Monk Parker, Clifford Lewis, Henry Grube, Fred Brown, and Bob Jones, Jr. They were all the officers, the movers, the shakers on campus. In later years, Ruth would hold up four fingers pressed tightly together and say, "We were like that. Best friends. We stuck together through thick and thin."

Clifford wrote in Ruth's album, "I am expecting great things from you in the future. I am looking forward to the time when Miss Ruth Mahan will be one of the greatest missionaries this world has ever known. Ruth, I believe that you have the determination, the high ideals and the faith to carry you through to this goal. . . . Remember that your friendship has been enjoyed and appreciated. May we pray for each other as we go through life.—Clifford Lewis, Red Level, Alabama." The Lord knew that she would gain more from these friendships than she ever would have had there been only one young man in her life.

Despite all the activity of college, the Lord still dealt with her privately, creating in her a hunger to be wholly His and to be used of Him. During the Bible Conference in her final year, Ruth wrote in her diary on January 30, 1931, "Have just listened to a sermon on the Second Coming by Billy Sunday, who is here for Bible Conference. I think it was wonderful, but somehow I was unmoved. I feel cold and somewhat discouraged with myself. I want to do things for Jesus! Oh, that I might win just one lost soul to the Master! Maybe someday."

A few days later she wrote:

> FEBRUARY 11: I have just finished reading *Borden of Yale*. Oh, that my life might amount to something. Bill was no more in the Master's Hands than I—who knows what God will do? Someday maybe I will win a soul to Jesus. The S.U. Band met today and James finished his report on Charles Cowman, another useful missionary. Yes, God has got to use me. I'm here and He can't get rid of me any other way!

But in an entry on March 31, Ruth shows another side of her personality.

> Oh, how tired I am! I crave beauty—expression of some kind—art! And here I tug and pull with "trig" till my head almost bursts! That is what I want to work for, slave for—Jesus, art, literature—the beautiful, fine things of life. If I had but two loaves, I would sell one and buy white hyacinths to feed my soul. . . . though I would also buy a Bible, a commentary and a book of poems!

Later, she surely laughed over this entry, but there came a day when all else was overshadowed by the unsurpassed beauty she found in her Lord Jesus Christ. For Him alone she was ready to "work for and slave for."

The last weeks of her college career were busy ones. Since Ruth had a double major in English and Speech, she had to give a recital. After much agony over gestures and expression and a great deal of coaching from her speech teacher, she was able to testify, "I have experienced the most glorious triumph of my life tonight! The stage was beautiful, the audience most kind, my dress stunning and my poise and calm were marvelous. I know Jesus did it all, for I am nothing. Everyone gave me gorgeous flowers. Oh, joy!"

The other two hurdles were the big debate with the boys and passing "trig". Her team lost the debate, but she comforted herself that passing "trig" was a whole lot more important.

On June 3, 1931, Ruth received her sheepskin and the same day headed home to Montgomery with no idea of what the Lord had in store for her—not realizing much of her education lay ahead.

I am so weak, dear Lord, I cannot stand
One moment without Thee;
But, oh, the tenderness of thine enfolding!
And oh, the strength of Thy right hand!
That strength is enough for me.

I am so needy, Lord, and yet I know
All fullness dwells in Thee;
And hour by hour, that never failing treasure
Supplies and fills in overflowing measure,
My least and greatest need, and so
Thy grace is enough for me.

It is so sweet to trust Thy word alone.
I do not ask to see
The unveiling of Thy purpose, or the shining
Of future light on mysteries untwining.
Thy promise-roll is all my own—
Thy Word is enough for me.

—FRANCES RIDLEY HAVERGAL

Chapter Four
Louisville and Arkansas

With a diploma in her hand and a lot of knowledge in her head, Ruth headed home. What would be next? She could help with Vacation Bible School at her home church and maybe at Clayton Avenue Baptist. The WMU always needed speakers. She knew she could help there, but that still wouldn't get her any closer to Africa, the country on which she now focused.

Later, while seeking the Lord's direction, Ruth visited the Baptist headquarters in town and saw her pastor there. As he congratulated Ruth on making it through college, she began to pour out her concerns to him.

"Pastor, I wish you would pray for me. I really don't know what to do next. The Lord is still speaking to me about the foreign mission field, but I feel I need more training. I don't have any idea of how to go about it."

"That's interesting you should ask me. Recently I've been hearing about the Women's Training School in Louisville. That's where you need to go. It's connected with the Southern Baptist Theological Seminary and is especially to train young ladies like you."

"But I have no money, no contact," Ruth interjected.

"Don't you worry about that. I'll contact the right people and even see if I can get you a scholarship. You just go home and get yourself ready." He spoke so confidently one would think it was a matter already settled.

Ruth thought the months of July and August would drag by as she waited to hear the results of her pastor's inquiry. Instead, several of her friends from Bob Jones College invited her to work with them on a summer gospel team. The teams scheduled their first evangelistic meeting for Electic, Alabama, a small town northeast of Montgomery. Clifford

Lewis, Ruth's "ole pal," was to preach. Ruth helped with children's rallies and youth meetings, took part in a weekly radio broadcast, and generally supported the young evangelist.

The weeks flew by. Soon it was time to get on the bus and head for the Women's Training School in Louisville, Kentucky. Entries from her diary give us a clearer picture.

> SEPTEMBER 22: Arrived here at 6:30. Girls are darling, faculty precious, house beautiful, roommate a dear. Went to Seminary this p.m. to opening exercises. Saw gobs of divine brethren!

> SEPTEMBER 25: Oooh, I like and yet I fear Dr. Carver. I love Dr. McGinty who teaches me Old Testament and New Testament. I'm finding *From Babylon to Bethlehem* rather difficult which shows me it isn't going to be easy keeping up. We have s-o-o-o many books to study.

> SEPTEMBER 28: We had a beautiful Y.W.A induction meeting tonight. We were all dressed in white and holding candles. I hope I can become gentle and refined as the other girls. Please, Jesus, help me.

> SEPTEMBER 29: I worked awfully hard today, but not as hard as I'm going to work.

> OCTOBER 8: Today I did a little bit of everything—studied, went to classes, practiced, walked and wrote letters. I feel the need of a quiet talk with the Lord. I realize more each day the failures I have made in the past. It was all through ignorance and I still want to be used of God.

At this point in Ruth's diary, entries stop. There is no more written record of her daily life at college. Perhaps she really did work hard and did find little time to write in her diary. In later years, however, she told her daughter Sheila about the amazing way the Lord provided the exact training she needed.

Ruth's Christian Education teacher was Dr. James Dobbins. For a reason she could never quite figure out, he took a special interest in her training. Perhaps he did so because there were not many other students interested in the foreign mission field. Perhaps he detected a teachable spirit in Ruth. Whatever the reason, Ruth felt that she had a sympathetic ear in him. When she explained to Dr. Dobbins that she was confident that it was God's will for her to become a missionary but that she was totally "in the dark" as to how to prepare herself, he had a suggestion.

About twenty miles from the seminary was a little country church that he pastored. The church needed help in the Sunday School for the term and someone full-time to organize the daily Vacation Bible School in the summer. And if Ruth would accept the responsibilities she would also have the opportunity to help with the Women's Missionary Society and in the cottage prayer meetings.

During the summer between her two years in Louisville, she chose not to go home. Instead, she tackled a full three months of practical Christian training.

She told the story this way.

> I went by street car to a certain point and there Dr. Dobbins would meet me in his car to take me the rest of the way. I was there both years, but also spent the summer working in the church. For the most part, I boarded next door to the church with an elderly lady (a real saint) and prepared my own breakfast. For dinner and supper I ate out among the other church members and in this way was able to get to know them pretty well and take an interest in their lives.

Tired but happy at the end of that summer, Ruth rejoiced that she had worked so diligently. Later, she realized that things would not have worked out as they had without Dr. Dobbins offering a wise word here and there, encouraging her, and gently guiding her youthful ardor.

Ruth returned to the classroom with a better understanding of why she needed additional training—a part of which was speech classes.

> You have to remember that I was born in Texas and brought up in Alabama and learned to talk in Alabama. I had a terrible Alabama accent. I say *terrible* because I have done quite a bit of traveling outside Alabama in my life! When I went to the Baptist Training School in Louisville to train to be a missionary, my speech teacher, Miss Suttles, began to discipline me concerning—not so much the method of my speaking—I had learned that at Bob Jones—but my accent. She wanted me to learn to speak so that anyone could understand me. She really had her work cut out for her, I can tell you.

> The first thing she had to show me was how not to speak. She made me hear myself as others heard me. In those days we didn't have tape recorders and I couldn't believe I really sounded the way she said I did.

"NO, NO!" she would say. "Try it again. 'Down' is only one syllable, not two!"

She gave me a part in the life of Ann Judson to read, and I remember to this day the first sentence. "Ann Hasseltine came in from her favorite walk by the river and sat down in the armchair by the window." The reason why I remember that sentence after all these years is the many times I had to say it before my teacher was satisfied.

"AnnHasseltinecameinfromher walk," I would say, running all my words together.

"No, no! You must say clearly every syllable," she demanded.

Say every syllable? That sounded dumb to me. I could never talk like that. But she made me practice every word separately and distinctly before she would let me go on to something else. Now, that was training. It certainly wasn't pleasant and there were times I would cry.

"Mrs. Suttles, I just cain't do it!" I'd wail.

"What did you say?" she would retort with a frown.

"I ca-ahh-n't do it."

"I didn't mean that. Never say you can't do it. Try it again—and again—and again. You can get it."

And so I learned to speak correctly and distinctly so that I can travel to foreign countries to speak and if they know any English at all, they understand me. I also learned what teaching and training means.

The principal of the Women's Training School was Miss Littyjohn. Regularly she would call the girls individually to her office and discuss with each the student's studies, practical training, and personal life. Miss Littyjohn was a wise woman, knowing how to advise and correct Ruth's spontaneous efforts without squelching her spirit. Having an excellent speech teacher, a caring principal, and excellent Bible teachers, Dr. McGinty and Dr. Dobbins, Ruth spent a profitable two years in Louisville. Looking back, Ruth blessed the Lord for providing such godly counselors in the days of her "youthful enthusiasm."

* * *

It was 1934. Ruth had been home from Louisville for almost a year and was working in her old job at the laundry. Her life seemed to be locked into a pattern. High School, what then? Along comes Dr. Bob. College . . . what then? Along comes the pastor who smoothes the way for her to attend the Women's Training School. Now she once again had absolutely no idea of which way to turn. At times hopes of going to the mission field seemed to be just a dream, an impossibility.

Ruth began to wonder if the Lord truly had called her or if she were simply imagining it. Reality was home—Montgomery, Alabama. She was smart. She could finish her business certificate and get a job as secretary to the Governor. Her father worked in the gardens at the capitol. One time he had even fixed the clock in the capitol tower. The governor owed him a favor. Besides, there was a young man interested in Ruth. He'd probably marry her and give her a good life. Such were the thoughts that ran through Ruth's head when her missionary vision grew dim.

Nevertheless, she stayed faithful to her work in the church and with the WMU, thinking that maybe that was all the Lord would want from her. She was oblivious to the fact that God was testing her.

One day, however, Ruth heard that a Baptist missionary conference was to be held nearby in Birmingham, Alabama. All of her old professors from Southern Baptist Seminary were to be there—Dr. Dobbins, Dr. Carver, and other outstanding speakers. How lovely it would be to see them again, she thought. But the Lord had more than just a reunion for her. During the conference one speaker after another challenged the congregation about foreign mission work. So fired up was she after one particular sermon, Ruth could hardly stay in her seat. As soon as the benediction was given, she literally ran up the aisle to the platform.

"Dr. Carver, the Lord has called me to be a missionary and I've got to go. What am I to do?" she blurted out.

At first she thought he had not heard her.

Dr. Carver looked at Ruth and then paused as though he were thinking. "Do?" he questioned. "Pray. That's what we'll do."

Ruth thought he was finished, but then he added, "I'll get to work on it."

Soon Ruth received a call from the Women's Missionary Union headquarters in Birmingham informing her that several of the professors at the Louisville school had recommended her. The caller then asked if she would be willing to take an assignment as a city missionary in Little

Rock, Arkansas.

As Ruth prayed, she felt the Lord directing her in this next step of her life. In Little Rock she organized daily Vacation Bible Schools, ministered in homes for unwed mothers, and trained workers in the black communities to minister to children.

A still-existing, battered family photograph shows a scene in front of an old church with Ruth and a number of other workers surrounded by 64 children. An inscription reads, "VBS at Liberty Hill Baptist Church, June 22—July 3, 1936. Sponsored by Immanuel Baptist Church, Little Rock."

At twenty-four years of age, Ruth found the work of a city missionary to be a big responsibility. Days were full and time raced by. She loved her work and settled in as though to stay. She made dear friends during this period, friends she kept for a lifetime—Ruby Heater, Thelma Bell, Mildred Cobb, and Lucille White.

Recently Lucille White reminisced about those days:

> I will never forget Ruth. We shared an apartment when she was working here in Little Rock. She was so full of life she could hardly hold it down! I never think of her walking into a room; she waltzed in! One time Ruth, knowing how hard up I was, brought some meat home with her. I had just made biscuits, so I whipped up some gravy, and what a feast we had!

Days were filled with her city missionary work, but "off hours" were another story.

> My roommate, Lucille, and I were out to have fun, and fun we had. We met up with some other young people, some medical students if I remember rightly, and formed a friendly sort of gang. It was all quite harmless, but I found myself just one of the gang, with no thought of being a witness or of being a spiritual leader among them. I'm sure most of them were not Christians. Good kids, but not saved. It was like I lived two separate lives.
>
> The thing is, I don't ever remember being taught about separation from the world or holiness of life. Could be I had been taught, but just didn't take it in. It wasn't that my instructors and pastors weren't godly people; it's just that they didn't teach me how to get that way. Oh, at Bob Jones College, we used to sing the little ditty:

> We don't smoke and we don't chew,
> And we don't go with the boys that do!

But that was the extent of my knowledge of worldliness. At church I learned there were two things Christians didn't do. They didn't dance and they didn't go to the picture shows on Sunday. If there was any further teaching on separation from the world, I missed it entirely. Spirituality was equated with Christian service. A dedicated Christian was one who was sold out to the Lord and out trying to get souls saved. My friends all considered me to be a really good Christian because I was preparing myself to be a missionary.

However, in her own heart Ruth knew something was wrong. One day she would be full of zeal, ready to set the world on fire, the next she would be dissatisfied and *blue*. Was this the normal Christian life or was there more to it? Ruth longed for what she later called a "fuller surrender." Again and again in her diary, she would write the prayer, "Lord, make me good."

The Lord did not leave her alone. Little did she know that He was using the barrenness of soul to create within her a great longing that He would one day fill.

Two years passed. In the back of Ruth's mind, there was a constant awareness that Little Rock was *not* the foreign mission field. She lifted up her eyes and looked past Arkansas, past Louisville, past Montgomery. There were other sheep who were not of this fold. There were other fields white unto harvest. Within, Ruth wrestled with a great restlessness. Finally, she became so burdened in spirit that she had to do something about it.

Oh, matchless honor, all unsought,
High privilege surpassing human thought,
That Thou shouldst call me, O Lord, to be
Linked in such work, O God, with Thee!
To carry out Thy wondrous plan
To bear Thy message unto man;
In trust with Christ's own word of Grace,
To each soul of the human race.[2]

Chapter Five
A Missionary Candidate at Last

If only they knew how torn in two I feel today, and how precious the home ties are, they would understand. . . . Oh, how could I leave you all, my own precious ones, and leave the joy of being of ever so tiny a bit of help to you unless the hand of the Lord were upon me . . . Oh, that we may die, not in mere hymn and prayer, but in deed and in truth, to ourselves, to our self-life and self-love. I never knew what it meant before—dead to all one's natural earthly plans and hopes, dead to all voices, however dear, which would deafen our ear to His— alive unto God. When I think of Christ's life in its utter self-death, and then think of our, of mine, the contrast is too terrible.[3]
    — AMY CARMICHAEL IN A LETTER TO HER MOTHER BEFORE HER DEPARTURE FOR JAPAN

   In May of 1936, Ruth joined a delegation going to a missions conference in St. Louis, Missouri. Among the missionary speakers was Dr. Charles E. Maddry, executive secretary of the Foreign Mission Board of the Southern Baptist Convention.

   With a determination that overcame her anxiety, Ruth walked up to Dr. Maddry and announced, "Dr. Maddry, what do I have to do for you to consider me as a serious candidate? I've done all this training and I'm ready to go."

   Instead of being offended, it appears the director took these words as they were intended. In her diary, Ruth records, "Hurray! Talked with Dr. Maddry, Mrs. Jones, Mr. Cloud, 'n the whole shebang. They smile on me. God grant an outcome to my surrender."

   Soon Ruth heard from Dr. Maddry. "I'm on my way out West and I'll be passing through Memphis. Can you meet me there at the train station?" he wrote.

   Ruth arrived at the appointed time and found the missions director waiting for her. He invited her into the train with him so they could talk. She began to tell Dr. Maddry her story. Since she had been a little girl, she had sensed the Lord dealing with her about going to the foreign mission field and she had spent all the intervening years preparing for this one thing. She felt strongly that now was the time to take that final step.

Dr. Maddry listened intently. Before Ruth departed the train, he assured her that she would hear from him in the near future.

Her head in the clouds and her heart aflame, Ruth returned to Little Rock. At last she was being considered for the mission field! After speaking with the executive secretary and hearing of the opportunities with the mission board, she was ready to go to China or to Africa or to anywhere she was needed. For the first time in her life, Ruth Mahan was now ready for anything.

Before long Ruth received a letter from the mission board asking her to travel to their headquarters in Richmond, Virginia, for an interview. She did. Following the interview, the board appointed Ruth as a missionary to Budapest, Hungary.

Seventeen years before Ruth's appointment to Hungary, one of the most important Baptist conferences ever held took place in London to consider the post-war material and spiritual needs of Europe. Representatives of most of the Baptist groups in Europe, as well as those from the American Baptist Convention and the Southern Baptist Convention attended. The Southern Baptists were asked to help the European Baptist groups in Spain, Romania, Yugoslavia, Hungary, the Ukraine and other southern portions of Russia.

Dr. Everett Gill, Sr., who had been a Baptist missionary in Italy, was appointed superintendent of the new European fields, a position he held for the next eighteen years. Though called *superintendent*, he recognized clearly that his board did not initiate the work in any of these lands and had no right to superintend or direct it. His convictions about missionary work became to a large degree the policy of the Southern Baptists in Europe:

> My strong feeling is that the main stress, in our missionary work in these new lands, should be laid by our Board on training schools, publications, colportage, and chapel buildings. We should leave the matter of evangelism largely to the native churches. If we take out of their hands that spiritual responsibility, they will die just as surely as the

butterfly dies when we relieve it of its struggles and pains in its birth from the chrysalis.[4]

In Hungary, the mission board purchased valuable property which was perfect for the seminary and large enough to be used also for the training school for girls. The seminary teachers were mostly Hungarians, though Dr. Gill did lecture from time to time. In the Women's Training School, however, it was decided that an American would be needed to organize and get the work established. That American was Ruth Mahan. Her diary in 1937 tells the story:

JANUARY 1 RICHMOND, VA: Here for examination. Appointed to Budapest, Hungary. If I pass—but I did pass!! A new life!

JANUARY 4 LOUISVILLE, KY: Conferences with Miss Littyjohn and Drs. McGinty, Dobbins and Carver. On my way back to Little Rock.

JANUARY 16: So many good-byes. So many lovely gifts. Sold poor Betsy (her car) for $90. On my way to Montgomery. So tired.

FEBRUARY 16: I finished packing, checked out, said my good-byes and left home for five years! I don't think I have faced reality.

FEBRUARY 17: With Dr. Jones and his family at Richmond, Va. They are so sweet, but I am sick with a cold. I don't feel much like a missionary.

FEBRUARY 18: Today I was officially appointed a missionary to Hungary. "Oh, God, let me die, and live Thou in me! Help me to be crucified with Jesus." Dr. Maddry came to see me off.

FEBRUARY 20: The Kemps came with me to the boat. *S.S. Deutchland.* I found many letters and flowers from Dot and Woodie. I'm sick and alone and blue. "God be my helper."

The preceding eight years had loosened the *apron strings* and somewhat prepared Ruth for being away from home. But Hungary was farther from Montgomery, Alabama than was Lynn Haven, Florida. Or Louisville, Kentucky. Or Little Rock, Arkansas. And this assignment was for life, not for a few months or a couple of years.

Ruth was a Southern girl through and through. How would she ever adjust to a new country, a new language, and the gigantic assignment she had been given? It is hard to imagine the doubts and fears that must have arisen in Ruth's mind as she saw the skyline of her homeland recede into a thin line on the horizon. Besides, as she departed from the United States she suffered from a dreadful cold, and during her voyage she became horridly seasick.

Those were not the only difficulties Ruth faced. She left part of her heart behind. For eight years she and Woodie had been friends. At first their relationship meant nothing more. Then—somehow—she found herself caring more and more. What was she thinking? She had surrendered her life to the Lord's work—to foreign mission work. And Woodie was not even a Christian! Yet, while all the other Christian boys had looked on her as a sister and buddy, Woodie was different. He brought her flowers and boxes of candy and took her for walks and rides in his car. Soon he was talking of love—and marriage. It just didn't make sense. How could the Lord place the burden of foreign missions so heavily on her heart and then let her fall in love with someone walking in the opposite direction? Ruth had cried to the Lord year after year to save Woodie, but to no avail. He listened to all her dreams and plans, kindly, politely, and then passed them off as though she'd grow out of it and come home to him. Those last days when it was settled that she was actually leaving for Europe were agonizing days.

Years later, in a letter to her granddaughters, Ruth warned:

> Never consider marrying a man, no matter what his other good qualities are, if he does not know the Lord as his Saviour. How can man and wife bow together under the authority of their Head, Jesus Christ, if one does not recognize him as Saviour? And how can you submit yourself to a man who is not under submission to the Lord?

> My advice to you is to never keep company with a boy or man who is unsaved. . . . As I was growing up I did not know the degree of separation from the world which your parents have taught to you. Thus, while I was attending business college after my senior year of high school, I worked during the day and took classes in the evening. At work I met a man whom I liked and who liked me. He used to meet me after work in his car and take me to town where I had to wait for classes to begin. It was only a friendship with no thought of future involvement. Then came my second call to the mission field and the six years of preparation in college and training school after that.

> Well, I kept company with this young man for several years off and

on, believing that just because I wanted him, the Lord would save him. Then we could be married and "live happily ever after." Now, of course, I know that the wisdom of God is greater than our prayers for He knew that if He saved this man at that time I would have been tempted to marry him—completely out of the will of God for my life! So much in love with him was I that I was willing to give up all my plans for the future—forget my call to the mission field, my years of training for the Lord's service—everything! My one consuming passion was to have this man near me the rest of my life. Foolish girl!

You can believe that I had no peace in my heart with such a state of mind. My Lord was deeply grieved over my having put Him aside in order to fulfill my own desires. So it was that when the day came in which I was pressed for a decision, and I prayed desperately for the Lord to show me His way, I found the heavens like brass. Why should He speak to me? I knew the way, and it was not the way I was contemplating in my heart. I knew that I needed only courage and determination to take the road which led to Him and His service, turning my back on all else that would hinder me. But He did graciously work on my behalf. I was finally and definitely given the appointment to Hungary. Oh, the wonder of His grace and His long-suffering with us! It was only by His grace that I was able to say to Him, "Yes, Lord." I cried all night, feeling the decision to leave my love would tear my very heart out. Shame on me! Still, God was faithful and strengthened me to choose and to go His way—to make a clean break. . . . . I was enabled by the Spirit to repent and confess my backsliding and to return to the Lord even before He took away that emotional desire for my friend. Then He worked in my life, replacing that love with the love and devotion of a man worthy of His blessing and a man too good for me, really.

We have to go—the Voice of Him, the dearest Lover of our soul, commands. . . . Let it once be fixed that a man's one ambition is to fit into God's plan for him, and he has a North Star ever in sight to guide him steadily over any sea, however shoreless it seems. He has a compass that points true in the thickest fog, and fiercest storm, and regardless of magnetic rocks.

— S.D. GORDON

Chapter Six
In Budapest for a Year

Europe has her beautiful cities—Paris, Copenhagen, Prague, Vienna. But like a precious jewel placed in a golden band, Budapest literally sparkles on the banks of the Danube. Buda on the one side and Pest on the other, these two towns were not joined until a Scotsman, William Tierney Clark, designed the Chain Bridge which merged the two together to form the capital city of Hungary. Today some of that beauty has been marred, first by the bombing in World War II and later by the stark utilitarian buildings built by the communists who occupied the country for more than forty-five years.

When Ruth arrived in March of 1937, however, the city was at its zenith. Its new Parliament Building glistened in the sunlight by day and in floodlights by night, as did many of the old church buildings. The seminary where Ruth and her co-worker were to live was housed in a building situated on the left bank of *Buda*. One can only imagine Ruth's delight the first time she stood in front of her living room window and looked out over the Danube and Parliament Building across the river. Enchanting was the word she used to describe the view to her family back in Alabama.

Ruth was delighted to find that her co-worker, Maude Cobb, a native of Statesboro, Georgia, had already been in Hungary six months and was well on her way to learning the Hungarian language. The two of them *hit if off* immediately, and as Ruth said, "It was a good thing for I was no more than a 'babe in the woods' and depended much on Maude to get me acclimatized."

* * *

After the first week of catching up on her sleep and unpacking her trunks, Ruth began tackling the language. The seminary found a Hungarian tutor for her. Dr. Kovacs soon became both a friend and a task-master to Ruth. Some days the lesson went well and the two of them would take a leisurely walk over the bridge and onto Margit Island. Other days things did not go so well.

"Dr. Kovacs was so angry with me today; I fear I was not such a good pupil," she wrote. Another time she moaned, "I'm sick and discouraged. This language is so hard!"

The Magyar language flowed from the mouths of children, old folk, street vendors, and clerks. Yet Ruth's tongue could hardly find a way around the difficult sounds her teacher asked her to imitate. And the grammar! It was the hardest task she had ever encountered.

Outings with young people from the Baptist church were much more fun. More than happy to show off their lovely city to the two American young ladies, they planned picnics and excursions to the museum and other historical sites. Patiently they would point out the names for various objects and laugh good-naturedly at Ruth's pronunciation of words. Sometimes they would go down to a local cafe for coffee after the youth meetings. Later, they would walk along the river, joking, laughing and singing, to the amusement of passers-by. Ruth had no trouble falling in love with the passionate, fun-loving Hungarians. The first three months in their company flew by.

Mission work in Hungary was not all language lessons and pleasure. From the very beginning, Ruth was asked to speak through an interpreter to the Women's Missionary Union in the Baptist Church and to the young people in various churches. The seminary president's daughter, Elizabeth Udvarnoke, better known as Boske, was appointed as Ruth's interpreter and they became inseparable.

As summer began, so did plans for the Women's Training School. The training school's section of the building needed much renovation. Beds and wardrobes were to be bought. Dishes and other dining and kitchen items were to be chosen. Dr. and Mrs. Gill came and went, giving advice and keeping an eye on the progress being made. With these obligations added to the intensive language study, Ruth soon found her schedule filling up. In August she attended the International Conference in Zurich with other workers, both Hungarian and American. Earlier, she and Maude had gone to Bucharest to the seminary and training school to see how things were done in Romania.

48

After only a couple of years, the Women's Training School was thriving with about thirty students. Maude and Ruth were fired up to return to Budapest and get started!

The Baptist Bible Girls' School, or Women's Training School, as Ruth called it, officially opened with twenty-two students in October, 1937. Ruth and Maude shared responsibilities for operating the school. Maude was the main teacher because she already knew the language. As the director, Ruth was responsible for keeping the books and other office matters, teaching a couple of classes and generally caring for the physical and spiritual welfare of the girls.

Though by this time Ruth was able to speak conversational Hungarian, she was still limited when it came to teaching. In classes, Boske interpreted for her. Later she said, "It was the worse thing in the world to try to teach through interpretation. But what was I to do? I was thrown into it after just seven months."

Entries in her diary in 1937 give only a hint of those first days of school.

OCTOBER 19: School opened tonight. All the girls are here except one. They are so sweet-looking. I love them already.

OCTOBER 22: Emil Bretz, a young Hungarian preacher, came and talked with the girls. They're scared and discouraged and want to go home.

OCTOBER 24: This afternoon we went to the orphanage and then to the church and the young people's program. I spoke in Hungarian—made a mess of it, but I'm going to keep trying!

Ruth settled into a predictable schedule—language study, office work, WTS classes, church-related meetings with women and young people, and combined outings with the seminary students and training school girls. Winter came early and with it came bouts of colds and flu. Nevertheless, Ruth felt at ease with her *dear girls* and other Hungarians who were becoming more and more an important part of her life. She was perfectly happy to put her roots down in this place and give her life to the cause of Christ and the gospel. She rejoiced that the Lord had called her to Hungary!

Ruth Mahan was really and truly serving the Lord on the foreign field, just as she had always wanted. The Lord was helping her to make many friends and to speak the language. But there was a dark spot in her spiritual life. She still sensed an emptiness, a barrenness. Only a month before school started, she had written in her diary after hearing two American preachers who were visiting:

> I get so disgusted when I can't understand anything, and then when I do understand, I begin to realize how wicked I really am! My soul is empty and dry and thirsty for spiritual food—after a whole summer of seeking. God, free me!

Ruth had always thought that once she was on the mission field, she somehow would feel really spiritual. Instead, the very opposite was true!

Ruth's spiritual quest reached a climax on a cold wintry day in 1937. For a month snow had blanketed Budapest, turning it into a treacherous fantasyland. Ruth's boots could not keep out the wet snow, and she found herself suffering from a severe cold. On the morning of December 3, Ruth entered her office and closed the door. The lock suddenly jammed, trapping her inside. No one else was nearby and no amount of shouting or banging would bring a rescuer. Wondering what to do, Ruth remembered that this was the Foreign Mission Week of Prayer and she had complained about not having any time to get quiet before the Lord. Unmistakably the Lord had now arranged a quiet time for Ruth to pray. Instead of praying for foreign fields and missionaries, however, she began to pour out her heart to the Lord for her own desperate condition.

"I became very dissatisfied with my spiritual condition and began searching my heart for the cause. I spent much time alone praying for entire consecration (even down to that last key!) and a greater power in my life," she later wrote.

God heard Ruth's prayer and in a few short hours He would answer His servant's cry in a way she would not have imagined in a thousand years.

One of the leading Christians of Hungary, a man who was head of the Hungarian railroad, carried a great spiritual burden for his country. On one of his travels, he had met the Scots evangelist, James Stewart, who was being used tremendously in revival in Czechoslovakia. The Hungarian, Dr. Csia, immediately asked Stewart to come and preach in Hungary. The evangelist accepted the invitation.

Because the spiritual condition of his country was so low, Dr. Csia decided to spare any embarrassment for himself and the guest evangelist. So he secured a *small* Methodist prayer hall for the meetings.

James Stewart was unknown in Hungary. He did not speak Hungarian. Still, Dr. Csia believed it was God's will for him to preach there.

Nevertheless, one evangelical leader admitted, "We had little faith that very much would be accomplished. God may work in other countries, we said, but not in Hungary. And our unbelief was only increased when the evangelist arrived, simple in dress and appearance, simple in manner, and very unassuming in character. When he greeted us with, 'I hope you have secured the largest hall in Budapest,' we answered in the negative, assuring him that the small Methodist hall was sufficient in size."

Yet there were those like Dr. Csia, who with a heavy burden, prayed to God for their city and their country. And God delights to hear the desperate cries of His people when the situation seems the least promising!

Only five days had passed since the evangelistic campaign began in the small Methodist hall, but the crowds had already overflowed to the larger German Baptist Church. After the meeting on Thursday night, Maude came home full of news. The guest preacher was an evangelist from Scotland. He really could preach and, furthermore, he was young and unmarried!

Whether it was because of this announcement or because of the prayer she had prayed that afternoon, Ruth decided to attend the meeting on the following night.

> I was sitting in the balcony with some of the Baptist young people with whom I had been dealing concerning salvation—with too little results. We all sat with rapt attention, our eyes fixed on the speaker. The Scottish evangelist was preaching on the text John 3:16. . . . Not a person in that jam-packed building moved until the message was finished . . . Then, suddenly, people began to surge forward, somehow forcing a path in the center aisle where the overflow crowd had been standing throughout the entire service. The young man for whom I had been so concerned and who had been sitting beside me during the service was one of the first to move. He almost ran as he left his seat, tears streaming down his cheeks, to find his way to the front of the church.

Soon the meetings had to be moved into the Reformed Church which seated 2,000 and whose pastor was a real man of God. Suddenly the entire city seemed to catch on fire. Prayer meetings were called at all hours of the day. Believers from every denomination became burdened for loved ones. Mr. Stewart held morning sessions teaching those who showed a special interest in further instruction about the person and work of the Holy Spirit, about the need for repentance and cleansing, and about the need for passionate, desperate prayer to prepare for what God wanted to do in reviving the country. Teachers and students of the seminary and training school were deeply affected. Few could fix their minds on anything except what God was doing in their city and personally in their own hearts.

"And my heart, too," Ruth added.

Soon doors opened for Mr. Stewart to speak in other places as news spread of what many were calling a mighty moving of the Holy Spirit. Probably of all the meetings, the greatest experienced by the Hungarian churches was in the city of Debrecen.

By this time, Ruth had become acquainted with the Glasgow evangelist, and he had invited her to accompany him to Debrecen to work with the young people and women. Ruth agreed, hesitantly, because of responsibilities at the school. During the Debrecen campaign she found herself going from morning to night, helping in meetings for the women and the children, in youth meetings, in prayer meetings, in inquiry meetings, in meetings for new converts, as well as in the nightly gospel services in which hundreds were being saved! They were all functioning as if on *spiritual oxygen*. How else could they take the pace?

After a few weeks James Stewart left for other meetings, and Ruth returned to her duties in Budapest. But not for long. Within hours she received an urgent phone call from Boske who was visiting a Baptist pastor in a town near Debrecen. In a letter to her family back home, Ruth recounts what happened.

> Elizabeth phoned me and said, "The people from all around here have been arriving all afternoon, coming to the Baptist church where they heard you would be speaking." I protested that I could not "preach'"and wondered what good it would do for me to join her, but she insisted that I could help deal with anxious souls. So I caught the first train to that town and was met by Elizabeth and the pastor with horse and

wagon to go the last five miles to his home and church. When we arrived at the church we could not get in at the back door for the crowd. And what a crowd! They had been coming in wagons and on foot over the frozen mud all afternoon and now many of them, especially young men, were standing in the aisle to allow the older ones to be seated.

Actually, we did not know what was expected of us. No one had advertised the meeting; the people had just come expecting, no doubt, that the American missionary would bring to them the same message that the English-speaking evangelist had brought in Debrecen. You know I can't preach! But I did make known to them Christ's saving power and His love for sinners. . . . I can still see the expressions on the faces as I spoke, especially those lads standing in the middle aisle before me! Most of them would have been Roman Catholics and were, therefore, hearing the true gospel for the first time. . . . . They came the next night, this time invited. The weather is clear, but very cold and the snow is melted leaving the roads a ribbon of black mud which freezes at night. How I pray these people may have found the Fountain of Living Water during these days.

Even while she had ministered in the earlier meetings with James Stewart, Ruth had found her own soul being fed and strengthened. Often she had gone to the meetings for young converts and had been amazed at Mr. Stewart's counsel—hearing things she had never before heard. He had taught that "a holy life is God's plan and purpose for every born-again soul, not an elective which is left up to the believer to choose or reject at will. The Holy Spirit not only transmits to the redeemed saint the holiness of Christ, but He makes him practically holy in Christ."

Ruth remembered the prayer she had prayed for years, "O, God, make me good." Here, she thought, is "someone who can lead me into an understanding of God's way to make me good." Certainly, she knew that when she had asked the Lord to save her, she had received Christ's robe of righteousness, but practical holiness? How little she knew of that.

Sit Still

Thou sayest, how will the matter fall,
   The thing God has begun to show?
Thou knowest in part, but knowest not all:
   Sit still, my daughter, till thou know.

Sit still, my daughter, there is One
   Who works for thee, who will not rest
Until the thing is wholly done:
   Sit still, my daughter, and be blest.

Be blest, as once was faithful Ruth,
   Who all for love of Naomi
Forsook the promise of her youth,
   But found a higher destiny.

O then sit still: Thee too awaits
   A like glad favour from the Lord;
Thy Boaz sits within thy gates:
   Himself shall be thy full reward.

Sit still, my daughter, be in health:
   A Ruth must have a Boaz still.
Oh, may this mighty man of wealth
   Thy expectation's coffers fill!

Sit still, sit still: be this thy strength,
   Thy joy, thy confident repose.
Sit still, my daughter, till at length
   Thy life into His likeness grows.

AUTHOR UNKNOWN (A FAVORITE OF RUTH'S)

Chapter Seven
James Stewart

Only one peace now possible to me:
To do Thy will, O Lord, whate'er it be.
Only one way, one way for me to go
I know it not. Enough, Lord, that You know.
Only one prayer that I hourly pray:
To do that will, Lord, and to go that way.

When James Stewart first began the meetings, Ruth did not attend because of the heavy backlog of work that seemed to always be before her. Finally, at the end of the first week of meetings, she went, and she was deeply moved by the Holy Spirit in the service.

Hearing that she would be attending the meeting, Dr. Udvarnoki, head of the seminary, had asked her to find out if James Stewart would speak to the seminary students the following Tuesday morning. At the end of the Friday night meeting, as everyone else was leaving, Maude and Ruth made their way to the front of the church where others were speaking to Mr. Stewart. Having met him the night before, Maude introduced her friend to the evangelist. Nervous at the thought of speaking to this famous preacher, Ruth took a deep breath and quickly blurted out her request.

Mr. Stewart looked at her and smiled. "I'm almost certain I'm free on Tuesday, and I would be pleased to speak to the students. But what about tomorrow? Could I come see you? I often take Saturdays off to relax."

Maude and Ruth looked at one another. It didn't take long for them to decide. "Yes, come for lunch. Have you seen Budapest yet? We could show you around after the meal."

In a flurry of preparation, the ladies agreed that Maude would finish the last minute touches to the meal while Ruth entertained their guest. When Mr. Stewart arrived, they found him to be relaxed and entertaining. What a relief to speak to someone who actually spoke English as his native tongue—even though it was English with a lovely Scottish "brrrr"! Later the three walked along Margit Rakpart beside the Danube and then across the Margit Bridge to Margit Island, a beautiful park in the middle of the river. Both Maude and Ruth had problems they wished to tell to a "disinterested party," and they found him a sympathetic listener. In fact, later in her diary, Ruth moaned, "Oh, I hope I was not too friendly. He is so spiritual and understanding—and human."

After James spoke to the students on Tuesday, the two young ladies again invited him for dinner. Ruth noticed that today he seemed distracted and a bit nervous. As soon as Maude left to teach her class, he came straight to the point.

"Ruth," he said, "I believe the Lord has assured me that you are to be my wife. Will you pray with me about this?"

It was the last thing in the world Ruth had expected to come from the mouth of this serious young man, and less than five days after first meeting him! One can only imagine her reaction. To read the sentences in her diary makes it even more shocking.

> DECEMBER 3: Tonight I went to hear the Scotch evangelist. I like him very much. He's coming tomorrow to see us.
>
> DECEMBER 5: I have had him in my mind all day—a lump in my throat. What is wrong with me?
>
> DECEMBER 7: I can't eat or sleep. James told me today that he loved me. I am so excited—and disturbed.

Then James explained to Ruth the Lord's dealings in his heart. At twenty-seven years old, he had never really considered getting married because of his many travels. But in the last few weeks, he had felt the need for a companion and co-worker in his ministry. The Lord had given him the Scripture, "Delight thyself also in the Lord; and He shall give thee the desires of thine heart." On the plane to Budapest, he believed the Lord had spoken to him clearly that he was to meet in this city the woman who was to become his wife.

"I knew as soon as I saw you that you were the one," he said.

How does one answer such an argument? Certainly, Ruth was attracted to James from that first meeting. And already he had been such a blessing to her. But love? How could she know if this was love? She thought that what she had felt for Woodie was love, and it was nothing like this!

Ruth stuttered some foolish reply, and it was obvious to James that she was both embarrassed and overwhelmed.

"Look, let's just pray about it. That way the Lord can show you what He has shown me." James was not in the least deflated. Had not the Lord spoken to him? Besides, he had become aware recently of smiling young ladies and aspiring mothers flocking around him wherever he went. The Lord was right. He needed a wife.

Suddenly a storm of emotions enveloped Ruth. One minute she was riding on the crest of love. "I really think I love him, but how much I can't tell." The next minute she was plunged into a dark pit of despair. "I am so upset. Studied some, but not much. He really loves me. What shall I do? I am so afraid."

The conflict was real. In the past the Lord had often kept Ruth waiting, but, then, in His time, she would find the next step so clear that she had no doubt, no confusion. Never in all her years of following the Lord had she been in such a fix as she now found herself. James was so sure that she was to be his wife. When she was with him and he painted the picture of how they would travel together throughout Europe and evangelize the millions who were outside Christ, it all sounded so wonderful! But when she arrived back at the training school and looked into the faces of the twenty-two girls the Lord had put into her care, she was sure it was all just a dream. This was her place. This was what the Lord had called her to do. She would have to send James Stewart on his way to look somewhere else for a wife.

On and on the internal conflict raged. If only this had happened at another place, in another time before she was so committed to her task at the training school. If only she could forget everything and just enjoy being in love!

Before Christmas and James' departure to Czechoslovakia, Ruth and he spent an afternoon on the island. The events of the day are recorded not in her diary but on a used envelope found recently in Ruth's cedar chest. The notations tell the story.

Sealed and signed this 18th day of December, 1937, at Cafe Ostende. I love you, Ruth Mahan (in his handwriting). I love you, James A. Stewart (in her handwriting).

Ruth added at the bottom of the envelope, "With a new fountain pen James just bought me for Christmas—we pledged our troth."

Five days later as Ruth said good-bye to James, the train had hardly pulled out of the station, before all the misgivings rushed back into her mind. Her greatest fear was writing Dr. Gill, the field director, and Dr. Maddry, the executive secretary of the board. She had tried earlier to explain to James.

> There are four million Baptists in the United States who are depending on me to do this job of training these girls. They've paid for my training; they paid for my ticket to come here; they've invested a lot in me. How can I just up and leave? Who else will do what I am doing?

Letters and phone calls flew back and forth over the Christmas and New Year holidays. Ten days later James returned and presented to Ruth what he called an *earnest*. It was a new five-crown coin piece with Czechoslovakia on one side and the head of President Masaryk imprinted on the other.

"Do you know what an 'earnest' is?" he asked. She shook her head.

"If you look up Ephesians 1:14, it talks about the 'earnest of our inheritance.' In the Greek that means, 'engagement ring.' I don't have the money for a ring right now but this is the promise of the one I am going to buy you one day."

Ruth accepted the coin though her mind was far from settled. She went as far as to pen in her diary:

> He came! Why should we not wait for the Lord's coming with such expectancy? I spent the day with him. He gave me the "earnest" and promises me a ring by April. I am not sure, but almost. I don't understand why I must make another change, but I am wholly in His hands. I have made the surrender with no conditions. I walk by faith. God, wholly consecrate me to my task and Thy plan.

James left again for meetings, but each week he would write Ruth a letter. On January 19, 1938, he poured out his heart to her in the following words:

My Darling Ruth,

Again this morning I received a letter from you dated the 17th. How lovely to hear your voice on the phone last night again! It sounded so sweet and melodious. Precious One, please do be yourself when you are sentimental and dreamy; please tell out your heart. I joke, but I do love my Ruth when she's dreamy because it is the opposite of my Scottish nature. I can never forget those haunting southern melodies you sang to me when I was tired and weary. Is not the Lord good to give us such a pure, deep, deep love for Him and for each other!

Our responsibilities are great, and we must be deeply spiritual and bound together in love. Only a deep faith in God and a deep love for one another will carry us through. Ruth, darling, you are all to me! In you, I clearly see my prayer answered! I could never dream of anyone better than you, the Song of my Heart! My precious counselor and friend, but above and beyond all, my Sweetheart.

I'm sure the Charles Cowman book will inspire you. . . . Surely this is all a woman could desire to be—a help to her husband. Mrs. Cowman only lived to help Mr. Cowman and when he died, she was more determined than ever to carry on the work laid down by her husband. Brave little woman! You ought to hear how she just mentions his name. Never was love so true and sweet as theirs. We must be a great comfort to her and be her daughter and son. Yes? How lovely it will be to live with her together for a short time in sunny California, yes?. . .

God is preparing you for a mightier work beyond all your dreams, Beloved! Yes, there is a sorrow in love—yet a happiness which is able to overcome anything. All I ask you to do is to trust me. God sustain and comfort you is my earnest prayer,

Yours and only yours, Jimmy

Ruth's next step was to write Dr. Gill. On January 25, with fear and trembling she composed a letter stating what had transpired and asking him what she should do. Three days later she received a letter written by him from Bucharest. "You have fallen in love, so what is to be done? I hear James Stewart is a fine man. Marry him. But you must contact Dr. Maddry right away."

On January 31, after many fruitless starts, Ruth finally wrote:

Dear Dr. Maddry,

A most unexpected, uncalled for, and yet unavoidable thing has come into my life, which has upset me very much because I had said that "it could not happen to me." Maude said that I was in love and advised that I talk with Dr. Udvarnoki about it. Instead of throwing cold water in my face, he just looked at me helplessly and said that I am in love and I had best call Dr. Gill over to see about me. I wrote Dr. Gill and thought that surely he would come over on the first train to give me a good shaking, but instead, he writes back that I am in love and that I had better announce it to you! Now what else can I do since I have the witness of all these expert doctors, but write to you that I am sadly stricken. It came like a thief in the night, but the result has been most disturbing. I have suffered brain storms, heart trouble, and several nervous breakdowns within the past month, but the solution was neither in the wind, the earthquake nor the fire. I have prayed constantly for more than a month, just clinging, clinging, and begging for deliverance in one way or the other. Then I was quiet, but the still small voice which came in the stillness only made me sure that it is all of God, and that I must reckon with it as such.

The trouble is that he is not a "native" but rather the young Scottish evangelist who has been used so powerfully of the Holy Spirit in Hungary. This is the way it came about. During the Foreign Mission Week of Prayer, I became very much dissatisfied with my spiritual condition and began searching my heart for the cause. Then on the day of prayer, I spent much time alone praying for entire consecration and a greater power in my life. That night I went to hear this young man, as I have told you, and again I dedicated myself to the Master. I wanted to be wholly consecrated, so my heart was open—and somehow, I don't know what happened, but in he walked. At first I thought it was a test of faith, but when I learned that he was having the same experience as I—well, it just happened. We agreed to pray about it at first—just to pray and to wait to see what God would do about it. The thing I don't understand is how could this happen on the day that I unreservedly surrendered my life anew to the Master and the day that thousands of women around the world prayed, "Lord, bless Miss Mahan in Hungary." How is it that on that day I should develop such a complication if God answers prayer?

I have waited a month to make sure I was not dazzled or the subject of loneliness or such. I would do anything to spare you. Day and night I have fought the battle for you and Dr. Gill against my own feelings, his feelings of assurance, and the leading of the Holy Spirit. I can fight no longer. . . . The only question now for weeks has been my own work and responsibility here. I just could not see how God could have a hand in leading me out of a work into which I have just entered— and that part is still unrevealed. Yet, I know that if I can "blame it on God" then He has another person to step into my place when the time comes, for He goeth before.

Sincerely, Ruth Mahan

Praise the Lord for Miss Gussie and the debate team at Bob Jones. Were there ever such persuasive powers demonstrated on paper? But Dr. Maddry did not appreciate her writing abilities or her news. He wrote her back a "hot missive" telling Ruth that he was extremely disappointed in her and that if she left they would close the school!

And Dr. Maddry was not the only unhappy person. Ruth and James met with a mixed reaction to their announced engagement. Except for Maude, who had announced her engagement at the same time, Ruth's co-workers and students were horrified. She couldn't just go off and leave them. They needed her, the school needed her, the churches needed her. Hungary . . . What of Hungary's need?

The dye was cast. She had thrown in her lot with James Stewart and the Lord, come what may! When Dr. Maddry's reply arrived, Ruth was able to write:

FEBRUARY 28: Letter from Dr. Maddry. Says they will close down the school, but God will not let them do that. I know my Father! What will He do? Wonderful how trustful and peaceful I am about it all—that I have made the right decision. Yet, I still cannot eat or sleep for sadness and grief. My heart is breaking. I keep thinking of the School, the girls, the Baptists, Anya, Bela, Boske. I love these people and my work so!

FEBRUARY 29: All, of course, are disappointed in me, but I still believe God is asking me to step out and trust Him. If I perish, I perish.

MARCH 1: Every day, I have a greater peace in my heart that my Father will work out this mess I am in. What a poor, weak, erring child I am. And how He loves me! Spoke to Reformed church girls tonight. Enjoyed it so much. Oh, God, if only I could live and die in Hungary. But not my will. . . .

Ruth's heart was torn between two loves. To say yes, to the one, no matter how clear the Lord's leading, meant rejection of the other. Even in that last month before Ruth and James were to be married, she agonized. At times she felt she was on a fast train to an unknown destination with a man whom she had only known five months. She was tempted to jump off the "train" if for no other reason than to slow things down. But with directing the school, helping in the revival, writing letters for James, and generally keeping him happy, Ruth seemed to have little chance to get quiet until it was all over. There were days that she cried and cried to the Lord until she had no more tears—just exhaustion. What was the Lord doing to her?

If only Ruth could have looked ahead and seen the future. If only she could have heard her Father say to her, "My child, why can you not love me, trust me? I see the end from the beginning. In the very near future, there is to be a war that will cover the face of the earth, and it will also come to Hungary. The forces that be will say to you, 'You are an American; you are the enemy and must go home.' The seminary and training school will be closed down, and the city and its churches bombed. All missionaries will have to leave and Hungary will be a locked door for many years under the Communists. Here, I am giving you an open door before all this happens. Trust me and walk through it."

But there was no such voice, no such vision, only a glimmer of light and a still, small voice telling her to go with this man.

When I say to my husband, I LOVE YOU meaning "agape love", I mean that no matter the situation, or how I feel, or how he acts, I am consistently committed to his welfare. I value him and his mission in this world and before God, and I will give my all to sustain, and help him.

In other words, I am making the following commitment: "I, Ruth Stewart, so love James Stewart that I am willing to give up all and leave all that I held most dear in the past in order to be able to make his life and work complete. His well-being is my first concern; his success is my highest joy; his need is my greatest responsibility. My husband's attitude ideally should be the same towards His Head, the Lord Jesus Christ, but, regardless, my attitude is to be the same to my husband, my head."

But that love is to be mutual. "Husbands, love your wives as Christ loved the church and gave Himself for it . . . and He is the savior of the body." This not only speaks of "agape love," but the word "savior" carries with it the idea of "preserver." The truth set forth is that the wife is kept, preserved, guarded, shielded, and provided for by her husband, even as Christ is the Savior and savior of them both.

This is God's design. And is there not built into each of us women the desire to be loved in such a way? And is it not built into the man to desire to be the protector and provider of the woman? Only the distortion and destruction of our foundation as a Christian nation has changed the natural instincts that God puts in men and women.

—RUTH FAJFR, (MANY YEARS LATER!)

Chapter Eight
The Lord First

Each day brought new surprises from this man. In April, James kept his word and gave Ruth an engagement ring. She tells the story in her own words:

> We walked again to Margit Island and sat down on a stone in that beautiful park where we had first talked together. James took out his New Testament and turned again to the letter of the Ephesians, this time to chapter five.
>
> "Wives, submit yourselves unto your own husbands as unto the Lord," he began, "for the husband is the head of the wife, even as Christ is the head of the church, and he is the saviour of the body. Therefore, as the church is subject unto Christ, so let the wives be to their own husbands in everything. Husbands, love your wives, even as Christ also loved the church, and gave himself for it. . . ."
>
> I waited for a little lecture about how he was to be boss and I was to do everything he told me to without argument, etc., etc. But it did not come out like that.
>
> "As head of my wife," he began solemnly, "I am responsible for your mistakes and your weaknesses and for all you do. It will be my privilege to help you, strengthen you and support you where you are weak and sacrifice for you, even as Christ did for the church."
>
> It was understood that I was to "honor and obey;" he never thought of questioning that part! And then I understood the reality of the words used when a woman in Hungary refers to her husband as "uri fejem," meaning "my lordly head." So that is what the head is for! Not primarily to "boss" but to oversee and care for and to get one out of trouble; to nourish and love the body as its own self.
>
> James went on. "You understand, dear, that the Lord comes first in my

life. Then the people to whom He has called me come second."

After I caught my breath, I ventured to ask, "And where do I come in?"

"We both put the Lord first—together!"

On James' last trip to Budapest before the wedding he and Ruth began seriously making their wedding plans for May 20th. James brought along his mother and Ruth found her to be a delight and comfort, almost like having her own mother with her. It did not take long for Ruth to find out where James got so many of his good qualities. When James asked his mother to address the crowd of a couple of thousand one evening, this quiet-spoken, reserved *queenly lady,* as she was often referred to, did so with perfect grace and a touch of boldness that was such a mark of her son's ministry.

Thoroughly involved in the blessed move of God in Debrecen which had been going on for months, James was running from one church service to another with little time to think of anything else except the messages the Lord had laid on his heart and the glorious thing God was doing. He had forgotten one very important thing. One afternoon, they were resting a few hours before he had to catch the train back to Debrecen, when he looked at her with an expression of consternation.

"Ruthie, did you know we have to have wedding rings for the ceremony?"

Surprised, Ruth nodded.

"Well, we had better go right away and get them." He grabbed her hand and pulled her in the direction of a nearby jewelry shop. Suddenly he stopped and looked at her sheepishly. "Do you have any money?"

If she hadn't been so amused, Ruth might have been angry. It was always like that. For an international evangelist, James certainly was impoverished. At first she didn't understand. On their few "dates" she seemed to be the one with a little change to pay for the coffee or the tea or a taxi. James explained to her that he seldom had any money; he just trusted the Lord to meet his needs. When he arrived in a city or country to preach, those who invited him paid for his ticket and his expenses while he was there. He insisted that all offerings should go towards the meetings, hall rentals, advertising, and such.

"The Lord meets all my needs, but this is a new experience for me.

I have seldom had any wants before," James explained.

The two purchased rings and, at James' request, the jeweler inscribed on the inside of each "Colossians 1:18," which was to become their life verse. "That in all things he might have the pre-eminence." Ruth agreed, thinking surely it was a great aspiration.

Only when they started discussing the wedding plans did Ruth get a foretaste of what this verse meant to James. She was content to have a small wedding service in the Baptist church she had been attending since coming to Budapest. She was not one for show or fuss. Maude would be her only bridesmaid and dear Rev. Udvarnoki would give her away. The church people and a few close friends would attend. Then they could slip away for a few weeks of rest that they each needed so badly. James had other ideas.

"But, Ruth, don't you see? People have been talking for months about this wedding—the Scots evangelist and the American missionary getting married! They will all flock to the wedding and we will have one more chance to preach the gospel. The very start of our lives together will be the greatest testimony this city has ever seen!"

"I really would like Maude to sing, *O Promise Me*," she interjected, remembering the times she had romanticized at other weddings that one day it would be her song.

He looked rather surprised at her. "I don't know that hymn. What are the words?"

When she repeated them to him, he was shocked. "There's not one word about the Lord. Let's pick a Christian song that tells people how to be saved."

Ruth knew by this time there was little use to argue, so the two decided that Maude would sing, *Oh, Love That Will Not Let Me Go.*

Things began to come together for the big day, though those last days were busy. James again preached to a packed house at the *Tattershall*, the largest hall in Budapest. During the day the hall was used as a famous riding school. At the end of the day, hired laborers cleaned the huge arena, put down fresh shavings, and set up 4,000 chairs needed to seat the crowd. Surrounding galleries were also available for use. In the middle of the long side of the building a huge platform had been erected on which the leaders of the Hungarian Evangelical Alliance took their places each evening. James preached to thousands each evening from this platform. On the last night of the meeting, a youth rally attracted 5,000 young people.

It is no wonder that in the midst of all the activity that Ruth should have forgotten a commitment she had made for her fiancé. When it dawned on her, she went to James.

"Do you remember that I promised that little Baptist church that you would come and speak at their festival?" Ruth asked. "And that is the same day as our wedding. I had better let them know that we will have to cancel."

The meeting was not to be a revival campaign. The congregation simply wanted James to be part of a day set aside for them to raise funds to build a new church building.

James didn't hesitate. "No, no," he said. "We'll go, at least for a few hours."

And so on their wedding day Ruth and James first went downtown to the civil courts for the official wedding. Then they went to the Scots Mission to the Jews for the regular ceremony. Seating was limited to 250 people and only those with printed invitations were allowed to attend.

The wedding was all Ruth and James had hoped it would be. Dr. E. L. Langston performed the ceremony. Professor Dr. Kis, who had been one of the chief supporters of the earlier evangelistic meetings, interpreted, and Dr. Udvarnoki gave away Ruth. She looked lovely in her borrowed wedding dress, Maude having offered her the dress she had worn at her own wedding to Emil Bretz, a Hungarian preacher, just a few days earlier. As the photographer was taking pictures after the ceremony, someone yelled from the back of the room, "Get a hymnbook for Jimmy to stand on!" Ruth, wanting to look the tall, graceful bride of her dreams, had put on high heels and now she was taller than her husband!

Following the ceremony, a small private reception was held for them at the seminary with pastors, students and friends of the bride and groom attending. From the reception the newly wed couple was taxied to the Calvin Ter Reformed Church where hundreds had gathered for a larger reception. So many people had been saved and blessed through the ministry of James Stewart that they wanted to be a part of this unusual wedding! James and Ruth each spoke, giving testimony of God's faithfulness. An hour or so later, after receiving congratulations and well wishes from a pressing crowd, the couple was again whisked off to the little church on the edge of the city. There the participants were just finishing their day with music and singing and speeches!

For better or for worse, in joy and in sorrow, in sickness and in health, Ruth Mahan and James Stewart were married.

Dear James and Ruth,

God needs two souls whom He can trust,
Two souls who fully trust in Him;
Who pine 'neath one great "Preach I Must!"
Whose order never groweth dim.
Two souls who never follow men,
And never flattery employ;
To all God says, they say Amen
Whose hearts are filled with peace and joy.

Two souls who for the lost do care,
With iron in blood, they never swerve;
Salvation news they gladly share,
And onward pace with steady nerve.
You two fulfill this need I know
From Europe's cry you cannot stay;
Go, onward go, while yet you may,;
God will be with you as you go.

Yours in His fellowship,
R. E. Neighbor
May, 1944

— Handwritten on the fly leaf
of R. E. Neighbor's book, *Gems of Gold*

Chapter Nine
Go with This Man

In lieu of wedding gifts, an offering had been received at the Reformed Church reception, and was just enough to pay for three tickets to Britain for Ruth, James, and Mother Stewart, with enough left over for the honeymooning couple to enjoy two weeks on the Adriatic coast in Yugoslavia. Ruth wrote her mother of those days:

> One week ago we were married. If every week is as perfect as this one has been, we can never complain. But, we are still on our honeymoon. We are so thankful for the rest and quiet of this place and our opportunity to get better acquainted.
>
> We take a walk through one or two of the surrounding villages each day. Today we visited two villages and gave out Scripture portions from door to door. The people are so friendly that we feel at home among them, though we know very few words of their language. . . . It is a joy to feel you are bringing light and salvation to benighted souls. . . . We are planning a future attack upon the darkness and superstition here later. . . . Oh, we are having a wonderful time!

It certainly was not your typical honeymoon, even if it was on the Adriatic! But, Ruth wondered if anything would ever be typical, being married to this unusual man! In just over a week, she was getting a clearer vision of what it was going to mean to be married to James Stewart.

She looked on it as an adventure. No two days were the same, either in work or in play! The first year proved that. No sooner had they returned from their honeymoon to Budapest than they joined Mother Stewart and traveled to James' home in Great Britain. At Glasgow, James was greeted by curious family members who wondered why he had chosen an American over all the eligible British Christian girls. Nonetheless, Nan, David, Douglas, and brother-in-law John, gave Ruth a warm welcome and did all they could to help her feel at home in Scotland. For two months Ruth followed James around, meeting family and friends, attending meetings and simply being his wife—and secretary, a job she had taken on since the first week they met! Later they sailed to Port Stewart, Northern Ireland, where James was given eight minutes to present the need of Eastern Europe at the Irish Keswick Convention. At that convention Ruth met Eva Stuart Watt. Eva would later travel with them to see for herself what God was doing through James' ministry and write about it in *Dynamite in Europe*.

Soon it was time to pack and catch the passenger liner, the *Europa*, for America! What thoughts were conjured up in Ruth's mind as she thought of the reunion ahead. Her tall, handsome brothers, her dearest friend and confidant, Gladys, her baby sister, Mildred, who would be a young lady by now, and her own dear mother and father. She could hardly wait to get there. And what would her family and friends think of her *foreigner* husband?

Much to her amusement, Ruth's American family and friends didn't know quite what to think. First of all James wore his heavy European-cut suit, and it was August in Alabama! Next, they could hardly understand a word he said. By the time he repeated himself three times, they had forgotten what they had asked him! At the first meal his mother-in-law served him—a specialty of fried chicken, mashed potatoes, gravy and biscuits—the family was shocked to see him help himself to a couple of biscuits, and then ask if he could put them in the refrigerator! He wanted *scones* to go with his hot tea, which he insisted Ruth prepare him every couple of hours despite a temperature in the 90's. Ruth had certainly brought home a strange one! In the end, James' openness and immediate affection for Mom and Pop Mahan convinced the family that he wasn't all that bad.

Besides, he didn't stay with them long enough for them to make a permanent judgment. For a couple of weeks in Montgomery, he preached in several churches that had had an interest in Ruth's foreign mission work. After that, his American friend, Dr. Neighbor, arranged meetings for him in Charlotte, North Carolina; Macon and Athens, Georgia; Columbia Bible College in South Carolina; and Charleston, West Virginia. Just before Christmas, he received a call from a Mr. N. A. Jepson in Seattle, Washington. Mr. Jepson was head of the Christian Businessmen's

Association in his area. He asked James if he would be willing to preach there in the New Year. James left Ruth to celebrate Christmas with her family and he went alone to Seattle, preaching and spending time with the Jepsons. After hearing the Scotsman's burden for supporting colporteurs and for providing Scriptures for the peoples of Eastern Europe, Mr. Jepson offered the use of his office to receive donations and send out receipts.

By February, James became restless. Rumors were rife about Hitler, his hatred of the Jews, his greedy interest in neighboring countries. Everywhere James went, Americans were asking questions about Germany. He was anxious to get back to see what was happening to his beloved Czechs, Poles, and Russians. Ruth, too, was concerned about her Hungarian friends. They agreed that it was time to return to Britain and then the Continent.

In March, 1939, Ruth and James, along with Eva Stuart Watt, crossed the English Channel on their way to Czechoslovakia. German troops had already moved into Poland and there was substantial evidence that thousands of Jews had already disappeared or had been removed to the *ghettos*. With both apprehension and anticipation, they arrived in the beautiful city of Prague, which in earlier years had become like a second home to James. The three were welcomed with embraces and kisses by the Stifter family, who looked on James as another member of the family. After a meal and time of "catching up", the guests were shown to their rooms.

Imagine their astonishment as they awakened to the news that overnight the Germans had invaded the country and were only hours away from the capital city. Miss Watt, Ruth, and James stood at the window and watched the tanks roll into the city. Behind them the Stifter family, with faces paled by apprehension, wondered what this would mean to their lives and the life of the church. They loved their prime minister, who was a close friend of Father Stifter and who was thought by some to be a real believer. What would he do now?

They all prayed and decided that the meetings planned for James Stewart should proceed as arranged. Could they have guessed that this would be the last time for such an open gathering—that this was the beginning of the end of religious liberty in Czechoslovakia for the next fifty years?

The meetings went unhindered, despite all the unrest around the city. The three travelers set out to complete a survey. James, with some premonition of what was to come, was anxious to push on to Ruthenia, Latvia, Hungary, and Austria. Everywhere confusion and unrest prevailed concerning Hitler's plans for the country. Few thought war could be averted.

James felt the pressure of the current events. In a whirlwind of activity he raced from place to place, looking for men who could carry on the distribution of literature and evangelism in his absence. And God sent faithful men—and women. James planned to provide Scriptures through the Scripture Gift Mission and to raise support for colporteurs through Christians in Britain and the U.S. Under the present circumstances, he decided, the work of God must not be abated. With this in mind he held two Bible Schools for preachers in Poland and Latvia under the auspices of the Russian Missionary Society, founded by James' dear friend, Basil Malof. Forty-five men attended and what a time they had studying the Word from morning to night!

Eva Stuart Watt gives further details:

Here were lonely workers, so constantly at the ploughing and so far removed from each other, that such retreats as this were impossible. James knew how hard-worked and poorly paid they were. . . . They needed rest, as well as spiritual refreshment; and the month at Radosc provided both at no cost to them. Indeed, when they arrived they looked just like tired missionaries from some far off shore—listless, pale and worn, they spoke little the first few days.

An old basketball turned up from out some dusty corner; and the first sunny morning James had a handful of students with him, filling in a short interval before lunch. One of the older men on a seat was overheard to remark, "Look, they're playing as if they were children! Did you ever see the like of them for missionaries!"

Five or six hours each day were spent in classes, which covered, first of all, the history of the Bible. . . . Then an outline of all the books of the Old Testament, followed by a detailed study of the Acts of the Apostles (which Ruth taught) and Paul's Epistles to the Romans (which James taught) . . . Two very powerful periods of the session were those giving an outline of the Old and New Testaments. At the close of the last of these, when prayers were invited from the evangelist, one brother broke spontaneously into an outflow of praise. "Oh, Blessed Lord! how we thank Thee for such a wonderful Book. Thank You for ever choosing me in my unworthiness to preach it to men!"[5]

This school was held twice, once in April and again in May. Though Ruth took part in the teaching and sympathized with these warriors of the cross, she was not able to enter into the enthusiasm of Eva and James. She was too tired and too discouraged.

Almost a year had passed since the wedding. For Ruth the adventure was wearing thin. She was beginning to feel displaced. At times she longed for her little apartment at the seminary overlooking the Danube River and the orderly life she had lived there. She was homesick for Alabama, for a quiet evening to sit in the front porch swing and simply be young Ruth Mahan once more. Her childhood nickname had been *Ruth Run*, but no matter how hard she ran now, she could not keep up with James Stewart.

Some of Ruth's discouragement could be partially attributed to the fact that she was expecting her first child in September. Instead of being coddled and receiving special care from a doting husband, she seldom saw him except late at night when they both fell into bed exhausted. Besides that, they seldom slept in the same bed for more than one night. Traveling by train was exhausting at the best and dangerous at the worst in this pre-war state. Milk, cheese, and meat, as well as many other necessities were luxuries. Believers in each place were so kind to Ruth and gave her the deference they thought she deserved as James Stewart's wife, but that only made her feel worse. If they had only known the feelings of resentment, irritability, and wounded pride she harbored in her heart, they would have been shocked. She was shocked! Could this be Ruth Mahan, the Southern Baptist Missionary admired by so many for her courage and commitment to go to Hungary? Where was the Ruth Mahan who had consecrated her whole life to the Lord just over a year earlier, ready for whatever the cost of marrying James Stewart?

There was no such person; just a pitiful, weary woman, tired of traveling, tired of poor beds, tired of poor food, tired of poor train carriages and roads, tired of a husband who seemed to not even notice the inconveniences imposed upon her in his drive to stay one step ahead of Hitler. All Ruth wanted was to find a safe place and have her baby.

Miss Watt couldn't help noticing Ruth's behavior and her spirit. Being a single woman, she may not have been as sympathetic as Ruth would have liked. But being a wise soul, she also knew that to sympathize too much would weaken Ruth and cause her to miss something the Lord was teaching her. One day, she took Ruth aside.

"My dear Ruth," she started. "I have had it on my heart to speak to you for some time. I realize that you have always called your husband Jim or Jimmy. That is all right when you are alone. But have you ever thought that people will respect James as much as they see you respect him? Which reminds me. I have noticed that often when you are in a group of people that you make little remarks of criticism about your husband. Oh, you probably don't even realize that you do it because you have a clever way of cloaking your criticism in humor. Even while your friends are laughing, you have put a question in their mind as to James' worth. Remember, people will respect James in the same way you respect him."

It was a hard rebuke for Ruth to swallow from this respected Irish friend for whom she felt both affection and much reverence, but the words were indelibly imprinted on her mind. From that day forward she referred to her husband as James when speaking to friends, and as Mr. Stewart when speaking to mere acquaintances. More and more she found herself checking her words before she blurted them out, to make sure that they were "with grace, seasoned with salt."

MAY 19 LATVIA: Went to the seashore today. Lovely lunch at the railway station and then a walk along the beach. Reminds me of the beach at the Gulf where we used to go swimming when I was a girl. I am still ill. So tired that when I came back to the house, I went to bed . . . "My strength is made perfect in weakness" says the Master. How to prove it in my own life!

In Poland, Ruth had been reading the lives of Jessie Penn-Lewis and Hudson Taylor.

Gave me a greater thirst than ever. But HOW can I be like them?!! I had to speak today again. Realized my powerlessness more than ever. Oh, that I knew what to do to get the unction of the Holy Spirit. I don't believe the Lord wants me to keep saying words, even about Himself, until He sees fit to bless me.

* * *

After the Bible school closed, the three of them made one last tour of their mission fields—Czechoslovakia, Hungary, Yugoslavia—and then started on their journey back to Britain. They arrived on July 10th. Thinking they had plenty of time before the baby would come, James chose a Christian boarding house in St. Leonards-on-Sea on the southern coast of England. There, he thought, they could rest a few days before traveling on to Scotland. The three weary travelers knocked on the door and were graciously shown to two lovely rooms overlooking the beach and the channel beyond. With one quick glance around the room, Ruth fell onto the bed. She could lie there for a week and not move, she thought. Oh, the luxury of a good bed and a bathroom with a bath right next door. And good food and plenty of it! She basked in the thought! She would not think of trains or travel or speaking engagements or making sure she created no trouble for her hostess. She would just lie there and concentrate her thoughts on the little one growing inside her and becoming more active with each new day.

It felt so good to just relax and think of as little as possible. There would be time enough to plan a layette for her little boy or girl and to decide on names and to bask in all the other joys connected with motherhood.

After a couple of days, Eva Watt said her farewells to Ruth and James and headed for home in Ireland. A week later, James announced that he would attend the Keswick Convention where his friend, Dr. Waite, the chairman of the convention, had offered to give him a few minutes to represent Europe as a mission field. The English had never before considered Europe as such, but they would be thrilled to hear what God had been doing, especially in Eastern Europe. Ruth would be able to stay behind and rest, and James would return in plenty of time to escort her to Scotland.

> July 19: We came here eight days ago to St. Leonards-on-Sea. Have been having a lovely time resting and walking, Went to the sea-shore today for tea. Wish I could hear from James as he is to speak at Keswick. We are staying in a guest house with lovely Christians.

The very next day the owner of the guest house went to Ruth. She expressed her regrets for bothering her, then asked her if she would mind moving down the road to another guest house where arrangements had already been made for her to stay. Unexpected guests had arrived and needed the room Ruth was occupying. What could she say? There was nothing she could do but pack her things and move down the road. Amazed at what an effort it was for her to do so, Ruth struggled on. Her whole body felt like a dead weight and every movement was a challenge. Christian friends helped her move by taxi, but in a short while she was left alone in a strange house with a strange landlady and surrounded by strange guests. Still feeling too tired to make the effort, she ate a quick tea and went to her bedroom to rest. With much difficulty, she eased herself in and out of the tub, dressed for bed, and lay down exhausted.

At three o'clock in the morning, Ruth awoke. Before she could gain full consciousness, she knew something was terribly wrong. The bed was soaked and when she sat up, a sharp pain took her breath away. James! She needed James! But she knew that could not be. Friends at the other guest house would help her, but she didn't know their number. She didn't even know where the phone was in this guest house. Another sharp pain pierced her abdomen. She gasped and fell back onto the bed. What was she to do? After an hour of agony she realized the pains were getting stronger and closer together.

Moving cautiously, she felt her way down the darkened corridor to the stairs and the floor below. She had noticed a door beside the reception desk. Hesistant but desperate, she knocked. There was no answer. She knocked harder. "Madame, please, I need your help." Twice she called out for help before finally hearing someone move around. Suddenly the door opened and a nightgown-clad older lady stared her in the eyes.

"My baby . . . my baby is coming and I need to go to the hospital. Please call a taxi for me."

Shocked by the unexpected intrusion, the proprietress, Mrs. Hollins, quickly recovered and in typical English fashion began giving instructions. "Now, don't you be bothered, my dear. Go back up and put some things in a suitcase. I'll call the taxi. "

When the taxi arrived, she offered to accompany Ruth. In only a matter of minutes, Ruth was at the nearby maternity home and in the hands of a competent staff. After examining her, the doctor expressed great concern. The mother-to-be was appallingly run down and had a very low blood pressure, and the baby was not due for a couple more months.

As darkness gave way to light and light to full noon, Ruth's first child entered prematurely into this world. Afterwards, the mother looked so weak and her blood pressure was still so low that things did not look good. The baby, too, was at risk. At a mere five pounds, she was not very responsive. The condition of the mother and child was so bleak that a nurse asked her priest to give last rites to each!

When Ruth was able to respond, nurses asked how they could contact the closest of kin. The landlady had been able to give no information except that Ruth was an American who had checked into her guest house. Ruth hesitated. She pictured James that very day, standing before the thousands who had gathered at Keswick. She prayed that a telegram would not arrive until after he spoke. It was such an important day for him.

Ruth recorded the occasion:

> Our little one arrived today at 1:15. I was up all night, pacing the floor alone—with God! I'm glad James wasn't here for why should he suffer too? Soon it was all over. She weighs five pounds exactly and seems to be in perfect condition. James spoke this morning at the big missionary meeting at Keswick. It is the first time Europe has ever been represented as a mission field. Thank God for the privilege. We are at Briar's Nursing Home. So glad it is all over.

The Lord answered prayer, and it was not until he had returned from the great tent that James received the telegram, "Wife ill. Telephone St. Leonards-on-Sea. . . ." James did not wait to even use the telephone. Grabbing his hat, he rushed to the railway station and caught a train from the Lake District to London, crying the whole way that the Lord would save the life of his dear wife. At London he quieted down enough to remember the telegram. He phoned the number in it and was told that his wife was out of danger and that he had a healthy, though tiny, baby girl. He rejoiced all the way to the south of England, praising the Lord for the opportunity to present the needs of Europe and still be on his way to his two loved ones. Ruth and James decided to name their daughter Sheila, after the nurse who had been so kind to Ruth in the maternity home, and Helen, after James' childhood friend Helen Ewan. Even while caring for Sheila in the Maternity Home, Ruth had a heart burdened for souls around her.

> James came this evening. My husband is so sweet. I am just crazy about him, and my "little rosebud." No wonder that these days I keep praying, "Make me a good wife and mommy." Dear Lord, use my testimony with Miss Clark. Make Thyself real to her. Give her joy and peace in her soul. Make me wise to say the right thing. Also do a lasting work of grace in Miss P.

Sheila and Ruth and James did make their appearance in Scotland in September, but by this time Sheila was already two months old!

God strengthen me to bear myself;
That heaviest weight of all to bear,
Inalienable weight of care.
All others are outside myself;
I lock my door and bar them out,
The turmoil, tedium gad-about.

I lock my door upon myself,
And bar them out; but who shall wall
Self from myself, most loathed of all?
If I could once lay down myself,
And start self-purged upon the race
That all must run! Death runs apace.

 I could set aside myself,
And start with lightened heart upon
The road by all men overgone!
God, harden me against myself,
This coward with pathetic voice
Who craves for ease, and rest, and joys:

Myself, arch-traitor to myself;
My hollowest friend, my deadliest foe,
My clog whatever road I go.
Yet One there is can cub myself,
Can roll the strangling load from me,
Break off the yoke and set me free.

— CHRISTINA ROSSETTI

Chapter Ten
Except a Corn of Wheat

When the Germans moved into Poland in September, 1939, war was inevitable. Britain and France stood by, watching Hitler and Germany take over the Sudetenland in Czechoslovakia. Even before, when Germans marched into Austria in March of 1938, Britain and the rest of Europe had stood by, sure that Hitler would now be satisfied.

Instead, just weeks after Sheila was born, the blitzkrieg overran Poland with tanks and troops on the ground and bombers overhead! On September 3, Britain and France declared war against Germany and the Battle for Britain began.

Glasgow, Scotland
June 7, 1940

Mom and Dad,

I am no longer a free American; I have a British family. I belong here. My duty is here with James and the work. If the Lord leads James to go on a preaching tour in America and opens the way for us to travel with him, then we will. The future is in the Lord's hands also. I should not want to be there if Britain loses this war! What Hitler would do to you all would be plenty. If Britain wins, then all is well here. This is a world struggle against you know what. We have been let down enough by Neutral countries in this struggle so that we can face up to anything now. I never saw such grit and tenacity, not even in America as these folk have. We are getting plenty to eat and so far feel little effects of the war except that prices are higher, etc. Yet, think of the 30,000 of Britain's young manhood destroyed in a day as it were because of the treachery of one man! The world will never be the same after the battle which is now being fought. (We feel this is a VERY IMPORTANT BATTLE.) I AM HEART AND SOUL WITH THIS COUNTRY IN

THEIR EFFORT TO DELIVER OUR BELOVED CZECHS AND POLES, as well as Danes, and to save THIS COUNTRY FROM HELL ON EARTH. There is little I can do except stand by and pray.

Later reading Alice Miller's poem, the *White Cliffs of Dover*, Ruth was comforted to know that someone felt as she. Only she, in her mind, substituted the word British for the word English because now the English, the Scots and the Ulstermen were all banded together in this war.

> I have loved England, and still as stranger,
> Here is my home and I still am alone.
> Now in her hour of trial and danger
> Only the English are really her own. . . .[6]

Ruth had written earlier:

Glasgow, Scotland
April, 1940

Dear Mom and Dad,

James is waiting to get a visa to go to Bulgaria and Czechoslovakia. If he is refused then we probably will settle here in Britain somewhere for a while so James can carry on the work from here. Meanwhile, this past week we have been up to our ears in work—type, type, type, wash, cook, feed and care for Sheila so that I am so tired at night I just fall into bed. On the whole, though, we are fine.

I told you before that I have no news except to tell you how wonderfully the Lord provides for my family every day. James and Sheila mean so much to me, but I do yearn to see you all at times. I do not know now when we can come home. As I have said before, if I happened to get across the ocean safely, there would be the question of getting back. We just pray that this war will soon cease and that all will be well again.

More and more I realize the tremendous task that is mine as James' wife. His vision is so large and takes in so much that I cannot keep up with him. James' wife must be so deep and broad and high—must be so much that I feel I am not. Every day I pray God will make me all I ought to be.

Five years ago today, I left for my work in Arkansas. And I think how God had to break my heart and tear it out before He could do anything with me. I thought it was the end of both life and love! Today I am thrice blessed with the fullness of love and devotion from the Lord, my husband, and daughter. How gracious He is when we trust Him!!

Still Ruth struggled inwardly. Should she take her daughter and flee to America, or should she stand shoulder to shoulder with her brave adopted people? On June 24, her birthday, she was hit with a personal bombshell. James wrote: "My dear, we must arrange for Sheila to go to America. You and I must remain here to carry on with others in the place where the Lord has put us . . ."

Ruth felt her world falling apart. She had come to the place that she was willing to stay in Britain. It seemed the only right thing to do. But to send Sheila, not yet a year old, all the way to America, and alone. . . . Ruth's heart almost broke.

The next day James phoned to say that America had sent the ship *S.S. Washington* to carry American wives and their children back to the U.S. and that Britain was requesting that Americans leave for their own safety's sake. That settled it. Ruth and Sheila would sail to the United States on the first of July.

Ruth's relief was accompanied by guilt. She was leaving the gas masks, the black-outs, the bomb shelters, the air-raid alarms, the rations, the daily fear and apprehension for a land of clear skies, plenteous food, and business as usual. Was she being disloyal to her husband to wish for the latter? And what of James? Would she ever see him again? She was so caught up in her own grief that she went about her preparation to leave with little thought of what James was going through.

James, Mother Stewart, and David went with Ruth and Sheila to the docks in Glasgow to see them off on a boat bound for Belfast. From Belfast the train took Ruth and Sheila to the south of Ireland where they connected with the *S.S. Washington* off the coast of Galway. It rained much of the trip and Ruth says, "It rained in my heart, too." But in her stateroom she found a letter from James, who in his own Scottish way, bared his heart to her on paper in a way he could not do in person.

My Dearest Treasures, How my heart goes with you as you go forth once again in His Name! Remember that your DADDY'S HEART beats every second of the day for you two. God alone knows what you mean to me. Nothing can separate us from the love of God which is in Christ Jesus our Lord. How I will be with you as your train comes into the depot at Alabama. Yours eternally in Him, Daddy.

The *S.S. Washington* carried 1,700 passengers though it was built to accommodate no more than 1,000. Ruth and Sheila were thankful to find that they shared a stateroom and not the swimming pool or mail room as so many did. A day into the crossing, Ruth contracted food poisoning and was bed-ridden for the whole trip.

But Sheila had a great time! Some of the ship's crew took over her care, even using large linen table napkins when her diapers ran out!

When the ship docked in New York, Ruth was still too ill to stand. The Mahans in Alabama received the following wire: "MRS. DORIS STEWART ARRIVING SS WASHINGTON TEMPORARILY ILL. CAN YOU MAINTAIN HER AND CHILD AND PAY TRANSPORT. Signed, American Red Cross." The money was wired and another telegram sent: "DORIS STEWART AND CHILD LEAVING NEW YORK TODAY TWO TWENTY-FIVE FOR MONTGOMERY. Signed, Home Service Red Cross."

Weak as she was when she and Sheila finally made it to Montgomery, Ruth relished the breath of fresh air, free from smoke, cinder and debris, the subdued quietness of a southern city free from the scream of fighter planes, air raid sirens, and constant ambulance wails! She recorded, "Straight to Alabama and home!! There's liberty, there's peace, there's contentment and rest."

After seeing Ruth and Sheila off, James rushed to London. Though he had been rejected for military service for health reasons, he thought perhaps the British Foreign Office could use him. After learning of his background and of his many years of travel throughout Europe, the Foreign Office assigned him the position of Goodwill Ambassador to America, representing both the British and Czechoslovakian war causes. The two governments considered James to be a great asset in attempting to convince America of the rightness of the Allied cause, especially since he was better acquainted with most of Europe than anyone else they knew.

Less than a month after arriving in the United States, Ruth received a shocking telegram from James. "Arriving tomorrow evening train from New York."

Now that the Stewart family was safe in America, Ruth dreamed of having a modest home in Montgomery where they would be close to her family, a place where they could rest between meetings and live a more normal life. After all, Sheila needed security considering what she had been through the past months. For that matter, they all needed a rest.

James had other plans. Following a couple of weeks of rest, the three of them were off to Greenville, South Carolina, then Spartanburg, Chicago, Charleston, Asheville, and Johnson City. Most days when Ruth awoke, it took her a few minutes to remember where she was. Early in 1941, James announced plans to travel to the West Coast. Along the way they stopped for meetings in various churches. In Texas they were welcomed by J. Frank Norris, and they experienced a blessed meeting in the church he pastored. From Texas they traveled to Arizona, to California, and to Washington, where they settled for a few months. The return trip to Alabama was just as hectic and by the time they arrived, Ruth was at the end of her tether.

This was to be her life. A different church every week. A different state every couple of weeks. Living in boarding houses and other people's homes might sound fun for a while, but for months? . . . for years? A life of this she couldn't fathom.

Christians were so kind to the Stewarts, fulfilling their every need. But the strain of always using other people's things, eating other people's food, and watching out that little hands didn't spoil other people's treasures—well, it was just too much. After a few months Ruth felt stretched out. Bone weary. Fed up.

Of the following two years Ruth never spoke in detail, but she did often drop a few hints when speaking to women.

> Some people seem to close their eyes, breathe a prayer, and shout, "Praise the Lord" and PRESTO—they are filled with the Spirit. But I am glad He brought me the hard way—that He dealt thoroughly with the "flesh" before He gave me any sign that He had filled me. I understand now the law of the holy anointing oil in the Old Testament, which is a type of the Holy Spirit. God said, "Upon man's flesh shall it not be poured . . ." (Exodus 30:32) and I was so very slow in yielding up my flesh that He might deal with it through the Cross. And He would not fill a dirty vessel.

Ruth often told the story of Isobel Kuhn who met the veteran missionary, Ruth Paxson, on her way to China. There were eight or so young women missionaries on the boat and Miss Paxson consented to give them an hour's Bible study each day of the voyage. One day, she looked out at the fresh young faces before her and, staring them straight in the eyes, declared, "Girls, when you arrive in China, all the scum of your old nature will come to the top!"

Isobel was shocked. They were missionaries, the cream of the crop! But she admitted that there came a day when, down on her knees in deep humility before the Lord, she cried, "Oh, my God, scum is the only way to describe me!"

Ruth felt the same, not so much when she arrived on the mission field, but when she had to learn to live with her strange Scottish husband. It seemed everything he did irritated her! She blamed it on their two-culture marriage. They seldom saw eye-to-eye on anything. Even those things about him that had attracted her before they were married now drove her up the wall!

Since arriving in America, matters were even worse. He seemed to be driven, a crazy man who could not rest. He had to go, go, go, non-stop—morning, noon and night. He was distracted, as if he didn't really see Ruth or hear her complaints and objections. He forged ahead with no thought of her condition or her feelings. She was sure he hardly recognized the sweet-natured woman he married, who now was constantly whining, nagging and irritable. But Ruth thought she had an excuse. She was expecting again, and everyone knows that a pregnancy wreaks havoc on a woman's emotions. But what was James' excuse?

After eleven months of a grueling schedule and two months into her second pregnancy, Ruth's health broke. James had to leave her in Little Rock, Arkansas, as he traveled on to Chicago, where he had promised to preach a week of meetings. A few days after James left, she wrote him:

> Honey, do not be alarmed when I explain to you the situation. We will just face facts and pray things through. I have been in the Baptist Hospital since Friday. I guess I am no worse than when I arrived, but on Friday, I had a sort of set back. The doctor is hopeful—doubtfully hopeful—that I will be able the keep our James [James had already chosen a name for this baby because he was sure it was a boy.] I am going to be practically helpless for the next few months. If I lose him, it will be even harder on me and I will be ill for a long time.

Ruth then asked her husband to allow her to return home to her family to recuperate when the doctor discharged her. Obvious to everyone but James, Ruth was on the verge of a nervous and physical breakdown. In the same letter, she later instructs her husband, "If I should die, you could settle Sheila with most anyone and go on with your plans."

Truly, Ruth had hit rock bottom. She really wanted to die. She thought it the only way out. In her eyes, she was a failure. The more she had tried to figure out what James Stewart's wife was supposed to be—look like, act like—the more frustrated she had become. She had tried and she had proved that she could not be that woman in a thousand years.

Finally, in absolute despair, Ruth cried out, "God, either kill me or do something with me. I can't stand it any longer."

How could two consecrated Christians, who loved each other and loved the Lord, come to such an impasse? It was as though they were traveling down parallel highways, going the same direction, but never converging. They slept in the same bed, ate at the same table, ministered together from dawn to dusk in the same churches, but each had wrapped himself so tightly in the cloak of his own individual pain, he could not see the other's pain.

James seemed totally insensitive to his wife's happiness and well-being. An outsider, who did not know James' heart and his total commitment to the Lord, would have gone so far as to say he neglected his wife. But in his mind James had meant it when he said that he and Ruth would be one in body, soul, and spirit in serving the Lord. If that were really true, he reasoned, then she would understand that any sacrifice was not too great in helping Europe. Daily he heard the reports of the bombings, of the death toll, of the refugees, of whole cities devastated, of children starving in the streets. His people—the very ones to whom he had ministered, among whom he had lived, and whom he loved—were dying by the thousands while he and his family had food, clothing, friends and freedom. James was overcome with sorrow for the suffering millions in Europe. In December of 1942, he wrote Ruth, "Do not buy any presents for Christmas except for Sheila. We cannot forget Europe's starving." All he could do was give himself tirelessly to solicit the help of the American people in general in his diplomatic work, and the church in particular in his missionary meetings. He was willing to go anywhere he found an open door where people would listen to his plea for Europe.

Added to this, in May of 1941, he had received news that his brother

Douglas had been captured by the Germans while he ministered in Yugoslavia and that he had been sent to a concentration camp. This was James' darkest hour. The devil even whispered in his ear, "You are the one who assigned him to Yugoslavia. You knew it was dangerous."

Of this time Ruth wrote in her scrapbook:

> Just before leaving Seattle, we learned that Douglas was captured by the Germans. James, who has been under a terrible strain for weeks, is upheld only by God's grace. The news in Europe grows worse daily. Who has a heart to preach to over-fed Christians here when Europe is bleeding and torn? James and Ruth find it almost impossible to carry on.

While Ruth was in the hospital, James wrote:

> Dearest Treasure, I know the past has not been rosy, but what we have endured is for Europe's sake. Ever since our marriage we have been under pressure and tension. . . . Darling, you have the will to pull through—you must for Christ and the gospel's sake. I need you desperately and nobody on earth could fill your place. . . . You will never know what I have suffered because of the war. Douglas was a terrible blow. I never realized how much I loved him! . . . Keep holding up. I love you, James.

Satan and all his forces of evil were bearing down on these two faithful servants of the Lord, and the outcome seemed to be hanging in the balance. Ruth's breakdown. James' sorrow over Europe and Douglas. And later, the horrible shock of a miscarriage. Would they break? Would the Lord hear their daily, though separate, cries for deliverance?

Still very weak and still concerned about the baby she was carrying, Ruth wrote on her birthday, June 24:

> I have renewed my dedication of this worn-out body and this turbulent mind, along with this willful will to Him. Oh, that He might be able to yet use them to His glory.

Behind the scenes, God was at work. Ruth had wanted to die. That was exactly what she was going to have to do. And God was bringing her rapidly to that end. To the end of Ruth Stewart. She was going through death struggles, a terrible thing to behold and an even more terrible thing to experience.

Look not for a true living strength in the life of the ME or the I.
With nothing to love but its selfhood, and fearing to suffer and die,
As thou seekest the fruit from the seed-planted grain,
Seek life that is living, from life that is slain.

Then hasten to give it its death-blow, by nailing the I to the Cross;
And thou shalt find infinite treasure in what seemed nothing but loss;
For where, if the seed is not laid in the ground,
Shall the germ of the new resurrection be found?

The soul is the Lord's little garden, the I is the seed that is there;
And He watches while it is dying, and hath joy in the fruit it doth bear,
In the seed that is buried is hidden the power
Of the life-birth immortal, of fruit and of flower.

'Tis hidden, and yet it is true; 'tis mystic, and yet it is plain!
A lesson, which none ever knew, but souls that are inwardly slain;
That God, from thy death, by His Spirit shall call
The life ever-living, the life All in All.[7]

PROFESSOR T. C. UPHAM

Chapter Eleven
Dead to Everything

In August of 1942 Ruth had a miscarriage. She had never really regained her strength after three weeks in a Little Rock hospital. She had stayed the summer in a Chicago apartment where she was joined by her younger sister. Mildred took care of Sheila and ran the household so Ruth could recuperate. James came and went as meetings allowed, but much of the strain of their way of life was still there. In September, James finally agreed that Ruth and Sheila should rent a small house in Montgomery where the two of them could settle down to a sane sort of schedule while James continued his meetings.

Back in Montgomery, Ruth had to face both the past and the future. At first she reveled in the present, the quietness, the closeness to friends and family, the enjoyment of taking care of her daughter and her home like other normal wives and mothers. But every time she got alone with the Lord, she started thinking of all her failures in the past. James was gone weeks on end and she missed him dreadfully. When he came home, she enjoyed the lovely first few days until she started dreading the time he would leave again.

I was not long married to James Stewart before I began to manifest a bad reaction to things that upset me and threw me into either a temper or a sulky mood. And to pour oil on the fire, my dear husband would quietly say to me, "Claim the victory, Dear!" That was not the response I had desired from him, and besides, I did not know what he meant by those words. I had never heard them before, but somehow I felt he was saying I should straighten up—without his doing anything about comforting me. (And actually, he was, but it was for my own good and the only answer to my need.) I was not even sure I wanted "the victory." What was there in life if one surrendered his right to himself—his right to feel sorry for himself and to claim all kinds of consideration from others? What was the fun of going about getting victory over hurts and slights, and the like without some pampering of the flesh?

I used to sit and listen to James preach about the person and work of the Holy Spirit in the life of a believer, and my heart would long for that freedom in the Spirit which he was enjoying. But another part of me argued, "Yes! And if I were the head of this marriage, I would be carefree too. Just give me the reins for awhile and I would soon be telling him to 'get the victory'—whatever that means."

A couple of months after we were married, we attended the English Keswick Convention where I began to hear messages of personal and practical victory in life by the power of the Holy Spirit. I heard much about the need of being controlled by the Spirit each moment of the day just to "keep sweet." I began to hunger for this life of liberty in the Spirit . . . But I was not yet ready to "die" for this freedom, nor to surrender my rights. . . . But I believe that the very first time I uttered a secret cry to the Lord for the Holy Spirit to work in my life, He began to work. He began to overturn and overturn, and pull the heavy furniture from the walls of my heart and turn up the rugs and open all the doors to my secret closets until I began to see and to be shocked at what I saw. Then I began to abhor what I recognized as the evil intents of my own heart. Really, it was a nest of snakes He turned out of my "inner man." I began to understand why Paul prayed for the Ephesians that they would be "strengthened'—or infused or permeated through and through—by His Spirit in the inner man, in order that Christ might settle down and be at home in their hearts. (Ephesians 3:16-17) It is the Holy Spirit Who prepares the heart for the Lord Jesus to move in and take full control, and He, the Spirit, does not spare us in the process of preparation. How faithful He is in His work of cleansing and of renewing as He applies to our hearts the death which our Lord wrought for us on Calvary.

Years passed—years of living that up and down experience of Romans 7. I was sometimes up and sometimes down, but always conscious of defeat and failure in my Christian life and always longing for deliverance and peace. But after four years of this kind of existence, the Spirit had me thoroughly convinced that ". . . in me (that is, in my flesh) dwelleth no good thing." (Romans 7:18). I saw I had been hugging to my bosom a self which was a complete rebel against God, while at the same time claiming to love Him! I was at last ready to admit what the Spirit had been saying to me for a long time, that I was a rebel, deserving to die—that is, the "old man" within me who still had such a strong hold on my life, was a rebel against the desires of God for my life.

About that time the Lord brought across my path a young woman. She was crippled and had very poor eyesight, but she had something on the inside that I didn't have. She had gotten the victory over all her circumstances and her incapabilities—the very thing that I needed. And she stuck with me. She'd talk with me and show me Scripture. And I'd pour out to her all my resentments and hurt feelings. I even told her all those things about my husband and how he had neglected me and how all he wanted to do was preach and get out the gospel. He didn't care whether he pampered me or petted me or not. She kept saying to me, "Ruth, there are no 'buts' in the grace of God; He is the God of ALL grace. That includes all your trials and circumstances, all your hung-ups, all your resentment too. Everything that is causing proud flesh to keep a sore spot in you—there is a place in God's grace for you to get rid of those things and cast yourself upon Him."

But, I thought, how boring! To be without any thought of myself? Not to be able to react to circumstances and feel sorry for myself when someone doesn't treat me the way I think I ought to be treated! What was there to live for? And I'd say, "But, but, but . . . ."

And she'd say, "Ruth, there is grace in the economy of God to meet all those 'buts' you are about to bring before me."

Finally, the penny dropped. And my machinery, my mind, my understanding woke up, and I realized that what she was saying was true. God will give grace to me to overcome all my "buts." He will grow me up and stop me from acting like a spoiled brat. Here I meet this young woman who tells me that there is grace for every need. Myself, my cares, and the Adversary himself were all taken care of at Calvary. "I am dead, and my life is hid with Christ in God, and the life I now live, I live by the faith of the Son of God who loved me and gave Himself for me." (Gal. 2:20). Not even my own faith, but His faith!

On another occasion she shared this period of her life with a group of women.

I remember how the first four years of my married life were so difficult because I had never been taught the facts on the victorious Christian life and very little on the Holy Spirit. I remember a missionary came from China and was giving lessons at the training school in Louisville where I attended and she told us very simply about the indwelling of the Holy Spirit and the privilege of having fellowship with Him daily because He is a guest in our hearts. But apart from that I don't remember being taught the necessity of being filled with the Spirit or messages about the basics of the Christian life.

So when I became married to a man who was filled with the Spirit and he had all the victory and all the joy and all the peace my own heart had been longing for down through the years, I just couldn't take it. And just because I didn't understand it, I would hit out at him. And immediately the Holy Spirit began to work on me. And all the dirt—well, I don't mean so much those outward sins—but my old self and selfishness and pride and doubt and fears and all the things to which the old nature held me hostage—came to the surface. And the longer I realized what was in me and the more I observed my husband, the more miserable I became.

For four years I battled this thing. If something went wrong, I was sure it was James' fault and I would hit out at him. He never answered me back. Oh, sometimes he would say, "Look, dear, I think you didn't spend long enough in your quiet time this morning." The truth was I sometimes hadn't even had a quiet time that morning and if I had, I had not really gotten quiet and gotten through to the Lord to receive anything from Him. And James would say, "You know, dear, I think I will take Sheila for a walk and you go on back and finish your time with the Lord."

That was worse than if he had hit back at me. Then I could have found some kind of consolation, but then the Lord finally answered the longing of my heart and I received the Holy Spirit into my life in such a realistic way. I knew the Holy Spirit had taken control of my life and had taken charge of all those things I saw within myself. That is why these truths, I feel, are more important than my giving you instruction on how to live quietly with your husband or how to get him to meet your needs. Discovering what the Holy Spirit is able to do when He takes control of your life—that is the real answer .

At the very end of herself, Ruth finally surrendered that final arch-traitor, Self, that last stronghold. About this same time, another friend, seeing Ruth in great distress of soul after a particular meeting, knelt down beside her. She took Ruth's Bible, opened it to Isaiah 58 and pointed out verse eleven. "And the LORD shall guide thee continually, and satisfy thy soul in drought, and make fat thy bones: and thou shalt be like a watered garden, and like a spring of water, whose waters fail not." The very cry of her heart! Oh, how she longed to be satisfied, to be like a watered garden, to be done with a dry and parched soul! In that place of desperation she claimed that promise for herself.

She explains:

> That night the Lord began to seriously "make me" what He wanted me to be, and nothing else mattered. I was all His and He was my Lord. From that time on He began to sort out my priorities. Until then I had clung to my husband—James was everything to me. If he came I was happy. When he left I was sad. When he wrote or phoned me and paid me attention, I was happy. When he was too busy to do so, I was miserable. But over the coming months, I realized I had been set free. I had the victory! The Lord was my all in all, my Satisfier; He was always with me, and He was the one I sought to please!

The strangest thing about gaining victory in her spiritual life was that instead of making her love James less, it made her love him more, unhindered by petty grievances and irritations.

One day, he confided in her. "It seems to me you have only now come to love me."

Ruth was shocked. She had loved him so much all the time. That was the trouble! He went away and spent too much time in his ministry and with his preacher friends and he didn't stay home with her. He didn't spend enough time with her—too busy serving the Lord to pay her much attention. And when she was with him in meetings, he was talking to everybody else and not to her.

She later commented:

> But he wasn't talking about that kind of love. He was talking about God's love that pays attention to the needs of somebody else. And it was true. Only as the Holy Spirit took control of my life did I become a real wife to my husband and did I begin to keep my eyes open to those things which would please him and so becoming a real wife, companion and co-worker to him.

Then she remembered all the times she had wished her husband were different, and had wished circumstances were different. How quickly human, possessive love wears thin. To her delight, she realized the Lord had given her an "agape" love for her husband, a self-forgetful, sacrificing, unconditional love, a Calvary love!

So much had she learned that in March of 1943, she was able to write James:

> Darling, we must find grace to stay apart, as you have said. I would not have you miss the plan of God for your every day, even for the joy of being with you. And I know you will not let your love for home take you from the fight one minute. We will stay in the fight and fight for His glory until He gives us a time together again. But please, God, that it will be soon.

Through the Spirit's eyes, Ruth began to see her husband and their life together in a different light. Circumstances had not changed. James was still James. The sacrificial life he asked her to share had not altered. But for the first time since the first year of her marriage, Ruth looked to the future with anticipation, and more importantly, with hope—hope strengthened by the knowledge she was once again pregnant.

Despite the fact there were no ultrasounds in those days, both James and Ruth were convinced she would give birth to a boy. She wrote James:

> Darling, it is all so different this time, somehow. I feel so confident in your love, your concern, and your care. I don't even have to have you here beside me because I know you understand the importance of this thing that has come to us—that another life is being added to our little circle and you feel with me the meaning of it all. I need so much a letter from you, but when I don't hear, still the realization that your love toward me and Sheila is perfect—that we are completely one—keeps us happy. I know you have said you want to call him John Bunyan Livingston Moody Sankey Frank Norris Oswald Smith Stewart, but Sheila and I have chosen James, after the man that we love with all our hearts!

And in another letter to him:

> I had hoped that with the distance between us, you would not suffer morning sickness this time! (Forgive me for laughing, for I can tell you from this end it is no laughing matter!) However, I might advise some dry toast and a cup of tea in bed each morning before rising, then something to eat every two hours! My heart tells me this little one is to

be our pride and joy—the Lord's chosen one. I never dreamed I could feel so wonderful about a baby at such an early stage—even while he is making me so sick! . . . Oh, Darling, the dreams I have of the future, God's work, two children to bless us and the Lord. It is all so different than ever before. It is God the Holy Ghost that makes the difference!

Life has taught us that love does not consist in gazing at each other, but in looking together in the same direction.

—ANTOINE DE SAINTE-EXUPERY

* * *

I am my beloved's, and his desire is toward me. Come, my beloved, let us go forth into the field; let us lodge in the villages. Let us get up early to the vineyards; let us see if the vine flourish, whether the tender grape appear, and the pomegranates bud forth: there will I give thee my loves.

— SONG OF SOLOMON 7:10-12

Chapter Twelve
Ready for Anything

One of Ruth's favorite books of the Bible to study and to teach was the Song of Solomon. In this beautiful love story she not only saw her relationship to her Lord unfolding, but she saw a picture of her own love story.

In the betrothal period, life is sweet and full of expressions of love and appreciation—the perfect beginning. The bride is delighting over her Cinderella romance—that the King should choose her, a nobody, to be his bride. She marvels at his grace and the precious times of communion as they enter into marriage. But after the nuptials are over, the feasting and the celebrating, she finds it is not as she expected. There are long periods of time that her loved one is separated from her. We find her in the palace, enjoying all the joys of being the King's bride, but he seems to be elsewhere most of the time. She becomes lonely and sad, missing his presence. Halfway through the story, she stirs herself, gets up and goes out into the streets to find her beloved. She goes about asking everyone where she can find him whom her soul loves. Gradually, the realization comes to her that he has a work to do, a kingdom to run, subjects to care for. As their relationship progresses, she finally understands that if she is to fully become one with her beloved, then she must join him, know his thoughts, his vision, his heartaches, and that can only be done by accompanying him on his long days and nights of toil. Not until she is willing to leave her own life behind—all her expectations of being the queen of the land—and enter fully into his business, can she honestly be "one flesh."

So it was with Ruth. She could stay at home and live a normal life—set up housekeeping, care for her children, help in the correspondence, take an interest from afar, or she could join her husband in the field. In her case, it would mean leaving all those things thought to be rightfully hers as a woman—protection, security, maternal joys and duties. How could she do this? Was the price too great? Who can know the agony of soul and what struggle and torment of spirit were experienced before Ruth literally died to all she had thought life would give her? Few letters are preserved and no diary tells the story of these struggles of Ruth. Only the obedience is known.

Once Ruth experienced spiritual victory, her life-style was changed forever. She presented a sacrifice never to be revoked. Into her life flowed that quietness of spirit she had so longed for—quietness that can only come from knowing the battle is over and peace reigns!

In his book *Beyond Humiliation*, Gregory Mantle says:

> Rest! Thousands of hearts are longing for it! And it cannot be found, as some vainly dream, by flying away on the wings of a dove from their surroundings. Rest comes through a true confession and deter-mined forsaking of sin, and through the cleansing of a nature from its stains, for sin in every form is "dis-ease", the opposite of rest. Mate-rial things are in a state of rest while fulfilling the laws and purposes for which they exist. . . . So rest comes to man through an adjustment of man's will to the total will of God. "Take my yoke (My will) upon you . . . and ye shall find rest to your souls." Rest comes through the subjugation of the whole being to Jesus. The perfect emblem of rest is God, and in proportion as man has his center in God, he becomes a partaker of His rest.[8]

Peace finally came to Ruth when she admitted that her problem was not James, not circumstances, not even poor health. The problem was Ruth Stewart in her natural, uncrucified state, a condition that kept her unhappy, resentful, and full of unrest.

With Ruth's victory so many pieces of her puzzling past fell into place. At Christmas of 1942, James returned home after spending months in Canada under the auspices of Oswald J. Smith. During this time, the Lord had been speaking to James, and when he arrived in Montgomery, he poured out his heart to his wife. As was their custom, they were tak-ing their evening walk when he shared with her the fresh vision the Lord had given him.

"The Lord now wants us to do more for Europe than just support national workers and send relief and literature," James explained to Ruth.

"We're going to start our own missionary society and send out Canadian and American missionaries to Europe. They can work alongside the national pastors and evangelists. If Europe was needy before the war, just think of her need now."

Ruth held her peace. She had learned not to argue when her husband said, "the Lord told me." Once he knew the Lord's mind, nothing could stop him. The matter was settled.

"We'll make our headquarters in Czechoslovakia and send out workers to Yugoslavia, Hungary, Poland, Romania—maybe even to Russia!" James mused. "Oh, Ruth, all these years of agonizing over our dear people, not really being able to do much for them. But as soon as this war is over. . . ."

Ruth hadn't seen James this enthusiastic since they left Europe, two and a half years earlier. There was a new bounce in his step, a holy fire in his eyes, an excitement in his voice as he laid his plans before her. Milton and Mary Lovering, a couple from People's Bible Church in Toronto, volunteered to join them and help get the mission on its feet. Though fifty years old, the Loverings were willing to leave everything behind and step out on faith simply because the Lord had laid Europe on their hearts.

In the summer of 1943, Ruth, three months pregnant, and Sheila moved to Buffalo, New York, to join the Loverings in the venture that was to become the European Evangelistic Crusade. If this was to be a faith mission, they were certainly starting out the right way! They had no building, no missionaries, and just enough money to pay rent on a small house and put three simple meals on the table. All they had was God and the word He had given James!

James Waite Stewart was born in November to the great relief of his mother Ruth and the great joy of his father James. An absolutely beautiful child, Jimmy, as he was called, was a fair, rosy-cheeked, chubby little cherub who captured everyone's heart as soon as they saw him. After the despair of her earlier miscarriage, Ruth knew just how Hannah must have felt when first holding little Samuel in her arms!

Now Ruth also had her hands full with a talkative four-year-old and a son to feed every four hours. A God-send during this time, Mrs. Lovering prepared meals, kept the men happy, and generally spread her radiant good-humor throughout the house.

In February of 1944, James found a house for the mission on Delaware Avenue in Buffalo. It needed much repair and re-modeling, but in James' usual optimistic way, all he could see was the finished product. The Stewarts and Loverings prayed together and James fired up everyone's enthusiasm. Soon, one friend volunteered to decorate the Hungarian room, and another the Russian room, until in just a few months, the Stewarts and Loverings were able to move into a spacious, bright, three-story headquarters.

With that move, the missionary candidates began to arrive—the Torbicos going to Hungary, Miriam Wheeler going to France, Margaret Friesen and Mary Sue Bucko, burdened for Czechoslovakia. Each candidate spent weeks or months at the headquarters before starting out on deputation work to raise their support for the field. Later, the Loverings gave themselves as missionaries to France and labored there many years before finally retiring!

When the war ended in 1945, the missionary recruits were ready to go to the field!

With a sense of awe, Ruth saw the whole thing unfolding before her eyes. This man she had married really did hear from God. Absolute, immediate obedience was his rule of life. To be a partner with James Stewart meant the same was required of her.

Following the surrender of Germany in May of 1945, and Japan in September, the Stewarts began to make plans to return to Europe. James was anxious to see his family in Scotland and then move on to Eastern Europe to visit the believers of Hungary and Czechoslovakia. His anxiety amounted to that of a father, forced to leave his family for a long duration, and eager to know how they had fared in his absence. Under the circumstances, James tried to visualize how many of the dear saints had been killed, starved to death, or been left homeless. He wondered if they had stood strong in the faith or if they had buckled under the pressure of Nazi occupation.

The Stewarts arrived in Glasgow in December of 1945. With tears of rejoicing they greeted family whom they had thought they might never see again. Times had been difficult. Coal, food, and clothes had been rationed. Scarcely a family in all of Britain had not lost a loved one to the war. But God had been with the Stewarts. Even Douglas had been released from the German concentration camp and though in poor health, he would soon recover. That particular Christmas became a season of much praise to the Lord for bringing the family together again.

By the New Year, however, James was off to London to seek an entry permit to Czechoslovakia. Ruth remained in Glasgow with the two children, all in one rented room with a single-eye burner, a coal fire and one bed. She tried to be thankful, knowing that she was only getting a taste of what James' family had suffered for five years. Still, the room was drafty, the children had colds and coughs, Jimmy was cutting teeth, and Ruth had become sick as well. For months she had anticipated returning to the mission field, but this was reality. Mother Stewart and Nan were helpful and did all they could to make things easier by taking the children a few hours each day. Either Douglas or David often came to carry the huge hopper of coal up the three flights of stairs. Still, Ruth found herself struggling with her spirit through that cold, wet Scottish winter.

A letter from James just before he left for Czechoslovakia brought cheer for a couple of days.

> My Darling One, Thoughts of great tenderness fill my mind and heart as I leave for Czechoslovakia. How I miss you dreadfully already and also my wee bairns [Scots for "children"]. Not only do I feel that my Heavenly Father is with me but also you. We go together. Amen! I love you with all my heart, my wife, mother, partner and sweetheart. How wonderful to know our love increases daily. It seems that we keep on discovering afresh new heights of love and fellowship in each other and in Him. . . . Think of me preaching in Prague this Lord's Day. GLORY!! Your very own, James.

By the end of January another letter arrived telling of his grand reception in Czechoslovakia:

> Our dear friend Senator Benes, the President's brother, welcomed me back to his homeland as did Brother Urbanek. Imagine the surprise of the saints when I walked into their Sunday afternoon service where they had gathered at the Lord's Supper. Meetings already planned for here, Kutna Hora and Brno.

A wire came a few days later. "Have just concluded the greatest revival meetings I have ever held in Brno. Now leaving for Budapest."

Then silence. Not a word from Hungary. One week, two weeks, three weeks went by. At first Ruth was angry, then worried, then depressed. What could be so important that he couldn't keep in touch? He knew how she worried. Besides, she was longing to hear about her friends in Hungary.

In her treasured, signed copy of *Streams in the Desert*, Ruth has left notations beside the readings for each day.

> FEBRUARY 21: "Rest in the Lord and wait patiently for him." Still, waiting, Lord!

> FEBRUARY 23: "And there came a lion." A lion did come today—discouragement. No news from James for 3 weeks. He should be in Budapest.

> MARCH 1: Still waiting, Lord. Four weeks since I heard from James; two and a half months we've been waiting for our trunks from the States; and two months for a larger apartment! The reading today says, "It is a platform for the display of His almighty grace and power!"

On March 12, five weeks after his last communication, a wire arrived, typically terse. "Arriving tomorrow morning, Love, James."

James came, and did he ever have a story to tell! Actually, he *had* written Ruth, but the letters arrived after he did! A fuller account of what he experienced is recorded in *Revival Behind the Iron Curtain*. Briefly, however, James arrived in Budapest and crowds flocked to the halls to hear him preach.

One of the allied forces in World War II, the Soviet Union occupied Hungary as part of the peace keeping process. The Soviets became suspicious of James' activities and arrested him. They interrogated James at their Addrassy Street headquarters—what was to become for the next 44 years the dreaded KGB headquarters in Hungary. After the interrogation, the Soviets accused him of being a British spy. They could think of no other reason people would gather to hear him. By a gracious act of God, James was not imprisoned but was put under house arrest. He was free to roam the city of Budapest, but he could not leave nor could he preach. Friends took him to a hospital run by Roman Catholic nuns. He only dared leave to find food and to seek an exit permit. The British consul had advised James to lie low until the permit arrived. They feared the Soviets would secretly nab him and send him away to Siberia. The believers also feared for his life and they told him of similar arrests of innocent people who later simply disappeared.

When American and British generals appealed to the Soviets to grant James a clearance permit, the Soviets politely refused. Even Hungarian President Tildy Zoltan was powerless to intervene. Under the Soviet domination he was only a political figurehead.

Of his situation, James later confessed to Ruth, "You won't believe it, but I was gripped with fear as never before in my whole life. I could hardly read my Bible or pray. It was terrible. I paced back and forth in that little room until I thought I would go crazy."

For a few minutes, her husband was lost in his thoughts.

"Then, one day, I picked up my Bible and this verse appeared before my eyes as though illuminated, 'For ye shall not go out with haste, nor go by flight: for the Lord will go before you; and the God of Israel will be your rereward.' Isaiah 52:12 told me that I should sit tight and wait for the Lord to go before me and work it out. And He did."

James pulled out an official piece of paper and waved it in front of Ruth's face. "My release was signed by Marshall Voroshilov himself. He is the Soviet general in charge of the Russian forces in Hungary! Nobody there could believe it."

Marshall Voroshilov was a powerful man who held life and death in his hands. Later he became president of the Soviet Presidium. But, "the king's heart is in the hand of the LORD, as the rivers of water: he turneth it whithersoever he will."

President Benes in Czechoslovakia, whose brother had traveled in America with James to win support for his country, was told of James' arrest. Being one of the chief leaders of the Allies in World War II, he knew Stalin personally. Though exiled in London, Benes sent a courteous, but clearly authoritative letter to Marshall Voroshilov, asking him to grant James Stewart a safe passage to Czechoslovakia as he was to be his guest in Prague. To everyone's amazement, the Marshall signed for James's release, and he was escorted safely over the border to Czechoslovakia.

It's all happening so fast. The Soviets are replacing the Nazis. They have been planning this all along. Germany was the one country hindering them from conquering all the nations of Europe. Now she is helpless, they are carrying out their plan. I saw the troops for myself in

Hungary and Czechoslovakia. Even Benes and Masaryk fear for their lives.

Then Ruth read the letter he had written to her before leaving the country.

Budapest lies in ruins. Buda must be one of the worst places in the world hit by the war. Just a city of ruins and yet people live where they can in parts of bombed buildings. I see men with haversacks over their shoulders going about trying to find a bit of food to feed their families. As the rubble is cleared, people are still identifying the bodies of loved ones.

It is terrible to see the people starving. I had $180 and was able to buy food for the believers wherever I went. During the war and even now old people and little children are dying of starvation. Oh, the sorrows these believers have gone through. Our Sheila's favorite song, "Some through great sorrow, but God gives a song," was always before me. "Comfort ye, comfort ye, my people." God help us in our lovely places of comfort to be true to Him.

Ruth looked about their room, now more crowded than ever with James there. They were all four together again with a roof over their head, clothes on their back, and fish and chips for tea. It was not exactly a "lovely place of comfort" in her eyes, but compared to the situation of her friends in Hungary, it was much for which to be thankful.

Every step that is taken in faith is tested. Samuel Rutherford's famous saying was true, "Grace tried is better than grace; and it is more than grace; it is glory in its infancy. . . ." Well, she had certainly been tested—the nasty winter in Scotland, James' long absence, and once again facing an unknown future. But the Holy Spirit still garrisoned her heart daily with songs of deliverance!

"When the children of Israel passed over Jordan, a picture of death to the old life and rising into the new Spirit-filled life, the first thing they came face to face with was Jericho. Life in the Spirit is one of battles. But we have the Lord of hosts with us!" she would one day say to the women when teaching Joshua.

The spirit of revival lived in Eastern Europe. Now James' mind was at rest about Hungary and Czechoslovakia, he set his thoughts on the European Evangelistic Crusade and its future.

We have to go—His last great word
Though so unheeded, unobeyed, yet stands.
When millions have no smaller chance to know,
How shall we tie to things He counted loss,
The baubles of the earth-life here below?
Yea, if we dally with their dross,
The joyance of the moment they bestow,
How can we dream of glorying in the Cross?

We have to go—although we die,
These temples bleaching on a desert sand,
Or in a distant lonely grave may lie;
Although with struggle and a brave stand
We fall before an unknown banditry.
But if such privileges now be granted men—
To view the martyr's crown with closing eye,
We shall remember, and you also then,
That though the orders were to "Go, stand by,"
We were not told that we must come again.

— OPAL LEONORE GIBBS

110

Chapter Thirteen
Into the Fields Together

Exactly a month to the day after arriving home from Eastern Europe, James went to St. Leonards-on-Sea, Sheila's birthplace, and the place where he felt the Lord wanted him to set up the British headquarters for the E.E.C. He arrived March 12th, went house-hunting on the 13th, and purchased a house on the 14th. As had happened so often with James after spending much time in prayer, the Lord led him directly and quickly. He led James to Mrs. Mills, a dear Christian widow, who sold her house at a very reasonable price so she could go to South America as a missionary.

Eight, Caple Gardens. It was a lovely concrete and frame house with a large front garden lined with nasturtiums and blooming fruit trees. The owner had left behind bits of furniture, several antique vases, some china, and kitchen utensils. Those gave Ruth a start in setting up housekeeping.

The Stewarts were only in their new home a few months before people began to come. At first it was friends from Eastern Europe. Brother Koukol from Czechoslovakia, recovering from the horrors of the Nazis, visited. Then Noemi Stifter from Prague dropped by on her way to Bible College in Glasgow. From America came the new missionaries on their way to the Continent. The Loverings passed through going to Switzerland to study French and to await their visas to minister in France. The Torbicoes arrived with their baby, Donna. They were on their way to Slovakia to live and labor until the door to Yugoslavia would open for them. Miss Bess Cornell, a courageous woman in her fifties who gave herself for missionary service after hearing a challenge by James, came also.

A year later, the first missionary candidate from England, Betty

Stevens, spent a few months at the headquarters before moving on to France. The following year two more missionaries from the North American Continent arrived—Miriam Wheeler, going to France, and Tena Blatz to Germany.

Meanwhile, the early ministry to Eastern Europe was not forgotten. After the war, it was still possible to help the associate workers of the E.E.C. in those countries which were so dear to both James and Ruth. Reports came from the Angeloffs in Bulgaria, Mr. Zrifka and Vlado and Jirina Fajfr in Czechoslovakia, and Oscar Abers in Latvia.

Vlado Fajfr sent the following report to the mission:

> I preach regularly in Zlin and the surrounding stations; also on free days take evangelistic meetings in several towns where I am invited. I edit the leaflet, "Pozdrav" (Greetings) which my wife, Jirina, and I publish quarterly. We began with 50 copies during the war and now print 10,000 copies. This leaflet is evangelistic for believers and goes to all parts of our country. Besides I have written several tracts . . . and write articles for several spiritual magazines. Last year (1947) I distributed over 45,000 different kinds of tracts. Please pray for our country, for the workers, and for the Lord's work in Zlin.

As early as the summer of 1948, James knew opportunities for supporting the ministries in Eastern Europe were rapidly coming to an end. By December 31, 1947, the mission had printed 200,000 tracts for distribution in Czechoslovakia. Reports of what God was doing were still coming from their associates. Within the next year, however, the door to Poland closed and literature and support could no longer be sent into the country. Some of the American missionaries who had gone to Hungary and Czechoslovakia were already having to leave and go elsewhere.

As much as the Stewarts rejoiced to see missionaries interested in Western Europe, they could not help but be heart-broken over the closed doors in Eastern Europe. They cried to the Lord night and day. What was to be done? Miraculously the Lord opened a wide and effectual door. Actually, it was to be the last such opportunity.

In August of 1949, James wrote in the E.E.C. magazine:

> Never in the history of our mission have we had such glorious news to announce to our loyal Crusade Family scattered throughout the world. We are now broadcasting the Gospel over Radio Luxembourg in the

three main European languages, English, French and German. . . . Radio Luxembourg is the most powerful long-wave radio station in the world. Eighty-two percent of the population of Europe are potential listeners. . . .

The final means of reaching the peoples of our original Mission Fields of Central and Eastern Europe is by means of a strong radio broadcast. Since the rise of Communism, we have had to withdraw our North American workers, leaving the sole responsibility in the hands of our national evangelists. One of our great objectives now is to comfort and strengthen the Church of God behind the Iron Curtain. . . .

For the most part, the Stewarts now turned their attention to Western Europe. Earlier some had thought it would have made far more sense to first evangelize France, Spain, and Portugal and then move eastward. How providential of the Lord to direct James to start in the east and move westward, and how important it was for him to be more sensitive to the Holy Spirit's directing than to human reasoning.

As missionaries arrived, they needed to be settled in their special sphere of service. They needed to find an apartment and arrange language study. And they needed to be introduced to local groups of pastors and believers. As the *Mama* and *Papa* of the mission, Ruth and James showed a great interest in these matters, often visiting the field first and paving the way for the missionaries.

Miriam Wheeler, a long-time friend of the Stewarts, tells how it was in those early days.

It was the policy of the Mission to cooperate closely with European evangelical leaders and pastors and for the missionaries to work under their leadership. In this way the Mission was unique. We found many open doors for service. James Stewart would introduce us to these men, "drop us off" and let us find our own way. It was a hard beginning, but it worked. At first the European pastors couldn't see a ministry for young, single women. I started off with flannelgraph for children, which was new in France. People were fascinated and soon I had more meetings than I knew what to do with, presenting the gospel with the aid of flannelgraph lessons.

Every year in May we had a conference in Switzerland for all the missionaries. There were Bible messages, reports from the various countries, and wonderful fellowship. No matter how large we became, we were like one family. One year, 1954, I think, 19 new missionaries arrived and were sent out all through Europe.

When the work was difficult, James and Ruth Stewart often arrived unannounced. In one place I was living in a room that had one window, and this window opened on to a narrow street with an open sewer. I hated the smell. Ruth said, "Just remember, Jesus has smelled those smells before you." Somehow that made it easier to endure odors after that. When they left, we usually felt we could "turn the world upside down."

They really knew how to encourage missionaries and give them renewed vision.

Only our present older generation can still picture the photos the newspapers carried of war-torn Europe after World-War II. In old E.E.C. mission magazines, every outdoor picture, whether of Italy, France, Norway, or Holland, has a backdrop of rubble and ruins. Germany, of course, suffered the most devastation. Physically and emotionally, the Germans were totally demoralized. Across Europe inflation was high. Money, food, supplies, and jobs were scarce. In a climate of hopelessness, the missionaries invaded Europe with a message of hope. During those early days after the War there was an openness, an eager interest, a pitiful pleading for help. With no place to go and nothing to do, people attended meetings inside and out in the open air. They received gladly the thousands of tracts and gospels given out.

It was in this distressful situation that God began to work. James was not only an organizer, but above all he was an evangelist. Constantly, he moved from place to place drawn by the great needs he daily observed.

He wrote:

Europe is a continent of tragedy and sorrow. Millions are destitute, homeless and hungry. Not only have millions lost their country, home, loved ones and professions, but they have lost their hope, courage, self-respect and character.

There are five hundred million souls in Europe, four hundred million of them who are non-Protestant, and few among the Protestants who truly know the gospel.

Wherever James went people flocked to hear his message of hope in the Lord Jesus Christ. Huge open-air gatherings were held in the southern French cities of Marseilles and Cannes. Later in the year he preached in Denmark and Norway. In Norway, there was such an ingathering of souls in 1947 that James returned in 1948, taking Ruth with him. They held five to six meetings a day, often hurrying from one building to another because the crowds could not be held in one hall. God had prepared a people!

How did Ruth fit into all this activity? She was "in the field" with her husband. A typical day saw the two arriving in a new town and settling into a hotel, guest house or a believer's home. While James rested and prepared for his messages, Ruth unpacked, did a hand-wash of her husband's shirts, set up the typewriter and wrote four or five letters, and found a cup of tea for James. She did all this before she was able to prepare her heart for the Bible study she was to give. It was no secret that on the physical side of things, Ruth carried the heaviest load. One friend jokingly commented that "Ruth carried the wood and James the matches." That was actually true, and at first she must have resented doing the *donkey work*.

Soon it became evident to Ruth that the Lord had put the two of them together for her to save her husband's energy and enable him to better carry the taxing spiritual load the Lord had laid on him. It was not unusual for her to write, "This morning as James spoke on missions, at the end, when he spoke of Christ's heart being broken for the millions yet untold, he broke down and wept—uncontrollable weeping." For days afterward, he would be too weak to continue and would be forced to go aside to recuperate. At other times, she saw him go days and nights hardly able to eat or sleep as he wrestled with God for the souls of men.

Perhaps this is why during the 1940s and 1950s, hundreds of people were called to the mission field through his ministry.

One such missionary wrote:

Your father was a speaker at a high school assembly at the Prairie Bible Institute in Three Hills, Alberta, Canada, in the fall of 1951. I made a clear commitment to the Lordship of Christ after his message and eventually served as a missionary to the Chinese people . . . for 18 years and am now the director of a mission with 600 missionaries serving in 45 countries. I share this information with you to let you know some of what the Lord of the harvest unleashed through a single message I heard in 1951. I owe your father a great debt.

Only eternity will reveal the answers to the heart-rending intercession of James Stewart.

But with such a burden came a price, not only for James, but for Ruth also. Often she was tired and weary and longed to rest for a while, but there was no place to stop. She had to be the strong one. James needed her. At times her flesh cried out, but even in day-to-day activities, Ruth had to learn the daily crucifixion of her own desires. She knew what Bishop Moule meant when he stated:

> Here is one inexhaustible paradox of this great matter; on one side a true and total self-denial, on the other, a daily need of self-crucifixion. This is a thing which I am content simply to state, and to leave it as the Lord's word upon the believer's mind and soul.
>
> But "daily"; without intermission, without holiday; now, today, this hour; and then tomorrow! And the daily "cross"—a something which is to be the instrument of disgrace and execution to something else! And what will that something be? Just whatever gives occasion of ever deeper test to the self-surrender of which we have spoken; just whatever exposes to shame and death the old aims, and purposes, and plans, the old spirit of self and its life.
>
> Perhaps it is some small trifle of daily routine; a crossing of personal preference in very little things; accumulation of duties, unexpected interruptions, unwelcome distractions. Yesterday these things merely fretted you and, internally at least, upset you. Today, on the contrary, you take them up, and stretch your hands out upon them, and let them be the occasion of new disgrace and deeper death of that old self-spirit. You take them up in loving, worshipping acceptance. You carry them to their Calvary in thankful submission. And tomorrow you will do the same.[9]

The quality that amazed those who knew Ruth best was her self-forgetfulness. She willingly waited on her husband hand-and-foot even when she appeared to be at the end of her strength. She had the ability to quickly pack and go at a moment's notice when James said the Lord was moving them on.

How could she do it? Was Ruth a *wonder woman*? Did she not have normal feelings and desires for stability and security? If you asked Ruth, she would smile, shrug her shoulders, and say, "That's life with James Stewart."

For those who pressed her further, she would share how she had learned the secret of drawing hourly quietness and strength from the inexhaustible supply of her Heavenly Husband!

* * *

From the first time James visited Asheville, North Carolina, he loved this town surrounded by cloud-encircled mountains. He was at home.

He loved to tell the story of George Vanderbilt who traveled all around the world before deciding to make his home in Asheville. He built what was to become America's most famous castle, the Biltmore House. Then James would say, "What's good enough for Vanderbilt is good enough for me!"

In those early years after the war, James had a vision of bringing his dear friends from Eastern Europe for a rest in the Smokey Mountains where they could regain their strength and health before going back to their labors. With this in mind he bought a house on a hill, overlooking the Smokies. But this dream never materialized. Instead, Asheville became the first home of the Stewarts. Finally, a place to come home to.

As Ruth looked across the mountains from her dining room window, she remembered all those years she had longed for a place of her own. The Lord had heard her cry. How strange that often when we give up everything for the Lord and His work, He returns to us "the desires of our heart." James was thrilled to have a final resting place for his books which he had carted from country to country in suitcases! Ruth was thrilled to be able to wash clothes and set up the ironing board whenever she wanted to. That in itself was a luxury.

Another reason they had purchased this home was because James insisted that the Lord had told him they were going to have a baby girl. He immediately picked out the name "Sharon Grace" and started advertising the fact. When asked when this baby was due, he would answer, "Oh, in a year or so."

His friends probably thought he didn't know the facts of life, but even though he didn't know the exact date, he knew Sharon Grace was on the way. That was 1948. Sharon did not make her appearance until January, 1951, but that made no difference. She was already included in all the Stewart plans!

When Sharon finally did arrive, her father was far away in Little Rock, Arkansas, preaching a meeting. By this time, Ruth was used to her husband not being around for the birth of a child, and she had made all the necessary arrangements. One Sunday afternoon, she was resting in her bed, and Sheila and Jimmy were showing an unusual interest in the antics of this little sister, still inside their mother's womb. They cuddled up to their mother, asking the usual questions about what it would be like to have a little baby. Suddenly a sharp pain gripped Ruth's back and she looked at the wide-eyed children and exclaimed, "Oooh, maybe she will come today."

Mother Stewart, who was living with Ruth and James at the time, tried to dissuade Ruth from calling the doctor on a Sunday. By this time, however, Ruth knew when things were getting serious, and she called friends to take her to the hospital. Sharon was born less than two hours later! When James was delayed because of bad weather, Ralph and Jacque Sexton transported Ruth and baby home from the hospital.

The Sextons love to tell the story of the procession going up the curved stairs to the bedroom—Pastor Ralph carrying Ruth, Jacque behind with the little bundle of Sharon, then Sheila, Jimmy, and Mother Stewart taking up the rear.

Later, James skidded and slipped over treacherous roads to get home to see his little *prophesied* gift from the Lord.

But a new crisis was arising. With a mother's heart Ruth longed to stay at home in Asheville with this little one. Sheila was now in the seventh grade and Jimmy in the third. Ruth had enjoyed being home for the months leading up to and following Sharon's birth. Now the thought of leaving her children tore at her heart, but she knew the time would soon come when James would say to her, "Ruthie, dear, I think it is time for us to go back to Europe. I have had an invitation from so many countries. . . . "

And that time did come. At a family meeting the Stewarts discussed the subject. Sheila was old enough to attend eighth grade at the Bob Jones Academy in Greenville, South Carolina. Jimmy would be closer to them if they put him at Emmanuel Grammar School, a boarding school for missionary children in southern Wales. Baby Sharon could travel with James and Ruth.

Ruth looked at the two older children. "How can you just sit there and not say anything—not show any emotion?" Tears welled up in her eyes. "Here we are talking about being away from each other for a year and you act like it is a week-end trip to Grandma's. Aren't you even going to miss us?"

Shocked, James and the children stared at her. They had never seen her like this before. It was a family rule that you didn't make a big deal of good-byes, simply because it didn't make it any easier.

"Of course, we'll miss you, Mom," Sheila answered matter of factly, "but this is our life. It's the way things have to be. What do you want us to do? Cry?"

" Yea," Jimmy added with a shrug, "You're the one who said if we are good while you're gone, we'll get a star in our crown for every person that gets saved."

Ruth saw that her children had been taught too well. The good-byes, the long partings, the lack of day-to-day communication, the surrogate families who adopted them—all these had become second nature to Sheila and Jimmy. That was the only incident in which Ruth allowed her raw feelings to show in front of the children, and after that she kept up her part in being strong and cheerful. Only if you read between the lines of Ruth's letters can you see the heart-rending that came with each parting. Once more, she was learning that the cross had to be laid on every object dear to her heart.

As Abraham willingly offered up his son for the glory of God, Ruth saw her need to do the same. She saw her children as gifts from the Lord to be held or loosed, as God willed. Like Abraham, Ruth had made the sacrifice. She loved no less than any other mother. Perhaps she loved more, because the reality of the sacrifice lay constantly before her.

This experience is what Isobel Kuhn called *harnessed affections*. She knew well this subject, as can be gleaned from her biography, *In the Arena*. The Communists for years separated Isobel from her young daughter who was in a boarding school. After much turmoil, she gained victory over her situation and she was able to write:

It does not mean that after such an experience all affection is gone.

119

Just the very opposite is true. But affection in its natural state is dealt with. Affection, especially with intense natures, as it comes to us from Adam, runs to excess if given free rein. "And they that are Christ's have crucified the flesh with the affections and lusts [strong desires]." (Gal. 5:24).

Uncrucified love runs to inordinate affection and selfish possessiveness which blights rather than blesses . . . When we allow the Lord to nail our affections to the cross, we do not cease to love. We love more widely, but it is a love stripped of corrupting influences. Love is not killed—only the seed of corruption in natural affection is killed . . . This brought me into a realm of unexpected freedom and relaxation. Human loves did not cease to delight but they no longer enslaved . . . Crucified affections lift you into a realm of child-like simplicity and relaxation. The little child takes each day as it comes. He does not waste time imagining tomorrow's woes. He lives a day at a time. In the days that were to be ahead of me, I would again have partings and separations from loved ones that cost heart agony but never again did they overwhelm me.[10]

If it were possible, the second half of 1951 and the earlier part of 1952 were fuller than any years before. The E.E.C. was just now becoming known in Great Britain and the Stewarts were booked for months of preaching, teaching, and deputation work throughout England, Scotland and Ireland.

While her parents traveled, Sharon was placed for a while with Omri and Dorothy Jenkins, dear friends in Barry, Wales. An invitation came from Germany where the Wittenborgs were getting a solid work established. While there, a call came from Norway telling of continued blessing and asking if the Stewarts would please come. The Holy Spirit had begun to move afresh, and they felt themselves to be on the verge of revival. Sharon stayed in Germany with the Wittenborgs while James and Ruth hastened to find the Norwegian report true. Churches were being revived. There was a great ingathering of souls in the ensuing months. The encouraging story of the E.E.C. and the Stewart ministry for the next few years is recorded in *James Stewart, Missionary.*

For all through life I see a cross,
Where sons of God yield up their breath;
There is no gain except by loss,
There is no life except by death;
There is no vision but by faith,
No glory, but in bearing shame,
No justice but in taking blame;
And that Eternal Passion saith
Be emptied of glory and right and name.[11]

— ANONYMOUS

* * *

Men may misjudge thy aim,
Think they have cause to blame, say thou art wrong—
Hold thou thy quiet way, heed not what men may say;
Christ is the Judge—not they; fear not, be strong!
Be brave, and dare to stand alone against the foe;
Thy Saviour stood alone for thee long, long ago.
Be not a coward in the fight, look up! be strong!
The morn of victory is near—the day of song.

Chapter Fourteen
Plowed Under

James was often misunderstood. It came with the manner of man he was. Once he heard from God, that was it. Like Paul, he "conferred not with flesh and blood," (Galatians 1:16) but followed through with the holy vision. Such is acceptable with a lone missionary or evangelist, but for a mission director—well, it simply was not teamwork. There came the rub. The problem was not with the missionaries on the field. They saw James Stewart's heart, his passion, his faith, and they were ready to follow. But on the homefront, misunderstanding arose—*understandable* misunderstandings. From where would the money come for this project or that far-fetched idea of the director? Who was going to implement the plan? The Board did not understand the days and weeks this man lay before the Lord, seeking His mind on a matter, before coming up with "crazy" ideas.

For this reason James resigned as director of the E.E.C., retaining only an advisory role. Again he was set free to pursue a ministry which, led by the prompting of the Holy Spirit, was as diverse as it was demanding.

Ruth knew James better than any other human being. She knew his devotional life. She knew his great faith and how often that faith had been rewarded. But there were times that even she did not understand. There were times she wasn't sure if she could trust James Stewart not to make a mistake. Those were the times she cast herself on the Lord and trusted Him not to let them go astray.

Such was the case in 1958. In many ways, it was a typical year. In others it was not. At the time Ruth would have judged 1958 to be one of the most difficult years of their ministry. Certainly, God was mightily blessing their ministry. Missionaries were being thrust out to the fields.

The European Evangelistic Crusade was growing by leaps and bounds.

The Stewarts had been in constant demand by churches on both sides of the Atlantic and though not yet in their fifties, they appeared to be at the peak of their ministry. At the end of 1955 James had had a heart attack and had been laid aside for a time before God gave him a fresh commission.

But in 1958 problems arose at the mission headquarters in Philadelphia, and some called for James to step in and do something about it. Because dear friends, family and co-workers were involved, it was a difficult situation to referee.

"So often I wished James would set the record straight. 'Let's write them a letter and tell them the truth,' I'd say. But James never would. His meekness was never so evident as when he was attacked," said Ruth.

Being one flesh meant that Ruth bore the shame and reproach right along with James. And how hard on the flesh it was! If only James had defended himself against his accusers, she could have gotten some pleasure out of that. But to have to suffer in silence was another thing.

The Stewarts' schedule for the month of February, 1958, was full. They said good-bye to Sheila at Bob Jones University and to Jimmy at the Bob Jones Academy in Greenville, South Carolina. Though Ruth showed a brave face before the children, she was greatly burdened.

Sheila says she never hated to see us go so badly as she does this time. I wonder how Jimmy feels—does he miss us? Oh, dear Father, don't let him feel lonely. And Father, please, please cause him to cast himself on Thee for his very life. Sharon is with Mildred. Seems to be happy there. God bless her too.

On their way to Europe, James and Ruth first stopped off in Philadelphia and then Washington, D.C. What happened in Philadelphia, she would never talk about. "It's under the blood," she would say. But whatever happened sent them both to their knees in confusion and despair. For months, "the situation" as she referred to it in her diary, bore as a heavy weight on the two of them.

Scanning through Ruth's diary for 1958 one only sees dark threads of confusion, loss, misunderstanding, and failure. At times, Ruth could see only the mass of unsightly threads on the underside of the garment of life, and she would lose sight of the Master Weaver and His great design for her. How lovingly her Heavenly Father carried her through. Her journal gives witness. It is a significant record because in it are constant cries to the Lord and the blessed promises on which her very sanity rested during those days, weeks, and months of the inexplicable.

FEBRUARY 15 PHILADELPHIA, PENNSYLVANIA: Oh Lord, our God, never let us cease for one moment our utter dependence on Thee! Never let us act in the energy of the flesh, to dishonor Thee by trusting in the arm of flesh!

The Stewarts fared much better in their trip to Washington D.C. In August of 1957, they had received word that their friend of Eastern European days, Pastor Basil Malof, had passed away, leaving the entire responsibility of the Russian Bible Society for James to carry on. Though his plate was already full, James, after much thought and prayer, agreed to continue the work of this mighty champion of the Russian people. Exiled from Eastern Europe, Brother Malof had spent his last years preparing and publishing a Russian New Testament with Helps that was already being distributed among Russian-speakers. He also had been involved in producing a Russian Bible with a modern Russian type in which archaic words would be exchanged for understandable words.

FEBRUARY 16 WASHINGTON, DC: James is now President of the Russian Bible Society. We had a very encouraging Board meeting yesterday. We feel that once we sell the Bible House in Washington, D.C. we can begin to move forward in evangelizing the Russians. Now may the Lord give us wisdom for the E.E.C., Gospel Projects and now the R.B.S. Not to speak of the book we are about to write. We can't do everything. We must know what to concentrate on.

FEBRUARY 20 LISBON, PORTUGAL: We are on the plane for Lisbon with all of our luggage, including James' huge bag of books and the material he is working on for the Book. Now, dear old cheap diary, every page of you is blank, waiting for the Lord to fill. . . .

FEBRUARY 28 NEAR PALMA, MAJORCA: We have come on to Palma on the island of Majorca looking for sunshine. Because of his heart, James needs warmth. Here we hope to settle down and write—on Revival, and Pastor Malof, etc.

MARCH 9 NEAR PALMA, MAJORCA: See the Daily Light for today. ABLE!!

He is ABLE to keep; ABLE to do; ABLE to make; ABLE to succour; ABLE to save; ABLE to subdue! "Believe ye that I am able to do this?"

MARCH 10 NEAR PALMA, MAJORCA: Lord, keep me full of faith at the time when the bread gives out and there is no firm ground underneath and I walk by faith. Amen . . . So be it! Yesterday I prayed. The Lord stood before me and said, "Ask what ye will." I told Him all about the situation, the problems. He took the load and said, "Leave it to me." I told him about dear friends and family who had such deep needs. Oh, I told Him many things, and He listened and took notes. "I will work," He said.

MARCH 13 PALMA, MAJORCA: The dear Christian lady with whom we stayed the first few weeks here reminded me that every time we go into a new hotel room, I need to cleanse it (consciously cover it) by faith, with the precious blood of the Lord Jesus. But today I forgot. James suggested we move to another hotel, (the fifth one in as many weeks) and we did. I suggested the only way we would get warm was to go to Switzerland where hotel rooms were heated. I snapped at James and he retorted back. [*One must remember that for weeks on end, even months, they shared a room 24 hours a day in which they studied, worked and slept!*] Then I remembered. Oh, Lord, keep me so close to Thee I will be conscious of these things. I only mention the above because it came so forcibly to my mind. Oh, to be clean and pure and gentle—like Thee, my Lord! Holy as Thou art!

MARCH 23 PALMA AIRPORT: I have been under such an oppression with the situation in Philadelphia. A guilt complex as if I ought to do something—but what? Was I in the Spirit at all times? Had I prayed enough before speaking? And so my mind has been pressed down and occupied and my spirit low. This is not from the Lord; it is from the Enemy. But how to get deliverance? I know the answer. I can plead, I can claim, I can have ALL that He purchased for me. (Hebrews 2:14, 15.)

Forgetting those things that are behind—under the blood—I press toward the mark for the prize—what prize? The high calling in Christ Jesus. Oh, Lord, help me to relax in Thee. I have been under such a strain and irritable. Twice I have been so ashamed at showing irritability. Dark-brown ugliness. Where is the light, the joy, the gladness, the sweet patience? I would be like Thee, Lord—without sin; strong, firm, sweet, gentle.

MARCH 25 SAN FELIN DE GUIXOLES, PORTUGAL: "The work of righteousness is PEACE; the EFFECT. . . . . quietness and assurance." Oh, Lord, my Righteousness, Thou dost expel guilt from the mind and heart—the feeling of guilt that Satan would hound us with day and night. Thou dost not just stand for us, leaving us with guilt still on us, but "if we confess our sins . . . He is faithful and just. . . . to cleanse us from all unrighteousness." No more guilt. The blood cleanses!

MARCH 31 PORT BOU, CUSTOMS, SPAIN: This past week has been good. The room was large, the food good, the weather changeable. The main thing is that we got somewhere with the book. We have the overall picture now and have worked at least some on every chapter. Our premise is that God has a standard—a pattern or mold for the Christian life. Revival is the awakening of the soul to attain to that standard or return to it. Therefore, revival is God's will—God's desire. So we can pray in faith! This is a new approach to the theme and indeed, the only approach!

And so it was under physical weakness, distress of spirit, and a continual attack by the Enemy to defeat, distract, and destroy, that Ruth and James saw the book, *Opened Windows*, take shape. Perhaps it could be said this message came "out of" those very things.

Later, in *Evangelism in Print*, Ruth comments:

In the early part of 1958, James began to feel that the Lord would have him write a book on revival, bearing in mind our friends on the mission fields. His health had improved greatly so that he felt he could return to our mission field in Europe and hope that somewhere in the midst of our journeys we could find a quiet place to work.

But Satan knew of this plan and determined to frustrate it from the beginning. Circumstances over which we had no control began to press in on us from every side until it was impossible for us to think clearly—certainly not sufficiently to write a book! Confusion reigned at every turn of the road. There was no possible way for us to get around the existing circumstances. Neither could we go through them. The only thing for us was to rise above them, in the Name of Jesus, and mentally and spiritually fix our eyes, our minds, and our hearts on the Lord alone. Then resting in Him, we could carry on the task before us. . . .

There were many things which James could write from his own wealth of experience in the revivals in Eastern Europe (and Norway). . . . Yet, each day when we sat down to write, he was aware . . . that only those words spoken by the Spirit were worth recording. It was, in this case, though, not necessary to wrestle with the Spirit for His message; our constant wrestling was to keep ourselves above circumstances and resting in the Spirit.

APRIL 2 VALENCE, FRANCE: Stuck for the last 24 hours on a side track in Valence, France, due to train strike. "My peace I leave with you, MY relaxed attitude I give unto you!" Amen, Lord! I take thy relaxed attitude, knowing there are no second causes—all things come through or by Thee, and for Thy Glory. Now help us to settle to study today, or pray. The train is now moving slowing toward Switzerland. This was all His will though our money is gone, but today I have been reading Hudson Taylor, "The Man Who Believed God!"

APRIL 3 GENEVA, SWITZERLAND: Have met with the Lamberts, who are the RBS representatives here in Switzerland. Left Russia three years ago. They want to go to the World Exhibition at Brussels. They hear there are to be over a million Russians to go through there in the next six months. Lamberts need Scriptures, tracts, etc. Another project for James.

APRIL 4 MONTREUX, SWITZERLAND: Good church services, but I could not be at peace until I wrote that letter of apology to E.M. It seems silly when there are such larger problems and misunderstandings, but I am responsible for my own sins of the flesh and of the spirit. When I express the flesh, I must repent and apologize! I wrote the letter. Now, Blessed Spirit, it is in Thy Hands to prepare the heart of E. to receive it.

There must be no shadow—no faint suggestion of shadow between my Lord and myself. All must be in the light; I must be clean and without guile, pleasing, pleasing, oh, Lord, to Thee!

APRIL 6 WEGGIS, SWITZERLAND: My meditation for today has been Phil. 3:10 and 21. I am convinced that we shall never know the power of His resurrection until we know the fellowship of His suffering—sufferings in reproach, in being misunderstood, in being slighted, in knowing hardship for His cause in the world. His sufferings were more than physical; they were mental—agony of mind and soul and spirit—sufferings caused by His perfect obedience to His Father—obedience in attitude and actions so opposed to the world.

APRIL 15 CLARENS, SWITZERLAND: With the Tchividian's family. Mr. T. wanted to give us a new American car and I knew the Lord did not

Ruth and Gladys, taken 1912 in Mobile, Alabama.

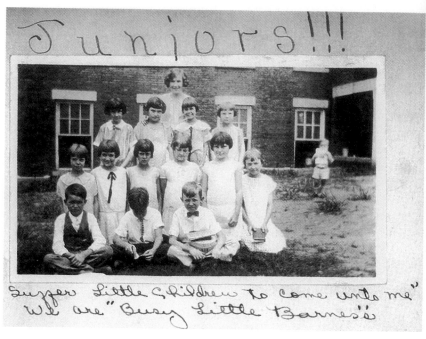

Suffer Little Children to come unto me"
We are "Busy Little Barnes's

Ruth's class of Juniors that she taught when she was fifteen.

**The last family photograph taken before Ruth left
for the mission field, 1937.**

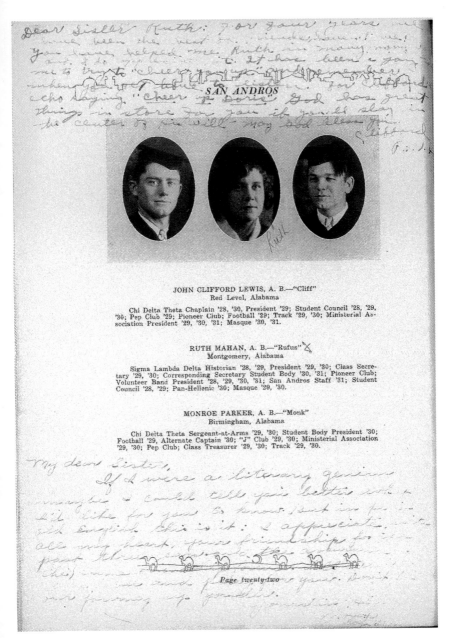

SAN ANDROS

JOHN CLIFFORD LEWIS, A. B.—"Cliff"
Red Level, Alabama

Chi Delta Theta Chaplain '28, '30, President '29; Student Council '28, '29, '30; Pep Club '29; Pioneer Club; Football '29; Track '29, '30; Ministerial Association President '29, '30, '31; Masque '30, '31.

RUTH MAHAN, A. B.—"Rufus"
Montgomery, Alabama

Sigma Lambda Delta Historian '28, '29, President '29, '30; Class Secretary '29, '30; Corresponding Secretary Student Body '30, '31; Pioneer Club; Volunteer Band President '28, '29, '30, '31; San Andros Staff '31; Student Council '28, '29; Pan-Hellenic '30; Masque '29, '30.

MONROE PARKER, A. B.—"Monk"
Birmingham, Alabama

Chi Delta Theta Sergeant-at-Arms '29, '30; Student Body President '30; Football '29, Alternate Captain '30; "J" Club '29, '30; Ministerial Association '29, '30; Pep Club; Class Treasurer '29, '30; Track '29, '30.

Page twenty-two

Ruth, graduating from Bob Jones College, 1934, pictured here with her "buddies" Clifford Lewis and Monroe Parker.

Ruth's engagement
picture.

"Yours because His"
Ruth
Col. 1:18

**The young man who stole Ruth
from the Southern Baptist —
James Stewart at age 27.**

Her girls at the Women's Training School in Budapest, 1937.

The wedding that became "an event," May 23, l938.

James, Ruth, Sheila and Jimmy — the Stewart family during the early days of the European Evangelistic Crusade.

With the birth of Sharon, the Stewart family was now complete. Taken 1953.

**Bess Cornell, Steve Torbico, and Ethel Kaye, early workers in the E.E.C.,
taken in Italy.**

David and Elsie Stewart, who played support roles both in the E.E.C. and later in Gospel Projects.

Gospel Projects workers in England and Scotland, 1967.

Vlado and Ruth Fajfr starting out together on an adventure that lasted 24 years. Taken near their cottage.

**Ruth speaks English with one of her "boys," Peter Hrubo,
over a cup of tea.**

**Jana Fajfr, daughter by second marriage, Ivana Tomalova, daughter by
spiritual travail, and Sheila Doom, daughter by birth seen here taking a
walk with Ruth. Her other daughter, Sharon took the picture.**

Surrounded by her "children and her children's children," Ruth rejoiced to see the church in Zilina, Slovakia grow.

Vlado and Ruth also rejoiced over the growth in the Fajfr family, here pictured during her 90th birthday celebration.

The Wilkerson children, Noemi and Chad, along with their mother Sharon, pose with Grandma during a rare visit.

Just before their grandma was leaving for Czechoslovakia, Susan, Robbie and Jamie Doom had this picture taken.

Ruth on her eighty-ninth birthday, 1998.

want it . . . so did James, but we only prayed. Now the Lord has told him to give us his black Pontiac. A good car, but not so imposing. HE doeth all things well. Money is coming in also to pay our publishers, also for personal needs. "Oh, that men would praise the Lord for His goodness . . ." Now we must pray as we will be meeting with our missionaries and they will be wanting to know about the situation at the Home Office. What to do? What to say? I wish I could get clear guidance as some do. But He has only said, "Christ in the midst of thee is Mighty." And, "The battle is the Lord's; he will fight for you and ye shall hold your peace." What more can we do than "Stand still and see the salvation of the Lord"? . . . I get no leading, no moving of the Spirit, about taking things in hand. Yet it seems awful to have power to act and not act, to stand by and see things "go down the drain," as it were. But I believe God that He is able to do, and He will do!

APRIL 21 CHATEAUX-D'OEX, SWITZERLAND: James has been to Germany to meet with Mr. Hallzon who prints Russian Scriptures for RBS. Arranged to print 20,000 N.T.s for Brussels. Now, how to pay? Mr. M. says no money is coming into RBS—a bottle neck. But we are shut up to the Lord. Also we have difficulty finding an interpreter for our meetings with Hungarian refugees in Austria next month. And the book. We must finish it! James feels we must trust the Lord for the book ministry now more than ever, for more and more this is coming to be our ministry.

APRIL 30 SALZBURG, AUSTRIA: Would you believe that when we went to pick up the new car from Mr. T., one of his girls had been down to the town and bought a camel coat for me, with hat and gloves to match! Oh, I can't stand too much kindness! We drove away in our newly-received car and me in a new outfit!

Now in Salzburg we made contact with a man who is key to contact with Hungarian refugees. Meeting the refugees, one feels so helpless. We have little money, no influence to get them moved out of the refugee camps, but we know the gospel and the power of our Lord Jesus and we can give love. James and I spoke to them and afterwards I sang a Hungarian hymn and they all joined in. Now the pastor has invited us for a week of meetings at the Hungarian School. We are visiting many refugee camps in the next few days. Dreadful conditions.

MAY 31 BRUSSELS, BELGIUM: We have been to the Fair in Brussels. The Lord has provided a place to stay for the Lamberts with a sweet Slavic family here. The Lamberts are elderly, feeble, but full of enthusiasm for the Lord and His work!

Ruth's next journal entry is shocking. In less than a month after writing a book, ministering to refugees, and preparing Russian literature for the World's Fair, they were now in Scotland! Well, that was life with the Stewarts. Why Scotland? One must go back to 1954, when James, on his way to a meeting in Chattanooga, felt such a heavy burden for his native land of Scotland that he was forced to pull over his car and pray. The next day after his meeting, a man with an obvious Scottish accent grabbed him by the shoulder and said with tears in his eyes, "Somebody has got to do something about Scotland. The gospel has died out of our beloved country."

James was startled, but the two incidents coming together confirmed to him the Lord's message. More than a year later, James and Ruth traveled to Scotland to personally survey the situation.

JUNE 4 PITLOCHRY, SCOTLAND: Beautiful day! After the long drive of the last few days, we are finally in the Borders. We visited Kelso, Yetholm, Kirk Yetholm, St. Boswells, Jedburgh, Selkirk, Galashiels, Peebles . . . We have gotten a pretty good idea of the physical situation of the Borders. Now we pray for a worker, an evangelist, a couple, maybe. One the Lord will raise up and equip for the task of evangelizing these places.

JUNE 8 BORDERS, SCOTLAND AND ENGLAND: The more people we see and talk with, the more depressed James becomes about the whole situation. There is such a deadness—such lethargy. James is almost despondent about it all. What can we do? Nothing. But God can do all things—and we can do all things through Christ. In one week of fasting and prayer with those who have been praying, the Lord can work wonders. Oh, Lord! I don't know, but surely you want to do something definite here—something lasting. This 8th day of June, we are baffled, perplexed, heart-sick. Give us some Word, some promise—a vision of what Thou art going to do. Lead us, Lord.

JUNE 13 BERWICK-UPON-TWEED, ENGLAND: We are here to look for a house for an evangelistic center. Our friend, Dr. Brown-Henry in Glasgow also has a burden for the Borders. He feels if we are to do anything definite, we must stay here until a work is established. But what of Gospel Projects and R.B.S.? And the book-writing? If not us, who?

JUNE 18 JEDBURGH, SCOTLAND: The Gospel Hall here will seat easily 250-300 people, has an organ, but needs a great deal of cleaning. Ten old ladies meet here to pray once a week, but this is mostly for fellowship. The place is dead. Many want to buy the building for secular purposes. We must get the title deeds and resurrect the hall and the work. As I looked about at the dirty Gospel texts, etc., I could have wept, like Ezra, who found the Temple destroyed and the people backslidden. Someone must weep over Jedburgh!

JULY 5 LONDON, ENGLAND: Have just heard disturbing news again about situation in Philadelphia. The Lord gave me earlier Mark 5:35 to prepare me. The comment on the reading was, "Another thing we learn from this passage is that Jesus never comes too late, never waits too long. It certainly seemed that He had tarried too long this time; but when we see how it all came out, we are sure that He made no mistake. He waited that He might do a more glorious work . . . So we have one more lesson on letting the Lord have His own way with us, even in answering our prayers." Now, Lord, may this be so in our case. Bring to nought everything which is not of Thyself. Thou hast a perfect plan. Do it for Thy glory.

JULY 25 YETHOLM, SCOTLAND: Moved into the house here on Saturday. It has seven rooms—five beds. We have our temporary evangelistic center here. Margaret Stenhouse, a candidate of the mission for France is coming to help. Also a Swiss lady under CIM will help with the children. Meetings are lined up for Evangelist Charlie Main. I read a quote from Spurgeon which said, "If one drop of the oil of the joy of the Holy Ghost should fall into hell, it would relieve the torment of all the inhabitants!" Oh, Blessed Holy Ghost, let one drop of that oil fall on me and on many here in the Borders. Oh God! Move among the people here—Convict of sin, of rebellion, of Thy righteousness, and of judgment. Come down and deliver.

AUGUST 24 NORTH BERWICK, SCOTLAND: There is to be a meeting in Holland with the missionaries concerning the situation in P. James is not going. He tells me that it is never the Lord's will for him to get into a controversy. He takes his stand and stands unflinchingly, but he will not fight back for his own reputation. It is in order to keep his soul and mind free for the messages of God for His people. I can see now how Satan would draw him in and get him involved and all stirred up so he cannot be a spiritual blessing to the saints. "The battle is the Lord's," I read again.

AUGUST 30 JEDBURGH, SCOTLAND: Saturday. Grand Opening of the Jedburgh Hall. We had spent days cleaning, painting, redoing the building. Then we knelt and prayed for Him to fill it. Now people came from all over the Borders. All wanted to give their testimony to bring James up to date on what the Lord had done for them since he was a boy and preached in this area. Afterwards we poured outside onto the town square for an open-air meeting. Tremendous.

AUGUST 31 JEDBURGH, SCOTLAND: Sunday. Our faith was weak but in the afternoon the place was full—over 100 children. At 6:00 the hall was packed with adults. We had visited every house in the town and given out a gospel booklet. Lord, cause them to read—to reflect on "Ye Must be Born-Again." Now, it is time for Thee to send a full-time worker for this field. Thrust forth. Expel laborers.

James had been asked to give a week of lectures on the topic of evangelism at Bob Jones University in Greenville, South Carolina, where two of his children attended. When he thought of the potential audience of over 3,000 young people, many of them preparing for the ministry at home and abroad, he was excited. But now, with those lectures less than six months away, the magnitude of the task hit him full force. Besides, he had more in mind than the current student body at the University. He had received letters from Christians in Nigeria, Ghana, the Philippines and other places begging for help in learning how to faithfully preach the gospel. These messages put into book form, he reasoned, could meet the urgent need of evangelical workers around the world. To help James in this endeavor, a dear friend, John Owens, provided a quiet room at Hotel Rosat in Switzerland. The setting was absolutely breathtaking and a perfect place for studying and preparing the messages.

SEPTEMBER 14 CHATEAUX D'OEX, SWITZERLAND: There was no place to get quiet for a minute in Scotland. We were in constant demand. We are back here to rest and James is seeking the Lord's pattern for the book—his lectures on Evangelism for Bob Jones University in February. Now, give Thy plan for the lectures. Make James to hear Thy voice; inspire him; come upon Him, O Spirit of Truth, with Thy message for the Church.

SEPTEMBER 19 SAME: Time flies. Arise at 6:30. Breakfast at 8. Walk and then work till noon. Lunch, a wee rest and work again till 5. Walk,

132

supper, work till 9, sleep, and repeat the process. The lectures are coming along fine.

SEPTEMBER 23 THUN, SWITZERLAND: We took the day off, but my heart and mind are in Holland where the missionaries have assembled for their conference. Daily Light for today promises the help of a Father who child-trains, but who is faithful to help. Ezra 9:9 "Our God hath not forsaken us." I Sam. 12:22 "The Lord will not forsake his people for his great name's sake; because it hath pleased the Lord to make you his people."

OCTOBER 2 'T BRUNDPUNT, HOLLAND: Missionary wife here tells me that the missionary body voted unanimously and the die is cast. Dear Lord, this diary witnesses to our cry of faith to Thee to work Thy will at any cost. Now, we ask Thy guidance in all things during the next months for Thy Glory. Continue to work and heal all involved.

OCTOBER 3 SAME: Oswald Chambers said, "One of the finest characteristics of a noble man is that of mature patience, not that of impulsive action. It is easy to be determined, and the curious thing is that the more small-minded a man is the more easily he makes up his mind." This helps me understand James—that "mature patience" which causes him to "wait on the Lord" about all matters. Chambers goes on to say, "To be strong is not the strength of activity, but the strength of being . . . to be dependable means to be strong in the sense of disciplined reliability." Paul says, "I do not frustrate (make void) the grace of God."

OCTOBER 19 OREBRO, SWEDEN: Came here to assess the RBS ministry here. Yesterday, my mind and spirit were concerned about many things . . . The Enemy would make it seem as if the bottom of our lives is about to fall out. But Lord, you have said "When a man's ways please the Lord, he maketh even his enemies to be at peace with him." Now, O Lord, accomplish Thy purposes in all this . . . Get beauty for ashes out of our sufferings. Give beauty for ashes for Thy own Name's sake. And . . . take away burdens Thou dost not want us to bear.

OCTOBER 25 SAME: "Why art thou cast down, O my soul? and why art thou disquieted within me? hope in God: for I shall yet praise him, who is the health of my countenance, and my God." Psalms 43:5.

In *Letters From Ruth*, she tells more of the Lord's comfort to her during this time.

133

One night when James was not with me, I received news of another blow against the Mission. I panicked. I was in great anguish of soul and confusion of mind. I awoke in the middle of the night with the problem still harassing my mind. I cried desperately unto the Lord for a "word" which would quiet my heart. "Show me from Thy Word that Thou art still on the Throne and that Thy hand is still upon the work which Thou hast wrought through us," I prayed. I took my Bible and opened it, trusting the Lord to lead me to just the passage from which He would speak to me. I was led to Isaiah, "Bind up the testimony, seal the law among my disciples. And I will wait upon the Lord, that hideth his face from the house of Jacob, and I will look for Him." Isaiah 8:16,17.

I understood the words, "I will wait" for that is what we had been doing for many months. And we had been really "looking to Him" to work on our behalf and for His glory. Still, until now things had grown only worse, it seemed. I noticed where Isaiah said over and over, "The Lord said unto me . . . The Lord spake unto me. . . ." Were these words which the Lord spoke to Isaiah the "testimony" which he was to bind together and tie with a strong cord, as it were, so they would be preserved for a future time? . . . Then, like a flash I saw it! When God speaks, whether it is for good or bad, every word is to be preserved, for it will surely come to pass. Therefore Isaiah said, "I will wait . . . I will look for Him (or I will hope in Him)." God's Word cannot fail and He will work according to plan. Why do I look for a new promise? What is wrong with the ones in which I have taken comfort already? . . .

Then a marginal reference to the verse led me to Isaiah 30:18 and I read, "And therefore will the LORD wait, that he may be gracious unto you, and therefore will he be exalted, that he may have mercy upon you: for the LORD is a God of judgment: blessed are all they that wait for him."

"So that is the answer," I cried. "All this time we have been waiting for You to work, You have been waiting for the proper moment to step in and settle the whole matter, a moment when the conditions will be such that through this settlement Your name will be exalted through Your gracious working." . . . All the time we thought He was asleep and doing nothing, He was actually studying the situation from every angle and moving behind the scenes to bring about just the right solution for the final move which would release us. Oh, why do we find it so hard to wait on Him? Is it not because we lose sight of His relationship to our needs and His concern for us in our problems?

Little more is said in the following entries of Ruth's diary except to show that at this point matters looked darker than ever before. Surely she would have despaired had not the Lord spoken to her. By November, she was back in the States and on her way to see her children and family in South Carolina and Alabama. James had promised to meet a friend in Israel after spending a few days in Turkey. So for a few short weeks Ruth and James were apart.

At night when the visiting was over and the house quiet, Satan would come again to tempt Ruth and try to confuse her. "Where is the Lord in all this?" he would whisper. "If you had just stepped in and done this or that. . . ." But as surely as the accusations came, so did her Heavenly Father's quiet assurance.

> O Thou Who art my quietness, my deep repose,
> My rest from strife of tongues, my holy hill,
> Fair is Thy pavilion, where I hold me still.
> Back let them fall from me, my clamorous foes,
> Confusions multiplied;
> From crowding things of sense I flee, and in Thee hide.
> Until this tyranny be overpast,
> Thy hand will hold me fast;
> What though the tumult of the storm increase,
> Grant to Thy servant strength, O Lord, and bless with peace.[12]

Fresh demands are placed on the Christian who travels to the rugged heights of the Spirit-filled life. Fresh demands of obedience. Fresh demands of faith. Fresh demands of commitment. The way up is down. The way to live is to die—to die not only to sin, but to one's reputation and to what other people think of you. The Lord says, "Them that honour me I will honour." The Lord was teaching Ruth that He would take care of His children's honor even while advancing His own. She could trust Him to do so, without fretting or questioning.

When you ripe fields behold,
Waving to God their sheaves of gold,
Be sure some corn of wheat has died,
Some saintly soul been crucified;
Someone has suffered, wept and prayed,
And fought hell's legions undismayed.

* * *

Not in vain the tedious toil
On unresponsive soil,
Travail, tears in secret shed
Over hopes that lay as dead,
All in vain, thy faint heart cries,
Not in vain, thy Lord replies:
Nothing is too good to be;
Then believe, believe to see.

Did thy labour turn to dust?
Suffering—did it eat like rust,
Till the blade that once was keen
As a blunted tool is seen?
Dust and rust thy life's reward?
Slay the thought; believe thy Lord,
When thy soul is in distress
Think upon His faithfulness.

But consider, was it vain
All the travail on the plain?
For the bud is on the bough;
It is green where thou didst plough.
Listen, tramp of little feet,
Call of little lambs that bleat,
Hearken to it. Verily,
Nothing is too good to be.[13]

— AMY CARMICHAEL

Chapter Fifteen

But If It Die — Much Fruit

The future is hidden from us. If we get any glimpse of it at all, it is usually through tear-dimmed eyes, eyes that squint and strain to see by faith what God is doing. The just do live by faith. The just must live by faith!

Hindsight is different. It sees more clearly. In later years as Ruth looked back on the Stewarts' ministry, the clarity of what God was doing in those excruciating days of 1958 hit full force. Oh, His way was perfect! All those heart-tearing experiences were important for God to get His servants just where He wanted them—to turn them in a new direction.

As Ruth and James had only begun to see in 1958, the book ministry was to become perhaps the most permanent and crucial aspect of their future ministry. The response to *Heaven's Throne Gift, Opened Windows,* and *Evangelism Without Apology* forced them to see the great need to put in print those truths the Lord had taught them and had used to change the lives of others. Those first three books were James Stewart's message to the Church.

In *Evangelism in Print*, Ruth tells the thrilling story of their literature ministry and gives the aim of their writings:

> The aim of all of our writings has been to promote evangelism by encouraging the saints to seek the fullness of the Holy Spirit for their individual lives and revival for the Church. When the Holy Spirit is at work through a revived assembly, souls are always saved through the effective witness of its members among the lost.

No matter how heavy the schedule or how inconvenient the setting, if a book was growing inside James Stewart, it had to come out! Ruth was soon able to recognize the *symptoms*. She considered herself a mid-wife who could not choose when nor under what circumstances a book should be *born*! Her business was to catch the baby! *Open-Air Evangelism* was written during a time of real blessing in Norway when James and Ruth were speaking five and six times a day. They wrote *William Chalmers Burns* while being detained with car trouble in a little village in southern Spain. *Heaven's Throne Gift* was actually typed out in Salzburg, Austria, and *Lordship of Christ* in Odense, Denmark.

About this time Ruth wrote to one of her daughters:

> Dad and I are so very much interested in your desire to write. This is an open field with unlimited prospects. . . . .Just now you want to learn the principles of grammar and expressing yourself in an easy, flowing, expressive way . . . Oh, there is so much I could say about this business of writing, for that is what we are wrapped up in just now. The Lord has given us the messages, and our task is to clothe them in words and sentences which will be alive—which will hold the reader so that he cannot let go—and when the book is finished or laid aside, the thoughts will go over and over in his head—gripping thoughts which will revolutionize the one who reads. Of course, in the final analysis, this is the work of the Holy Spirit, but our part as human instruments is so important.

Ruth's old friend, Dr. Bob Jones, Jr., often teased her that James Stewart might have a ghost writer, but that she was a very substantial ghost! It is true that James could never have written the books by himself. Though extremely well-read and well-spoken, he only had an eighth grade education! How like the Lord to bring together a future author with an ardent student of Miss Gussie! To watch them work was to witness a study in two working as one. James would give a few sentences, then he would pause. Ruth would suggest a better wording of a phrase or a more suitable word. Then they would go on, stopping here and there to decide if a thought should be placed in the front or at the end of the paragraph. Ruth was always aware of the necessity of unity, coherence and emphasis! And when a book was finished and read over, a sense of awe would settle over them.

> At the close of each chapter, when we read back what we had written, we could but marvel. Not only was the message there which our own

hearts felt, but there was little need to change anything! The Holy Spirit had exchanged our impotence for His ability

Ruth's description of their work on *Heaven's Throne Gift* was repeated over and over.

Often the question is asked, How do the writings of James and Ruth Stewart speak so powerfully and relevantly today? They were written forty and fifty years ago, and most have no more than a hundred pages. There can be only one answer. They were written under the leadership and the anointing of the Holy Spirit. Many of the books were written during, or just following, times of spiritual awakening. They breathe the very spirit of revival to the extent that the reader himself longs to see God do it again.

James encouraged Ruth to write books with messages especially for women and she did. She wrote *The Prototype Church: Studies in I Thessalonians, Book of Numbers, Our Heavenly Inheritance: Studies in Joshua, Better Than Wine: Studies in Song of Solomon,* and *Evangelism in Print.* Writing was second nature to Ruth and she joyously set down in words the precious truths the Lord revealed to her from His Word. As an author she is probably best known for her studies on the Song of Solomon. In it she taught the vital relationship of Christ with the believer, enabling women to easily grasp the correlation between the Heavenly Bridegroom and His redeemed Bride.

In commenting on the passage, "Who is she that cometh up from the wilderness leaning on her beloved," Ruth explains:

> To the Bride, her Beloved has come to mean more than her Saviour who has lifted her out of the pit of sin and shame—out of the wilderness of darkness and death—and given her a new name and a new nature. She has come to know Him now as her High Priest, Who has divine ability to help and sustain her and whose love makes Him willing that she should lean wholly upon Him for support. She finds Him not only willing, but pleased when she casts herself upon Him, delighting in Him and strengthening herself on Him.
>
> She has at last learned to relax in the love of her Beloved and trust Him fully for all things . . . Leaning on her Beloved implies sweet fellowship, mutual understanding, perfect confidence, and a blessed oneness which was not evident in the beginning of their life together.

She has known His forgiveness and restoration. She has come to appreciate His plans and purposes for herself and for the world. She has learned discipline through suffering and she is now conscious of her own weakness. They walk together as one; He in His strength and she, in her weakness, drawing from Him grace and strength for each step. There is perfect peace and rest now in this union.

Years later, evangelists, pastors, and ordinary Christians hungry for communion with the Lord and for revival are still reading James and Ruth's books. Yet, whenever she would go back and read one of their books she would always feel totally detached, as though she had nothing to do with it. In her mind, the Lord wrote through them to meet the hunger of His people. She and James were only channels.

* * *

From the moment the Lord laid Scotland on his heart, James pushed forward. He first tried to interest British Christians in the need. Many came to help evangelize, but all passed on to another sphere of service. Few seemed interested in tackling pioneer work such as would be necessary to bring the gospel back to a hardened and indifferent people. James' heart, as Ruth's, was broken. He had glorious memories of his own early ministry in the Borders of England and Scotland where the gospel had been bright and the believers fervent. When he talked to the scattered groups of believers here and there, he understood it was going to take more than a few summer evangelistic meetings to turn the situation around. Scotland was ripe for missionaries, and if the British would not answer the call, he would appeal to the Americans.

In 1959, Sheila, a junior at Bob Jones University, made a trip with her parents to Scotland. Her father arranged for her to have children's meetings in some of the towns where there was no gospel witness. The response among the children was so great that Sheila caught the vision and burden of her father and resolved to return when she finished school.

Meanwhile, James talked, ate, and dreamed of Scotland. No matter where he was ministering, the burden never left him. After a stirring challenge given to a group of preacher boys at Bob Jones University, four young men stepped forward to go on a summer team: Phil Porter, Ken Bender, Ray St. John, and Bob Doom. At the end of that summer the team returned to the States, but Sheila remained to start a work among the children in the towns and villages of the Borders.

A year later, one of the team members from Indiana contacted the Stewarts and told them that the Lord was calling him back to the Borders. He was ready to go immediately, stepping out on faith and believing that as he obeyed, the Lord would meet his needs. That young man was Bob Doom. Seeing Bob as an answer to their prayers, James and Ruth encouraged him to go and agreed for him to be sent out under Gospel Projects, the name they had given to their new ministry. Bob sold some cattle he had owned jointly with his father and paid for his ticket. With only a couple of hundred dollars more, he boarded the boat for Britain. When he arrived, the immigration officer didn't quite know what to do with this young man who claimed he was going to "live by faith."

"We'll let anyone in for three months," the immigration agent told Bob, as he stamped his passport and let him go.

Before leaving home, Bob had contacted a couple of dear older ladies in Berwick-upon-Tweed, a town just across the Scottish border and inside England. The two ladies bravely maintained a witness in their town by keeping their mission open and inviting guests to speak. Bob told them of the Lord's call, and they immediately wrote back giving him an invitation to come to them, and work out from their place evangelizing the area.

Meanwhile, Sheila was back in the States for health reasons. She also had gone to the Borders under Gospel Projects. Jokingly, Bob wrote to her, "You may be the Number One project, but I doubt they'll ever get you off the ground!"

During that first summer of working together they had come to know each other, but now, as Sheila returned, they found a special joy in discovering how the Lord had given to both of them a burden for the Borders and a desire to see the Lord pour out His blessing in revival. As they prayed and opened up their hearts to one another, they discovered the Lord was dealing with each individually about knowing the fullness of the Holy Spirit. After much prayer and seeking the face of the Lord, both together and separately, they saw the Lord gloriously answer their prayers.

Sheila wrote her mother who recorded in her diary:

A letter from Sheila tells of the Lord doing a new thing for both her and Bob this past weekend. She is like a ready flower opening to the sun! I must pray that this will be a new beginning for them and the ministry there in the Borders.

In the coming weeks as Sheila and Bob ministered together, they shared with each other their joy in allowing the Holy Spirit to take control of their lives and how everything was different, even in how each saw the other. By the end of the summer, Bob had a word from the Lord that Sheila was to be his wife. She already had been drawn to this young man who was sold out to the Lord just like her father. In August, Sheila and Bob announced their engagement.

When the Lord brought Sheila and Bob together, Ruth wrote them:

It is so sweet to hear Dad daily thank God for His love gift of a new son. He has prayed for so long, as you know, for the one whom the Lord was preparing for you. Now his appreciation for this answered prayer is really touching. He talks, plans, prays, and lives the Borders so much that God surely will do a special work there above what we have seen yet . . . we had a lovely letter from Jim which made us rejoice for he seems to be happy (at Birmingham Bible College in England). With all the interests we have in the Lord's work, our greatest concern is for our three (four now!) children and if things are not right for and with you, then things are not right period. We love you in the flesh, but our desires for you in the Lord are far greater. That is why you are such a comfort to us and rejoice our hearts so greatly.

The intensive evangelistic thrust made in the Borders was the beginning of a work that spread to Stirling, Glasgow, and Aberdeen. In 1968, the Stewarts were able to write a newsletter, showing how in just four years the Lord had expanded the ministry of Gospel Projects from being a support agency, helping seasoned missionaries with various projects necessary for evangelism, to being a sending agency for a fresh flow of missionaries.

The past months have been the best in the history of the work, for which we praise the Lord. We traveled in Great Britain and almost all the countries in western Europe except Portugal and Italy. Here is a brief summary of the work of Gospel Projects during the past few months.

Edinburgh: Bob and Sheila Doom carry on a very active ministry in the capital city. They have started the John Knox Memorial Baptist Church (later known as Bellevue Baptist Church), hold a monthly Truth For Youth rally, and evangelistic campaigns in different parts of the city. Open-air meetings are held in the center of the city where hundreds hear the gospel nightly. Besides this, Bob has a ministry called Light and Life Films.

Also in Edinburgh are Barbara Kehoe and Archie Martin who help in the various ministries and outreaches both in the city and in the evangelization of surrounding areas.

Eyemouth is a fishing village of 4,000 people. The Benders have labored here for five years. They have started the Free Baptist Church and built a church building which seats about eighty people. The Benders have about five children's classes a week in Eyemouth alone, and also visit four other towns each week for classes.

Kelso, where Spenser and Earlene work, is the scene of expansion through the gospel book store and the purchasing for themselves of a small hotel which they are making into a Christian Center. This house is situated in the moors, near the gospel hall where Spenser pastors in the village of *Yetholm*. "Peniel" will be used for evangelism and Bible teaching for youth.

Haddington, the birthplace of John Knox, has a population of some 8,000 people. There is only one known believer in the entire town. David and Susan Straub labor there and are praying for money to be able to buy a building for an evangelistic center where they can have a Bible book store and coffee bar for young people as well as a meeting place to start a church.

Hawick: Barbara Finnemore continues with all her classes in Hawick, one of the Borders larger towns. Remember the rally each Sunday night after the services in the churches.

Lauder, Greenlaw and Berwick: Jan Bunting and June Mullinix live in Edinburgh but travel to these towns for children's classes. God is really blessing their ministry.

Norwich, England: Jimmy and Jennifer Stewart are busy among the teenagers in Norwich and East Anglia. Norwich, a city of 100,000 is the capital of East Anglia. Jimmy goes each day from coffee bar to coffee bar and cafe to cafe in his task to reach young people. As you know, his is a difficult and sometimes dangerous work. They also have a Bible study and prayer meeting every Monday night in their home. Jimmy is teaching the book of Ephesians. He also conducts a Bible study every Wednesday night at one of the Railway Missions and on Sundays works with the Free Evangelical Church at Blofield, the village in which he lives.

France and Austria: The same triumph can be told of the work of Miriam Wheeler in France and Nell Pearson in Austria. They report that this past summer has been the greatest yet as they have been busy with their helpers in camps and evangelism in the needy towns and villages. Miriam Wheeler has a Colportage Camp in northern France from which she and her workers evangelize the surrounding towns and villages. As you know, Nell Pearson has the Church on Wheels which is pulled by a large truck to different locations. Nell has set up some glorious campaigns this summer in Salzburg and other towns, using evangelists to come in and do the preaching.

In U.S.A., we would value your prayers for Elsie Stewart and Bernita Ellis that God will give them the physical strength and spiritual wisdom in all their heavy duties. All of us who are missionaries know that we could not do our work on the field unless they were holding the ropes back home.

When James and Ruth Stewart's ministry was incorporated into Gospel Projects, James' older brother David and his wife Elsie offered to serve in the ministry as secretary and treasurer, and even more importantly, as prayer-partners and encouragers. Their enthusiasm for mission work was equal to any of the missionaries on the field. To these they wrote encouraging letters along with the business concerns. David often sent to supporters unforgettable poems that were sometimes comforting and sometimes challenging.

> God's thanks to you, our Christian friends
> Who to our work give wings.
> Without your aid we could not do
> So many precious things.
>
> We could not give God's word of truth
> To those in other lands
> Unless we first received from you
> Support of loving hands.
>
> You give to us the prayerful heart

That calls God's blessing down
On all our humble efforts to
Add jewels to Christ's crown . . .

For some must go—while others give
And more must hold the rope
As God sends forth His messengers
With words of life and hope.

So let us sow the gospel seed
Through weather foul or fair,
And we shall see the harvest grow
In answer to our prayer.

When the Lord took David in May, 1967, Elsie and Bernita Ellis carried on his duties faithfully until their retirement in the middle 1980s.

Workers continued to come—Roy and Valerie Williams, Clyde and Nancy Hiseler, John and Margie Schuch, James and Ruth Hughes, Lillian Shafer, Vickie Todd, Steve and Janice Worth, and Merle Ventrello, who later married Barbara Kehoe. These were some of the long-term missionaries. Every summer, teams of college and university students would come from the States to help in evangelism and often found themselves being ministered to as much as they ministered.

Ruth looked on these young missionaries as her own children, to be counseled, to be prayed for, to be encouraged, and even at times to be rebuked in her own very special way! In return, they loved her as their spiritual mother and in person and in letters poured out their hearts to her. Her diaries reveal the burden she took seriously before the Throne of Grace.

NOVEMBER 29, 1967: Barbara Kehoe needs someone (of Thy choice) to work with her. Surely Thou hast such a man or woman for her and Thou wilt reveal in due time. Have been reading F. B. Meyer who says, "The ideal servant" in Isaiah 49:2-6—even he must be hidden for a while and see apparent failure. Even so, Lord, Thou wilt bring forth Barbara into a glorious ministry for Thy Glory. Thank you, for this promise. And Lily is not doing well physically. Oh, Lord, touch her and heal her body.

DECEMBER 23, 1967: From Isaiah 52:13-53. Our Lord (from eternity) was radiant in the dazzling beauty of perfect moral excellence. What condescension! That he should have come to breathe our tainted air! Lord, Thou shalt see of the travail—or through the travail—and shall be satisfied—in Edinburgh, in Glasgow, in the Borders. Men and women shall know Thy power and Thy holiness and shall bow before Thee in deep contrition. Though it tarry, wait for it, for it shall surely come. O Love which sorrows after the souls of men, Love through ME.

OCTOBER, 16, 1968: Learned today that Sue Straub has a "bone deposit" and can't afford the expensive operation. If this is a testing or discipline time, O Lord, hold her and Dave steady and DO THY PERFECT WORK. Only keep them in Thy will and bring them back to Scotland in Thy time.

JULY 25, 1969: Praying much for Sheila in her ministry of intercession. I cover her by faith with the blood of Jesus for protection. For Jan in all her needs physical and spiritual. Blessed Spirit of God, break through as Thou didst in me. Cause her to say, "Yes, Lord, Anything!" For the Shellmires, the Benders and the Straubs. For Barbara Finnemore, meet her afresh with faith and courage and physical health. May she bow to Thy dealings in her life.

SEPTEMBER 20, 1969: Bob is at the present working with young men who are drug addicts, drunkards, parasites, if you will. Oh, Lord of the harvest! Guide Bob in the right path laid out for him. Give grace and wisdom. Save, oh, save for Jesus' sake. Guide the Walshes. Thank you for the Hughes in Dunbar and Judy in Morpeth and Lilly in Edinburgh.

From 1963 to the 1980s the Lord used these young people to blanket Scotland and the Borders with the gospel. There did come a time when many returned to the States or went to other fields of service, but through disciples left behind the work goes on.

* * *

Because of James' great love for the Russian people and his love for Basil Malof, he agreed to assist the Russian Bible Society by becoming its honorary president. But James did so with the assumption that the Lord would raise up a deputation secretary to make known the ministry and to raise the money for special projects.

James visited Sweden and with the help of Ingamar Hallzon, who was the director of the Russian Bible Society in Sweden and the president of the largest evangelical printing press in Sweden, he arranged for the printing of material for the Soviet Union.

> We began to turn out one edition of the Russian New Testament after another, in varying sizes and covers, printed a large edition of the Ukranian Bible with a soft cover as well as Russian Bibles . . . These were handed over to other societies for distribution, in particular the Swedish Slavic Mission.

The Bibles were smuggled into the Soviet Union, a few at a time. Through the RBS the Stewarts were able to help Eastern European refugees.

The Russian Bible Society ministry was not without its problems. Four years after James became president, Ruth wrote in her diary.

> The great prayer burden just now is the RBS. When James took this on he did so on the condition that the Lord would raise up a man to do deputation. Four years have passed and the RBS is in debt. There is opposition from the Enemy, and there is no man and no money coming in. James thinks of resigning. We had such hopes at the beginning, but the Lord has not provided. Now, Lord, undertake. It is Thy work. Thou knowest the end from the beginning. Hold us steady. Hold together this work until it is accomplished.

James remained president of the Russian Bible Society by default. There was no one to take his place. Gradually money began to come in, first for Hungarian refugees in Italy and Austria, and then, as James spoke in churches across the United States about the possibilities of getting Scriptures smuggled behind the Iron Curtain, for the printing of Bibles for Eastern Europe. Finding her workload overwhelmingly multiplied by her RBS responsibilities, Ruth began to pray for a secretary to send out the receipts to RBS donors. The Lord provided a dear friend from England, Miss Ethel Kay, who had retired as the mission secretary, but was happy to have the opportunity to work with the Stewarts again.

Ruth rejoiced in God's faithfulness to them—in everything! On May 23, 1961, she wrote:

> Twenty-three years ago today I married James Stewart with much fanfare—and much confusion in my own mind because of the Baptist work I was leaving in Hungary. Here I raise my Ebenezer. Truly, hitherto hath the Lord helped us.

On May 23rd of 1965, she wrote in her diary.

I must record here that God is faithful—has been faithful in all things each day of these twenty-seven years! I hereby record some of His blessings: 1. Love—perfect love and understanding—a oneness only God can effect. 2. Children—in fellowship with us and Him. All three wanting to serve the Lord. 3. A Home—a place to call home and to feel free, a place to leave things! 4. Supply of all our needs. 5. Guidance and Provision in the Work.

MAY 23, 1970: Thirty-two years ago today I married James Stewart. It was the smartest thing I ever did except trust my Lord Jesus to be made a part of His Bride—to follow Him whithersoever. . . .

Through the years the Lord has been faithful to meet the needs of the Russian Bible Society. In His providential arrangement and under the direction of Bob Doom, the society was ready when the Iron Curtain fell, a surprising event that few people other than RBS founder Basil Malof had believed would ever happen.

As far back as 1926 Malof had said, "But the Gospel will triumph over the Soviets. . . . The spiritual 'Wall' around Russia will become a smooth, level and wide highway, along which there will move from Germany, England, Australia, and other evangelical lands, caravans carrying Bibles and Gospels and other spiritual books."

A true prophet he was. In June of 2000, the RBS Bible Journal gave the following report:

The Lord has given to us in the last 12 years $3,182,168.85 in contributions from American Christians. We have put this into Bibles, New Testaments, gospel portions, and spiritual books for pastors, adults, children, and the unconverted of all ages. About one and one half million tracts have been printed and distributed in Russian, Ukrainian and Georgian. We've held campaigns in various churches and cities where the Lord Jesus Christ has been preached. Many have professed faith in the Lord Jesus Christ.

* * *

Fruit springs out of death. Selfishness is always solitary. It is the lives poured out in sacrifice that abound in blessing. The way of conquest is the way of the Cross. The names that are honored in history are the names that stand over graves where self was buried long before the body died.

Will not the End explain
The crossed endeavour, earnest purpose foiled,
The strange bewilderment of good work spoiled,
The clinging weariness, the inward strain,
Will not the End Explain?

Meanwhile He comforteth
Them that are losing patience; 'tis His way.
But none can write the words they hear Him say,
For men to read; only they know He saith
Kind words and comforteth.

Not that He doth explain
The mystery that baffleth; but a sense
Husheth the quiet heart, that far, far hence
Lieth a field set thick with golden grain,
Wetted in seedling days by many a rain;
The End, it will explain.[14]

Chapter Sixteen
Buried Years

For several years we had dreamed of taking a trip around the world to visit the many lands where our books had been distributed and from where we had received such urgent invitations to visit. However, each time we considered an extensive journey and began to inquire about the cost of the plane fare alone, James would shake his head and say, "For that sum we could print another book and send it to the pastors and evangelists in those countries." We seemed to always have another book in the making and were conscious of the need for money to publish it. Finally, in 1970, James was convinced that it was time for us to make that desired journey to Southeast Asia to arrange for having our books printed and distributed right there instead of having the expense of sending them from America. We made preparations for this long-desired visit and thanked God for supplying the money from the different churches to meet our expenses.

— RUTH STEWART

In Ruth's biography of her husband, she said:

One morning while we were spending a few weeks in Edinburgh, Scotland, the first leg of our journey to India, James awoke with a bleeding ear which sent him to the doctor. He had an inner ear infection (cholesteatoma), he was told, which required an immediate operation. On February 16, two days after his 61st birthday, he went into the hospital with complete confidence that all would be well. And indeed, the operation on the ear was a success—"a beautiful job" they all said—but the shock from the experience affected James' whole nervous system. He began to develop Parkinson's, arteriosclerosis, and mental depression. Although he lived another four and a half years after the operation, he never recovered sufficiently to resume his work for his Master. He was simply "called aside" to wait, to trust, to prove the Father's sufficiency. This he did until he was called Home on the 11th of July, 1975.

In one paragraph, Ruth compresses together four and a half years of darkness and perplexity. From the day James was discharged from the hospital in February of 1971, he was a different person. The man who had been bubbling with personality, full of energy, bold and fearless was now timid and retiring. Ruth's former companion of great faith and exploits was suddenly trembling with doubts and fears, his keen mind clouded, his smiling face creased with worry.

It happened so suddenly, so unexpectedly. One week James was writing to Bob in Scotland, "I continue to have the best meetings I have had for years. We are flooded with invitations from every quarter." Two weeks later he complained of an excruciating pain in his head and canceled all meetings.

It was so untimely. Ruth had written Sheila in November of 1970:

> It is almost frightening—if that is the right word—to see how Dad is continually anointed with the Sprit and what the Lord is doing through and for him. Surely these are momentous days! But it all drains him, "virtue is gone out of him" as it were. If anybody lives the supernatural life both physically and spiritually, it is he. But do keep praying.

More than anything it was unexplainable, baffling. How could such a thing happen? Certainly, Ruth had seen her husband again and again so give of himself that he would land in bed and would spend weeks regaining his strength. It happened in Norway in 1947, just before God sent revival. The same thing happened in 1953 after which the Lord gave another great time of reviving. Even at the time of James' heart attack and during his slow recovery in 1955 and 1956, when he and Ruth went to Morocco for rest, God gave them *Heaven's Throne Gift.*

Was God about to do a new thing in His servant? As time dragged on, Ruth realized this time was different.

The busy mission headquarters in Edinburgh was no place for James to recuperate, so at the invitation of dear friends on the west coast of Scotland, Ruth took her husband to their Conference and Retreat Center. Christians surrounded them with love, care, and prayers, as well as advice. Their host was a medical doctor who was anxious to see James on the way to recovery. But after some weeks it became evident that James was not recovering. He was actually regressing. Ruth watched as he lost weight at an alarming rate, but worse, she saw his agitation of spirit and turmoil of mind.

> March 6: I can't get a "word" to claim immediate deliverance. If only
> He would say to me, "Now!" or "Today!" or "Immediately!" but in-
> stead He only says, "My grace is sufficient." See *Daily Light* for to-
> day. "The steps of a good man are ordered by the Lord; and he delighteth
> in his way. Though he fall, he shall not be utterly cast down for the
> Lord upholdeth him with his hand . . . Many are the afflictions of the
> righteous: but the Lord delivereth him out of them all."

Another invitation came from friends, the Len Moules of WEC mission headquarters in southern England, who had heard of James' illness
and felt they could be of some help. In desperation, Ruth transported
James there, only to have him land back in the hospital despite all the
special attention given him by these godly leaders. The doctors explained
that part of the problem was a violent reaction to the newly-developed
medication for Parkinson's, *El-Dopa*, which had been prescribed to
James. But that explanation did not account for James' refusal to eat or
drink. It was July 3.

> Took James to the hospital this afternoon—the best in the country for
> nervous disorders. Today was the end of me, but not the end of our
> Lord. James is still in His arms—engraved on the palms of His hands—
> and in His loving care. I am baffled, perplexed, but not cast down or
> defeated. This is not just about James, but I believe the Lord has some-
> thing spiritual in it for me too.

Much to Ruth's shock, the doctor found James to be so dehydrated
and depleted that she was given little hope that he would survive. James
was unconscious and totally unresponsive. After much prayer, however,
the little group who had rallied around Ruth saw a gradual improvement. A few days later, the doctor met with Ruth to discuss her husband's
condition.

"Really, we have done all we can for him," Dr. Whitehead informed
her. "At this point what your husband needs is to be at home in his familiar surroundings—his own bed, his books, his garden, his friends. That
will hopefully speed up the process of healing."

Scarcely a week later, Ruth was making plans to have James discharged and to have Bob book tickets to America when she received a

sobering phone call. The Stewarts' lovely home of twenty-three years, their welcoming refuge at the end of each missionary journey, had burned to the ground. A neighbor's boy had entered the house through a basement window and had stolen a tape machine and a few other items. To hide the evidence of the break-in, he set fire to the house.

"Sister Ruth," she heard on the other end of the phone line. "I simply don't know how to break this news to you, especially knowing the condition of Brother Stewart, but your house on Brevard Road has just burned down."

"Say that again," Ruth replied. She was sure she had heard wrong. He repeated his message. "I'm so sorry."

There was a long pause, then Ruth, with a quiet but firm voice, added, "Brother Ralph, that's okay. Our Lord doeth all things well."

In her diary, Ruth did not record what had happened. She simply recorded the Scripture the Lord must have given her for those days.

"God is our refuge and strength, a very present help in trouble. Therefore will not we fear, though the earth be removed, though the mountains be carried into the midst of sea. . . . The Lord of hosts is with us. . . ."

Ruth knew of one refuge where fire and thieves could not reach, and there she would make her dwelling place.

Arriving at the airport in New York City, the Stewarts were met by friends, Pastor Ralph Sexton and wife Jacque, who drove them to Asheville. Providentially, the mission several years earlier had purchased a small house to be used as an office for the Russian Bible Society. The Stewarts moved into this house. They were delighted to be home among the familiar mountains and their precious mountain friends. Yet, there was little change in James' condition. Days, weeks and months which had rushed by in previous years now crept by, weighing heavily on both of them. At times James would seem better. He would smile, eat well, and take an interest in his books or in going for a walk. More often, however, he did not fare well and Ruth found it a challenge just to get through the day. Worse yet his condition finally deteriorated to the place that Ruth needed a hospital bed or a nursing home where she could place him for a few weeks.

James was diagnosed with chronic lymphocytic leukemia, Parkinson's, and arteriosclerotic heart disease. That could explain his physical condition, but surely not his other problems.

After a Christian doctor in Atlanta was recommended to them, Ruth made an appointment for James, and the Sextons drove with them to the doctor's office. The whole morning they waited. Finally, they were called into the examining room. The doctor spent a full five minutes with James, then turned to Ruth and curtly said, "Mrs. Stewart, there is not a thing I can do for your husband."

Five minutes! No tests. No thorough examination. But a bill for $50! That made Ruth as angry as the doctor's coldness and indifference! Well, that is what we get by looking to a doctor for deliverance, she thought.

Another Christian doctor gave his personal opinion on James' condition. "Mrs. Stewart, your husband has driven himself to a breaking point. And then came the operation. It simply was too much for his nerves to handle. This is a physical problem, not a spiritual one."

The doctor's words were comforting, but he offered no remedy for James' problems. Again they were locked up to, "But God. . . ."

Ruth could not have functioned without her friends who stood by her. Her sister-in-law Elsie Stewart had moved to Asheville during this time and was a great help. James felt comfortable in her presence and that gave Ruth an opportunity to slip out and do needed shopping or make a visit to the dentist. The Ditchfields, the Shoffs, Marjorie Jones— all longtime friends—kept in contact. Ralph and Jacque Sexton loved James and ministered to him as tenderly as though he were a child— *their* child. Friends were Ruth's lifeline, her sanity and comfort in a time of great need.

> I couldn't have made it without them. They would come by and sit with Dad, or take us out for a drive in the mountains, and we'd stop to eat. James usually was quiet and unresponsive, but it saved my mind.

At the very moment when Ruth felt her burden to be more than she could bear, she was hit with more bad news. Suddenly she knew how Job must have felt when one servant after another came bearing a story of further calamity. She tells in her own words what happened.

> Soon from each of our children came the news of health problems.

One was diagnosed as having an incurable disease, another faced almost certain blindness, while the third was in a desperate emotional condition. In each of these cases I was totally helpless to do anything, but I knew more or less how to take these matters to the Lord in prayer and receive comfort from Him. We had lost our home through fire and were, as it were, living out of a suitcase in our office in Asheville while I tried to salvage what I could from the ruins, and look for another place to live. Then the greatest blow of all fell when an un-thought-of situation arose among our workers on the mission field, which threatened to destroy the whole work so dear to our hearts. In the past I had been content to trust James's wisdom and instructions from the Lord in such matters, but now James was worse than unhelpful; in his state of depression he saw everything from a dark and gloomy standpoint, doomed to fail. I felt strongly that in the case of the work I must take some action, but the situation was such that any action I thought of taking threatened to bring certain disaster. Confusion reigned in my mind and heart, while the Enemy came in like a flood to play on my thoughts and imagination and to taunt me concerning the future.

Needless to say, I cried to the Lord. Oh, how I cried! And eventually He heard me and spoke to me with a verse from His Word—Isaiah 26:3. It was not something new; I could quote the verse from memory and had done so many times: "Thou wilt keep him in perfect peace, whose mind is stayed on thee: because he trusteth in thee." But this time my attention was directed to the margin reference which said, concerning the word "mind," *thoughts and imagination.* You see, my imagination had been running wild through the suggestions and intimations of the devil about what was going to happen. . . . My brain was on fire it seemed, ready to explode. And now I am told that He will keep him in perfect peace whose thoughts and imaginations are stayed on Him. I wasn't sure of the meaning of "stayed" so I looked it up. To "stay" means *to stop and stay there.* If I could bring all my imaginations into captivity and present them before God; yea, more! If I could bring each situation before Him with all my thoughts about it, and hold it there, He would give me perfect peace.

I made an effort. I told Him about the confusion on the mission field among the workers, but at first I could not "stay" my thoughts on God. They bounced off into my own apprehensions and imaginations. But I determined with His help to let GOD be the goal and end of all my thoughts: but God!—the All-powerful, All-knowing, All-wise, All-loving GOD. When the Enemy would interject a "yes, but . . . what if . . ."

into my thoughts, I learned to say, "God knows. I refuse to let my thoughts go further than God." It worked! Of course it worked, because God's Word is true and God is true to His Word. And He not only gave me peace and quietness, but He began to work in each of the situations which I had presented to Him.

And that's how Ruth made it through those dark, trying days—trusting the precious Word of God. At the end of each day, she recorded the Scripture she had trusted to give her strength and courage for that particular day. Some verses promised deliverance; others simply promised grace and faith to endure.

JANUARY 11, 1974: Here is the secret of rejoicing and of being glad: first of all, recognizing that our Father's hand is behind everything, every circumstance of the day—that He permitted every detail before it reaches us, for there is no power but of HIM. Second, choosing the circumstances (stretching out our hands to them), however undesirable they may be, because His will is behind them. But it is He who chose God's will and He chooses through us. "When the burnt offering began, the song of the Lord began . . ."

JANUARY 14: "And ye shall rejoice before the Lord your God . . . Bring all that I command you; your burnt offerings, and your sacrifices, your tithes and the heave offerings of your hand . . . and rejoice . . ." Deut. 12:11,12. Oh, Lord, only Thou canst cause us to rejoice when we sacrifice. James grieves so because he cannot get on with his missionary work . . . but now I should be the one to grieve (I who am well) before the Lord to beg for the fire of God to fall on my life.

MARCH 12: This morning I read a paper of illustrations of deliverance through praise—thanking God for all things. I now thank Him for James' illness and all that has followed it. Who knows what He has helped us to avoid, or what He has saved us from? "I will praise Thee with my whole heart."

JUNE 15: James refuses to eat at all. Says he must fast three days like Paul. Oh, Lord, he loves Thee! He wants to do Thy will—Thou knowest! "Hear me, O Lord, for Thy lovingkindness is good . . . for I am in trouble: hear me speedily . . . I will praise the name of God with a song, and will magnify him with thanksgiving. . . . This also shall please the Lord better than an ox or bullock . . . For the Lord heareth the poor . . ." Psa. 69.

The spiritual battle was a daily exercise. Sometimes these conflicts were caused by well-meaning friends.They phoned and sent letters and cards to let Ruth know of their prayers for the two of them. So often the messages were full of advice. Many said that she just needed to have faith and learn how to claim victory over the enemy, then deliverance would come. Others felt James needed to deal with sin in his life, that he had stepped over some boundary and that God was chastening him. Preachers from far and near dropped in to pray for him and went away shaking their heads, shocked to see the change in a man they had always honored and revered. Sometimes following these prayer sessions, James would appear to rally for a few days, and Ruth would be sure that he was on the mend. Then, he would plunge back into despair and weakness, often worse than before.

What was Ruth to think? What was she to do? In the secret place late at night after she had settled James, she would agonize over the how and the why and the what. So many of her friends were convinced that if she just knew how to lay hold of the Lord, and claim healing, James would be restored. But she had done that time and time again to no avail. Was James' healing contingent on her faith? Was even his daily existence dependent on her hope of his recovery? More than anything, that hope had kept her going, kept her praying, kept her from going under.

The only answer that brought her any peace was what she already knew about her God. First, He was faithful. Up to this point He had never failed her. In no way would He fail her now. The second thing she knew was that He loved her and He loved James. But possibly the greatest comfort was to know that the very God Who controlled the universe was in control of their lives. Nothing could happen to them without being filtered through His loving hand and then passing on to them. Nothing was by accident.

A dear friend who had passed through a similar experience sent Ruth a note and comments on verses from Daniel 3:17,18. "I had to learn to say with the three Hebrew children ' . . . our God whom we serve is able to deliver . . . and He will deliver. But if not . . .'"

At that time, Ruth admitted

I rejected the thought that possibly God would not deliver my beloved soon, and in the way we both expected. Had He not given instant healing many times before and set James again in the midst of revival?

158

God could not possibly delay the desperately needed deliverance for long! But He did. And in the fiery trial of the following years He dealt so tenderly with me that I, too, learned to say, "He is able to deliver, but if not—" I will still trust Him. I can testify that while the trial was long and the fires were hot, my Lord was there in the furnace with me! . . . So real was the Lord's presence with me that once when I felt I could not bear another minute of the pressure, I literally placed my head on His bosom and felt the comfort of His heartbeat, even as a child resorts to his mother or his father in a time of deep distress. This experience one does not know apart from desperate need.

> All else may go if I may have but Thee;
> My heart, though desolate, be unafraid,
> Through depth of loneliness still undismayed
> If Thou be with me, guiding, holding me;
> The loss but now sustain'd is no more loss;
> No burden any longer is this Cross.
>
> All else may go if I may have but Thee,
> For Thou art the beginning and the end
> Of my desire, dearer than any friend,
> Closer than all in spirit-unity;
> Deeper than tenderest human trust shall live
> Within my soul Thy Changeless Verity.[15]

Throughout her life Ruth had a habit of pulling out her diaries when she was having a *faith failure*. She would read how the Lord had given specific answers to prayer and had provided again and again when they were at the end of their resources—all tokens of His special love and care.

> Looking over old diaries, I see it was in 1955—20 years ago—that James had his heart attack. I stand on Mt. Horeb and look away back— ALL THE WAY my Savior has led. Yes, from the beginning, how faithful Thou has been. And wilt Thou leave us to sink at last? No! a thousand times, No! Thy love and grace will sustain us. Only, do Thou for James what Thou desirest.

And what was God doing with His dear ones? He was working out the truth that "Except ye eat of this bread and drink of this wine . . ." It is true that this passage primarily speaks of our partaking of Christ in salvation, but in the context it also speaks of entering into the "fellowship of his sufferings."

> Just as my Lord was made broken bread and poured-out wine for me,
> so I must be made broken bread and poured-out wine in His hands for
> others. What is meant by "in His Hands" is seen in the kind of things
> that bruise me—tyrannical powers, misunderstanding people, things
> that ordinarily I would have resented . . . The question is, is there be-
> ing produced in me, through the crushing of His disguised feet, the
> wine that is a real quickening of other lives.[16]

In Ruth's mind, these were desert days, days of being set aside. She
was totally unaware that the wine already was flowing forth from the
crushing. Ralph and Jacque Sexton's son, Ralph, who at that time lived
a few houses down the street and was struggling with his call to preach,
often dropped by to visit the Stewarts. He would always find *Sister Ruth*
cheerful. Whenever he would ask how she was doing, she would always
reply, "Just praising the Lord!" Then she would share with him the Scripture the Lord had given her for that particular day. If her husband was
having a good day, she would disappear to write letters while this young
man sat with James.

> Just to sit in his presence was a blessing to me. Sometimes I would
> pray with him and I would see his lips moving. I would lean down to
> catch his words, "I must tell, I must tell, I must preach." I would go
> away awed that here was a man whose tabernacle had been consumed
> in zeal for the Lord's work until there was little left of the frame. All
> that was left was a vibrant flame on the inside, still yearning for souls,
> still wanting to tell the Story! I can't tell you what an impact the two of
> them had on my life.

Four and a half years passed—slowly, painfully. In 1974, the
Stewarts' son-in-law, Bob, who was already the field director in Scotland, was asked to become director of the mission. Gospel Projects had
already suffered greatly from loss of its leadership, and the board felt
they could wait no longer to fill the position. At the end of 1974, Ruth
wrote in her diary:

> So many things have happened this year. Bob has arranged to come to
> the States and the family with him—in the New Year. God also gave
> us a new grandchild, James Stewart Doom. Sharon and Benny

(Wilkerson) have found God's will for their future—together. They love one another. God has done so much in them by His Spirit. Jimmy has done well in his course in London, and the Lord seems to have His hand on their staying at Seven Oaks. James has been "kept' according to Gen 28:15, "And behold, I am with thee, and will keep thee in all places whither thou goest, and will bring thee again into this land; for I will not leave thee, until I have done that which I have spoken to thee of." God has blessed me beyond all I could have hoped for.

Sacrifices of praise continued to be offered up as Ruth entered the New Year. Bob and Sheila and their three children arrived and settled into their new home. Bob lifted some of the load of the mission responsibilities from Ruth's shoulders. Always a bright spot for Ruth, Sharon and Benny visited every few weekends. They were always full of what the Lord was doing for them and asking questions about the ministry of the Holy Spirit in the Christian life. In England, Jim was still having problems with his eyesight.

James was in and out of the hospital, still weak, still low in spirit. Life went on and, still, Ruth believed God for James.

On July 10, 1975, Ruth visited James and he seemed no worse than before. The following morning she received a phone call from Pisgah Manor Nursing home. In the early morning hours, her beloved husband had passed quietly into God's eternal presence.

JULY 11, 1975: This is the day of His final Home-call to James. At 7 a.m., he slipped away. He "was not, for God took him." His sufferings are over. No more, "I'm afraid." No more torment of mind and pain of body—only praise to His God.

After James' death, Ruth wrote:

All during the long illness of my late husband, James, he used my little copy of Daily Light devotional book, which is all Scripture. I wish you could see the promises James underscored with heavy marks all the way through, and the notes he placed beside them in the process of believing and trusting hard in them. Yet, it seems few of these promises were fulfilled—at least not as we had expected. James never questioned the Lord nor complained, and I didn't then, maybe because I was so sure the whole thing would come out right in the end. But that which I had thought was "right" did not come to pass and now James

161

is with His Lord where all things have been made plain. But here I am year after year going through my Daily Light and seeing again these marks of hope and faith. I confess to you I still don't understand the relationship between these wonderful promises and that which really took place, but I do know there was VICTORY then, and there is victory now when His perfect will has been done. And I find myself contented.

God's ways are unpredictable, inscrutable. He reaches down and picks out a man, obscure, unknown, of humble origin—one of the "not many mighty, not many noble"—and uses him in a significant way for 45 years. Then He quietly sets him back into a place of obscurity and humiliation. Surely all His purposes are wrapped up in Himself—that He alone might get the glory and honor and praise! Ruth and her family rested in that truth.

John Bunyan believed God to be sovereign even over the temptations of the soul as well as the sufferings of the body.

> Now I saw that as God had His hand in all the providences and dispensations that overtook His elect, so He had His hand in all the temptations that they had . . . not to animate them to wickedness, but to choose their temptations and troubles for them, and also to leave them for a time to such things only as might not destroy, but humble them—as might not put them beyond, but lay them in the way of the renewing of His mercy.[17]

"Bunyan saw suffering as a means that drove the saint to 'live upon God that is invisible'."

In her tribute to her husband Ruth wrote to praying friends throughout the world:

> While the world felt the impact of James Stewart's drive, his sincerity, his urgent message and his uncompromising spirit, the thing that affected my own life most was his inner love-life with his Lord. Going through his things the last few days, I came across this poem pasted in his Bible.

> > 'Set apart'—His special treasure,
> > To His heart how dear!
> > Joined to the Lord, one Spirit,

162

Thou art more than ever near.
'Set apart'—to lavish on Him
All my heart's rich store,
And with His heart to enter
Deeper evermore.

HE IS FAITHFUL THAT PROMISED

There hath not failed one word of His good promise:
His hand hath guided on the unknown way:
He hath upheld, and comforted, and gladdened;
He hath been near—the promised strength and stay.
There hath not failed one word of His good promise:
Needs, claimant needs, He ne'er did one forget:
If ravens came not,—means undreamt of answered
His faithful word, that all our needs be met.
There hath not failed! nor shall there fail His promise
To guide, support, to succor and sustain;
Thus, with our spirits on His Word relying,
We shall but find that Word to ne'er be vain.[18]

— J. DANSON SMITH

Chapter Seventeen
Fresh Surrender

On the day of James' funeral, Ruth wrote in her journal:

> This morning the Lord spoke to me through Oswald Chambers. "The initiative of the saint is not towards self-realization, but towards knowing Jesus Christ. The spiritual saint never believes circumstances to be haphazard; he sees everything he is dumped down in as the means of securing the knowledge of Christ." Lord, I would see THEE and know Thee as James did, and be used of Thee as he was. I give myself to THEE ALONE. Work out Thy plan and purpose in me.

Suddenly she realized that though the future was a blank sheet of paper to her, it was not to her Heavenly Father. To Him the future is the present and in that she could rest. On July 21, she wrote the simple sentence, "The Lord thinketh upon me. Psalm 40:17. Amen!"

Soon after the funeral, Bob asked her what she planned to do, thinking perhaps she would take a much needed rest after all she had been through. Characteristically, she answered him, "Bob Doom, this is not the time to quit. I've served the Lord all my life, and I am not about ready to stop now."

Amy Carmichael penned the words, "The vows of God are upon me. I may not stay to play with shadows or pluck earthly flowers till I my work have done and have rendered up my account." They could just as well have been written by Ruth Stewart.

One of Ruth's dearest friends, Elizabeth Ditchfield, visited a few weeks after James had gone to be with the Lord. As she was saying good-bye, she put her arms around Ruth and whispered, "Mrs. Cowman suffered with and said good-bye to her dear one—then she saw the best years of her ministry. So it will be with you, dear friend."

That night Ruth recorded those words and added, "I wonder. O, Lord, Thy way—for Thy glory—the future is in Thy hands."

Invitations began to pour in asking her to visit various friends and churches. Often she was requested to hold women's meetings as she had done so often in the past. She accepted a few of the invitations, but it was on her heart to visit her son, Jim, and his family in England. They had been unable to attend the funeral, and Ruth had not seen them in a long time.

In October of 1975, she flew to Scotland and met with missionary workers and their wives. She had a delightful, though hectic time. As James Stewart's widow, Ruth wanted to take the same interest as James had always taken in the missionaries, to encourage them and to pray intelligently for their specific needs. While in Scotland she also visited James' sister, Nan, and her daughter, Joan.

But soon it was time to go to England where Jim and his wife, Jenny, were on the staff of a home for troubled teens in Great Offley. Five years had made a great change in her grandchildren. She hardly recognized them! To Ruth, it was a joy and relief to once more sit, relax and enjoy each member of the family. Observing the great responsibility her son had taken on gave her a whole new appreciation of his ministry with troubled young people. One particular night while Ruth was visiting, the whole lot of teenage boys ran away from the home and had to be rounded up!

Prior to leaving home, Ruth had received a letter of condolence from a Czechoslovakian friend of James. Converted during the Czechoslovakian revival of 1939, Vladimir Fajfr had become a faithful worker with E.E.C. He and his wife had been associates with E.E.C. until channels between the East and the West were cut off by the Communists. Over the years they kept in contact, but only sporadically.

Vlado's letter, written in September, told of his wife's death the previous year. He then asked Ruth if she would be traveling to Czechoslovakia any time in the near future. She replied negatively, but said she planned to visit her son in England in October. She was somewhat surprised to receive a reply from Vlado saying that he was planning to visit a mutual friend in England at the same time. He also asked permission to meet with Ruth at her son's home.

Vlado traveled to Great Offley and visited with Ruth, mostly speaking of James and of the revival in Czechoslovakia in 1937. Vlado was an unusual man. He had trained to be a lawyer before he was saved, but after receiving Christ as his Savior, he felt the call of God on his life.

I told my lawyer friends, "Czechoslovakia has enough lawyers to protect man's laws, but God needs men to protect His law!" My friends said I was crazy. How would I live? I told them I was willing to risk it . . . "It is the gospel that creates a new man, not communism. We will never have a perfect society without Jesus reigning."

As skeptical as his friends were, Vlado received permission from the Communist government to be a pastor and an evangelist. Such was unheard of in Czechoslovakia at the time. He was the only person in Czechoslovakia with permission to travel as an evangelist, and he used the privilege to the greatest extent.

When Jirina, Vlado's wife, became seriously ill and when for the second time he lost permission to preach, he moved his family to Usti nad Labem in North Bohemia. There he was allowed to live in the church's parsonage.

When Vlado arrived in England to meet with Ruth, he had only recently regained his permission to preach.

Ruth questioned him about friends she had known long before in Czechoslovakia. They also spoke of the intervening years and the ministry the Lord had given each of them. The hours flew by. Just before saying good-bye, Vlado brought up the subject that had been on his mind for weeks.

"Have you thought about marrying a second time?" he asked.

Hesitating for a moment because she was not quite sure how to answer, Ruth replied, "I can see how you as a pastor really need a wife, but as for me, I haven't—"

"You don't understand. I am asking if you will marry me," Vlado interrupted. He began to explain how the Lord had dealt with him.

"I am convinced you are the Lord's choice for me," he said with conviction.

Later Ruth confided to him that she had been so taken back by his proposal that she had hardly known what to say.

OCTOBER 17: Today I had presented to me one of the most unthought of considerations I have ever had. My mind goes back to 1937 for there was such a similarity. Dear Lord of my life, I have said all—all is Thine and I am Thine and I am willing to do and to suffer for Thy sake. Is this to test my sincerity? Is this to prove me? Everything within me cries out, "Nay!" But, Lord, I surrender all as I did 40 years ago. Am I ready to be emptied—again?

OCTOBER 26: This morning the preacher preached on "By faith, Moses . . ." He spoke to my heart. So much of our dedication is so shallow. We don't think we will be called on to really forsake all. Lord, I must face this matter with V. and of forsaking all that is a part of me, and by faith, like Abraham, be willing to go out, not knowing whither. I know I can trust Thee, Lord, to work out details. But I must know Thy way—that this thing is from Thee; then, all else will fall in place.

OCTOBER 29: I have been counting the cost—thinking of the ease I could take now with time and money of my own. (?) But can I forsake the hard road and be put on the shelf while I have strength to still give my Lord. If I discipline myself health-wise, I can expect another ten or fifteen years of profitable service for my Lord. And shall I not suffer for Him? Dear Lord, take full control of this flesh which tends toward ease and comfort. Give me wisdom to know and grace to do. Most of all, give me Thy mind.

NOVEMBER 14: Back home. Lord, they keep asking me, "What will you do now?" And I answer, "I shall follow on, picking up where I left off 5 years ago." But how? Shall I collect material for a biography of James? Or prepare messages for a women's ministry? Or get back into deputation work? I shall wait on Thee. Now, on this day I yield myself, my all to Thee, my Lord, my God.

NOVEMBER 19: Today, I cease from my own thoughts—the busy traffic of both about James' illness and Homegoing, and about the impossibilities that lie in the future. Today I rest down in His perfect will for my life, by His grace.

NOVEMBER 21: My mind is too much on V. I am so very lonely and perplexed. Lord, what are You saying? What is this Thou art doing to me? Emptying me into a new vessel? Or do these deep longings come from a natural cause . . . Lord, Thou art my all. Do Thou meet all my need. Make me truly satisfied in Thee.

NOVEMBER 24: I am convinced that these great waves of loneliness which roll over my soul come as a delayed reaction to James' Homegoing. This dreadful loneliness often chokes me.

In spite of often praying "Thy will be done," Ruth could not keep back the doubt. Her friends, her home, her beloved mountain churches—how could she give them up so easily, perhaps to never see them again? But even more dreadfully difficult was the thought of leaving her children and grandchildren. After many years of being separated, Sheila, Bob and the family were now with her in Asheville. She could finally be a regular, ordinary mother and grandmother. And Sharon. . . . How could she bear to tell her what she was considering since she had spent her life going off and leaving Sharon? Now more than ever, Sharon needed her. How could she just walk away?

> NOVEMBER 25: "Let my soul live and it shall praise Thee." Today I have poured out my soul unto my Lord in a way not before—with strong crying and tears for protection in the matter at hand. Lord! Thou hast said, "Great peace have they that love thy law and nothing shall offend them (or be a stumbling block to them)." I claim this for myself. I fix my eyes upon Thee. Now I rest in Thee to show me—teach me—Thy way—at any cost.

> NOVEMBER 26: "Ask of me and I shall give thee the heathen." This is the verse God gave Vlado after much fasting and prayer concerning his future. He is restless to get the gospel out—and his interpretation includes me! As his team-mate. But how? But that is not to be my concern. Mine is to say, "Yes, Lord," and to prepare my heart and follow Him. Tell me, blessed Spirit, is this truly from Thee? That is all I need to know. Yesterday I wept for the first time since James' going—I wept before the Lord, desiring greatly to know the truth concerning His will. I can think of nothing else.

The same day, she wrote Vlado:

> At last my mind is quiet. I confess to you that I have been in a real turmoil of mind and exercise of soul. Tell me, how can one make a cool decision about a matter which involves the emotions as this does? And besides, one does not "make a decision." This is not a matter of my choice, except that I choose His Will above all things. As it was with me in November, 1937, so it is now. I have said to myself that the matter does not rest on how I feel, but what He wills. But such a matter is not treated "in cold blood," as it were; it involves the emotions. Then one cries, "Are these emotions true? Are they from the Lord Himself, or are they a mere response to loneliness?" But I cannot be-

lieve it is so with me. I only know you have touched my heart and shaken my tidy little nest!

Now we must wait quietly on the Lord for His plan, if indeed He does have a plan for our future together. He will not fail. Still, because I am a "normal woman" I have so many questions racing at once through my mind; how I wish I had a recording of the things you said to me during our few hours together at Jim's when I was thrown off-balance and could hardly take it all in! I remember you quoted that Scripture, and your interpretation of it, but I can't quite remember where I personally come into it. Tell me that part again.

Soon after this, she received a letter from Vlado, explaining to her how the Lord had dealt with him:

One week in 1942, I was praying and fasting about my future when the Lord gave me the verse, "Notwithstanding, the Lord stood with me and strengthened me; that by me the preaching might be wholly known and that all the Gentiles might hear; and I was delivered out of the mouth of the lion." II Timothy 4:17. God spoke to me so clearly that I never doubted that it was the special voice of God speaking to me. All the following years under Communism when it has been impossible to travel out of my country, I have held these words in my heart.

Now it is 1975, and you sent to me word that your dear husband, my dear friend, James, died, and so soon after my own dear wife, Jirina, was called Home. I began to think often of this woman in Asheville, North Carolina. Could it be that this woman would be the answer to this promise God had given me? It was September 10. I fasted and prayed. In the end, I must pray, "Only let my life bring glory to You." You know the rest of the story. I was able to get permission to leave the country and meet you in Great Offley in England. I am still amazed that you did not say, "How foolish you are, you gentleman from Czechoslovakia. My plans are quite different than to be wife of a man from a socialist country! I know nothing about you and you know nothing about me. You are either stupid or impertinent. Good-bye!" But you said very gently, that it was something new for you to think about and you must pray about what you have heard. I find this to be a very intelligent and courageous woman.

As Ruth pondered his letter, she suddenly realized that what Vlado needed to fulfill God's promise to him was her American passport! Because he lived behind the Iron Curtain, traveling outside his own country was almost an impossibility. In fact, when he had received permission to meet her in England, it had been an absolute miracle. His own secret service agent had said to him, "How is it that you, a pastor, are able to go to England and never has it been possible for me?" But, in the scheme of things, if Vlado married her and she was an American with liberty to travel wherever she wished, then the authorities would have to give him the same privileges!

He wanted to marry her for her passport! Or she could take it that way. This would have thrown a woman less experienced in God's ways, and as Vlado said, she would have reacted with, "What impertinence! Good-bye!" Instead, she realized that if this was God's plan for Vlado to preach outside his own country, then, as part of that plan, she would be in a place of great blessing.

Truth was, Ruth knew that Vlado had been attracted to her when he met her. He certainly made it clear in all his letters that he could not get her out of his mind. Could it be love at second sight for both of them? As she had said in an earlier letter to Vlado, when emotions are involved, it makes finding God's will the more difficult. Again she went to prayer—and the Word of God.

> DECEMBER 4: I read today "You need to know that you have a God Who is watching and guiding you and working out in you a character fit for heaven and eternity. The one great mark of that character is absolute surrender to God, to let Him be all. This requires a deep humility that only wants to trust and obey." Lord, at any cost—at every cost—and in any way, I am ready to obey! As Andrew Murray says, "He will never disappoint the trust of a soul fully committed to Him and His will." Lord, I know that and I love Thy will because I love Thee.

> DECEMBER 6: "In quietness and confidence shall be your strength." Quietness is expressive of submission to the holy will of God, and presupposes a waiting upon Him as directed by His Word. All things will be made plain by relying on the Lord's wisdom, love and ability. My Lord, I thank Thee for giving me this quiet confidence in Thy loving purpose for my future. I do trust Thee. I will trust Thee with my life and step into the unknown. I asked the Lord to give me a token tonight

concerning Vlado. He did!!! Even while I was speaking to the Ambassador Class at church.

At this point, Ruth was able to sit down and write the letter for which Vlado was anxiously looking. He always loved to tell of Ruth's reply.

This letter arrived in time for Christmas—the most wonderful present I could receive. She told me, "My answer is yes.' And she quoted the verse from the Book of Ruth, chapter one, ". . . For whither thou goest, I will go; and where thou lodgest, I will lodge: thy people shall be my people, and thy God, my God: Where thou diest, will I die and there will I be buried."

Excerpts from Ruth's diary reveal the feelings of her heart at the time:

DECEMBER 8: I have been reading the life of Mrs. Boardman. Strange how I went into the library the other day and came across it for what I thought was the first time. Inside, it was inscribed by James, "To my Wife and Great Heart, December, '47." Apparently at the time, it meant little to me. Now, it has become the very thing to minister to my heart— from the exact passages James marked for me!!! As I read her story, I felt the Lord said to me He would never allow me to know widowhood. I accepted this with deep thanks—believing He meant He would be my Husband. But now I think He meant more—He will be that, but He will also give me another husband, even at my age (!) to live out my days in loving, serving, and sharing my life. Lord, I trust Thee, and I bow before Thee!

DECEMBER 20: Today it suddenly struck me that my Lord has been silently planning for me in the "vision" that Vlado has. Me! I, who am the least and only a "handmaid" to God's servant. I am overwhelmed with the thought that all the past, especially the last five years in the desert has been discipline for the future years. I will praise Him Who doeth all things well.

DECEMBER 15: Today I got a rude awakening and I realize my head has been in the clouds! I helped fold the booklist for Revival Literature only to discover an announcement that "A new biography of James Stewart will come out in 1976, written by Ruth Stewart." I came out of orbit and down to earth with a thud! I now clearly see that I must concentrate with all my power on that one task until it is accomplished. I will relive James Stewart until it is in print. Then, I shall be free to give myself to the future, whatever that holds.

Ruth realized the only way to close one era of her life was to write her husband's biography and record how and why God used this very ordinary servant in such an extraordinary way.

Someone said to her, "There are too many Christian biographies where these Christians seem to be perfect. None of us can relate. You need to paint him warts and all."

Later, after much thought, she gave her answer. "I want you to know, I haven't spent my lifetime covering up James' faults to expose them now!"

In fact, as she began the writing, she found:

I am not getting very far fast, but I am working—soaking myself in letters, etc. James is so very near and real to me. Today I cried as I realized how far short I came to being all that James needed when we were first married. But I think the Lord helped me make it up to him later. But I still can't remember faults; I can only see how faulty I was those years. And how sweet and wonderful he was. So I have a hard time making him anything, but wonderful.

Reading James' letters and his constant expressions of love for her, Ruth reflected on those early years.

Last night I was under inspiration to write—typed pages and pages about when I first met James. As I write, the central thought of James' life seems to be "This one thing I do." But, as I went back over those days, I realized afresh that so many things he did to me that I could not understand and I thought them so "cruel," it was because I didn't understand. His attitude has always been that WE ARE ONE, in it together. So if he made a decision about what the Lord wanted us to do, of course, it would be all right with me. Or if he had to make a sacrifice which involved my having to make a sacrifice, it would be fine, because we were doing it as one person. Oh, if only I had grasped this truth as he did early on in our lives together.

As Ruth began to plan out what she was going to write, she was not able to forget Vlado and their future.

Letters flew back and forth across the Atlantic as the magnitude of the decision they both had made began to register. Ruth and Vlado agreed that she needed to make a trip to Czechoslovakia to see her future h and meet her future family. The three Fajfr children were still at home. Jana, the oldest, had a good job as a secretary-translator since she could speak Czech, English, Russian, and some German. Daniel had recently been drafted into the army and Mark was working in a factory and already had advanced in his department. Vlado wanted his children to meet the woman who was to become his wife. The visit was planned for Easter.

From the Fajfr home in Usti, Ruth wrote Sheila enthusiastically.

Daniel came to Prague to "fetch" me with my luggage and traveled with me by train to Usti nad Labem in North Bohemia where they have their home. He speaks English very well, having studied it in school. Here at the station we met Jana as she got off from work . . . I had a very warm welcome. Jana baked a cake and put "WELCOME" on the top. Mark and fiancee, Jani, were here when I arrived. He is a pet. I love every one of them to death already and I think they accept—even—like me! About Vlado. It is as though I have always known him, and in our relationship—well, the reality is far better than my imagination of these past months. The home—typically European— has a lovely garden, central heating, plenty of hot water, a gas stove, plenty of books and pictures and music! My room, the guest room, looks out over the mountains and I am content—almost at home. . . . I was never more convinced than now that I am on the right track for my own future. These past weeks have been very sweet and blessed and I am thankful!

In her faithful old diary, a few days later, Ruth recorded more intimate thoughts.

APRIL 25, 1976: A day to be remembered! We were in the home of Dr. & Mrs. B. I spoke on I Peter 5, the Lord helping me. Traveled to Stara Tura where there was a packed room of country folk—my kind of people! Spoke on John 15. Oh, the hand-shaking afterwards and the warm greetings. I love these people! Now, Lord, what will you do? Vlado keeps warning me, "Usti is not like this, not so responsive or exciting." But there is our vision, our love, our willingness to let our Lord have His way, and our determination to keep our love fresh. This morning when I said good-bye to our friend, Noemi, I said, "Before the snows begin, I shall come again."

Describing this visit, Noemi said, "In Bratislava I was interpreting

174

Ruth—we were one spirit—I was drinking her words! It was from Isaiah 12. Every word was powerful. Especially I started to understand how it is to 'draw water from the wells of salvation'—with joy! This involves the will and is not easy, but it can be with joy."

> APRIL 26: At Vlado's "family home" in Brno where he was born and lived as a child. Tonight a large number of friends came. Each gave testimony to what James' meetings meant to them. Stirred my heart. Determined to pray more—to seek His face. I have got such a vision for revival NOW under these present circumstances. Oh, how I love that man, Vlado. How one I feel with him. Lord, help me to hurry back!

> APRIL 30: I believe I have taken the first step of the rest of my life— this visit to CSSR. I am seeing possibilities for the future—a new church building, a center for evangelism. Lord, give the vision to Vlado and give wisdom step by step to know and do Thy plan. Today I give myself again to Thee to fulfill in me and Vlado Thy will. Give a renewed vision and re-commission Thy servant. Anoint him afresh for the task.

> MAY 9: Father, I abandon myself into your hands. Do with me what You will; whatever You may do, I thank You. I am ready for all; I accept all. Let only Your will be done in me—I wish no more than this.

Upon her return and in the intervening months, Ruth had much to do. First, she had to finish the biography about James. Next, she had to decide what to do about her house in North Carolina, whether she should rent or sell. Then there were her belongings to sort and decisions to be made about what to carry and what to discard. She had to take care of business at the bank, and there were many good-byes she needed to say.

One of Ruth's friends, Marian Shoff, even gave her a bridal shower, something she had missed out on the first time around!

But one of Ruth's great remaining concerns was Sharon. Jim and Sheila had families and could manage with their mother being at a distance. On the other hand, only the year before Sharon had graduated from Southland Bible Institute. Though she was now working in Pensacola, Florida, she was far from settled. Doctors had diagnosed Sharon as being manic depressive, and surely this was a difficult time for her. The entire year leading to Ruth's departure from her homeland, she cried to the Lord to work out the situation with her daughter. The

Lord abundantly answered her prayers. Not only did He touch Sharon's body, but He gave her a Christian husband who would care for her.

JANUARY 12, 1976: Sharon phoned tonight, absolutely desperate. I don't know what to do. Lord, I stay myself upon Thee. I will not doubt. I will depend on Thee. Undertake for Sharon. Oh, help me to resist Satan for her.

JANUARY 21, 1976: Today I talked with Sharon. After meeting her at the airport, I told her, "I am suffering, too. God is the judge (the controller). He is going to take Benny and you and everything dear to me until there is nothing left except Himself, but I submit to Him. Why don't you submit to Him too?" She said to me, "At the moment I can't feel His love, only His sovereignty."

JANUARY 29: Arrived home after a safe trip from Florida. I reason thus: since God is sovereign and knows all things concerning me and mine, and since He has chosen my way, He will overcome . . . Since Sharon is a chosen vessel, a child of promise, our all Wise God—EL - SHADDAI, THE ALMIGHTY—will undertake for her all the way. He will attend to her health and her mental and spiritual needs. O LORD THOU WILT DO IT! I trust Thee and I am helped.

FEBRUARY 8: Faith is substance and what is—is. Because God says it is. Therefore I claim these things for Sharon: 1. Healing of her body 2. Filling of the Spirit 3. Providing of work for her. These things I claim, I take in Jesus' Name.

MARCH 14: Sharon is under depression—maybe about . . . my going away. But Lord, draw near to her to find her comfort and stability in Thee and Thy Word, Amen.

MARCH 20: Spent much time with Sharon—just talking. But maybe that is where I have failed in the past—too busy to talk and listen. I go back to Hebrews 6:13-15. Andrew Murray says, "Faith may accept, but only long-suffering inherits the promise . . . "

MARCH 23: Praying through might be defined as praying one's way into full faith.

MAY 22: O My Faithful God! Guide . . . Benny and the deacons in W. Va. about his going there as youth pastor. Don't let him go out of Thy will. Make him certain.

JUNE 19: Sharon's wedding to Benny Wilkerson. So beautiful, so simple, so sweet. And the Spirit was there!

SEPTEMBER 3: Sharon phoned from W. Va. They are happy. Thank you, Lord, for Thy Faithfulness!

SEPTEMBER 29: Reading through my diaries. I see desperate cries to God which have been answered. Thank you, Lord, for the way you have worked especially in Sheila and Bob's life and in Sharon's. Now Lord, help me!

Even until July, Ruth was still struggling with her move to Czechoslovakia, even though the Lord had assured her that if she would step out on faith, He would be with her. Perhaps it was that reality was setting in.

JULY 27: I have been thinking that I have no gift I can use in CSSR since I can't speak Czech—Now I read: "Some of us have been given special ability—have a gift for caring for God's people as a shepherd does his sheep, leading and teaching them in the ways of God . . . that God's people will be equipped to do better work for Him till all be come grown in the Lord . . . Yes, to the point of being full of Christ!!" Lord, let this be my gift.

In the middle of July, Ruth realized that in the rush of things, she had forgotten to apply for a resident visa into Czechoslovakia! She panicked. Would she get it before the date set for the wedding in October? The Lord would just have to tend to it!

And the Lord did! After a flurry of good-byes and a long plane ride, Ruth arrived in Czechoslovakia the beginning of October. By October 16, all permissions and arrangements were in place for the wedding. Most Americans would have felt the wedding day strange, but Ruth already had had one European wedding, though many years ago. She took everything in stride, writing a long letter to her family back home.

Everything went off in a wonderful way. The wedding dinner at 2 p.m. was at the Bohemia Hotel which gave first class service. At 4:30 we all went to the Town Office where the official wedding was to be held . . . A court interpreter was present so that I could understand all that was going on. The ceremony was very good as far as it went (of course, no mention of God) . . . Then it was over and we went across the street to a church used by the Presbyterians and the Hussite Brethren. They were happy to loan it to us for the day, our own hall being too small. The church was full even though the announcement of the wedding had only been made on Wednesday night. This service was called the "Blessing" at which we again exchanged vows and rings. The same pastor who preached the "Blessing" also married us. Joseph sang as did some of the youth groups. After the ceremony, we sat on the front row while a long line of people came to us with gifts and speeches, each gift and speech representing a different church or youth group! After that, we came back to our home for the reception in the church hall which is in the basement of the parsonage. There we sang and prayed and gave our testimonies of how the Lord brought us together. No one seemed in a hurry to leave so we ate and drank some more and enjoyed the fellowship. What a day!

October 16, 1976: One year ago today Vlado Fajfr came to Jimmy's home to visit me. Today that man will become my husband and I shall be his wife. I love him with all my heart.

October 17: We stayed for the Sunday morning service and Joseph, Vlado's brother, sang and preached. The whole family had dinner together after which we took Daniel to his military post and Noemi to Vysoke Myto. Weather was bad—dark and rainy—so we spent the night with the Cernys where Mother Noemi had prepared a wedding feast for us fit for a king and queen. Then we were taken upstairs where she had prepared a "bridal chamber" with her best sheets and pillowcases, until the Hilton would have been ashamed to compete! How sweet is such friendship and love . . . And how sweet is our love— the love the Lord has given Vlado and me for each other! Our life together even in these first hurried days and nights is so established! So sweet!

This was the same Noemi Stifter who had visited Ruth and James in St. Leonards-on-Sea immediately after the war. She was now married to a pastor, Stana Cerny. Their daughter, Noemi, had lived with the Dooms in Scotland for a year during the Prague Spring. The younger Noemi agreed to be Ruth's one attendant at the wedding, a role she counted as a great honor.

Noemi later wrote to Sheila, "I was so proud to represent your side of the family in the wedding. I felt so close to your Mom when she let me help her get ready, and then to stand beside her during the ceremony."

The honeymoon couple traveled to a cottage which a friend had given to the Fajfr family. To her family, Ruth wrote from the honeymoon cottage:

> There isn't much to say since the wedding because there isn't much exciting news around here—not even the news of who won the election last Saturday! We are really happy doing things together—walking in the forest, cooking on the wood stove, eating what and when we please, studying and praying together. This is a real vacation and rest time and I am enjoying every minute of it! You would love it here at the cottage. Oh, it is primitive, all right, but at the end of May it won't be so cold. The water comes from a flowing stream just below the house. There is another stream nearby where Vlado takes a bath each day, while I stand inside shivering, with all my clothes on! Still, the room we live in is cozy and warm! By the way, the toilet is down a little path in the garden! The seclusion makes it a perfect honeymoon haven.
>
> What more can I say? I am so happy with Vlado Fajfr and my new home. Last night we talked about future prospects and my vision became more clear—and my feeling of inadequacy stronger. But God! Of one thing I am sure. I am deeply in love with Vlado Fajfr! And that helps!

The seed must fall. The cold, dark
earth entombs with tough embrace
the hardened case. The soiling
and the softening, the stark
stripping away, removes all trace

of former shell. The germ of grain,
now free, bursts forth. The tender shoot
takes solid root. Relentless
sun and drenching, greening rain
produce abundant harvest fruit.

— SHARON STEWART WILKERSON

Chapter Eighteen
Starting All Over — New Crop

After the excitement of spending her first Christmas in Czechoslovakia with her new family, Ruth was left to consider what her role would be in helping Vlado's ministry. For the first time in her life, she was already finding herself at a loss for words—*Czech* words! She had picked up languages in her many travels, some Hungarian, some French, some German, even some Greek. But the Czech language was not like any language she had ever studied. How long would it take her to learn it?

On New Year's Day, she wrote:

> Last night in the meeting, I drew for my year's verse, II Corinthians 4:17,18, "For our light affliction which is but for a moment worketh for us . . . While we look not at the things which are seen, but at the things which are not seen!!!" Amen. Now, Lord, I must trust and believe that a quiet, unconscious influence—unseen by man—is at work through me for Thy glory.

In the coming weeks and months, Ruth began to experience an onslaught of feelings she thought were long gone from her life—irritability, self-pity, and even depression. It did not take her long to recognize the fact that her "old flesh" had come back to haunt her. Such a possibility had never occurred to her. Had she not fought and won that battle scores of years before? She had come to believe that anyone who could maintain victory living with James Stewart's lifestyle could be victorious in any situation! Now she was utterly dismayed to see all those old enemies with which she had grappled in her early years of marriage to James were no longer defeated. She was defeated. And she was stunned! The flesh and the Devil attacked Ruth at her point of weakness—her loneliness and tiredness. Weariness set in. In her new environment, she found that the least exertion taxed her strength. She suffered attacks physically, mentally, and emotionally. They were enough to make her despair.

The loneliness was no one's fault. Ruth was surrounded by people and everyone went out of the way to be kind to her. She loved her new family and the church people. But she longed to sit down with an old friend and communicate freely, pour out her heart, laugh, joke, tease! Ironically, in the past Ruth's whole life and ministry had been a matter of talking, counseling, writing—using words. And people constantly pulled on her from every direction. She had often longed for such a time of silence and solitude. Now that she had it, she was actually sulking.

Ruth had not been neglected. In May, Sheila and Sharon and their husbands, along with six other friends, visited for five days! At first sight Ruth's daughters and the four Fajfrs fell in love with one another. It was as if they had known each other all their lives.

In September, two of Ruth's close friends visited, Tena Blatz from Germany and Edith Weeks from America. Their visit brought all the memories of old times, and Ruth dreaded their departure from the minute they arrived.

Ruth was so ashamed of her feelings, but she simply couldn't seem to help herself. She was in a period of adjusting. Years before when asked what was the most important thing a missionary needed to know, she would say, "There are three things. Number One: Adjust. Number Two: Adjust. Number Three: Adjust!"

Ruth had spent her life adjusting to different people, different places, different cultures, and different languages. In each case, however, she had been the guest, a short-term guest, at best.

This adjustment was different. For years she had been counseling pastors' wives. Now she was one! She was not the guest, she was a permanent fixture. At this point she was no longer required to give Bible messages, counsel those who stayed behind, or talk about the mission fields she had visited. Now she was Vlado's wife. Her duties were simple: cook, clean house, wash clothes, and go for late-night walks with her husband. She was not sure where she could fit in to the scheme of things spiritually.

November 13,1976: I read today, "Oftentimes we allow loneliness to prey upon our own bodies . . . this lack is surely intended by God to drive us closer to Him. Let us revel in His love and closeness, keeping ourselves in the consciousness of His love. (Jude 21)" "My Beloved is mine and I am His," Amen. And He speaks to me in English! . . . Now, I refuse to be lonely. I will exercise myself in His company.

Two months after their marriage, she felt, "hopelessly helpless," as she says in her diary.

One day Ruth ventured to ask Vlado the thought that plagued her mind. "Why am I here? What is it I should be doing?" she asked.

He looked at her somewhat surprised, "Why, your job is to be my wife." He could not understand why there was a question about it.

Until the last five years, Ruth had lived at a whirl-wind pace, traveling from state to state and from country to country with seldom a minute to herself. She had been active—teaching, counseling, writing letters, writing books, and being James Stewart's secretary and office manager. Go, go, go, every minute of every day had been the rule of her life. Suddenly, she had come to a full stop. Her hands were still busy, and she went about her daily tasks willingly, but something was missing. She lacked a sense of calling, a clear understanding of what her ministry was to be in this place.

Ruth wrote home:

The main struggle I have had has been because of the language barrier—being constantly "lost in a fog" from not understanding what was going on and being unprepared mentally. Also it has not been easy getting used to living with others after all those years alone with James. I am experiencing a normal home and family and it is taking some adjusting. But it is getting easier.

She often wondered if her mental and emotional state caused her weariness and tendency to catch colds and flu, or if it was the other way around. Vlado was a great comfort. He was kind and gentle and forgiving. He told her that her situation was her "Arabia" and that she would soon come out to a new ministry just like Paul. How wisely he spoke!

In late summer of 1977, Ruth wrote:

Now, Lord, you have to show me the secret of how to minister to these people. I am here; I have a message, but I don't know how to get it over to these people. . . . "There is no grace equal to the resignation and humility that always leads to instant obedience and self-efface-ment . . ." Have I laid aside humility—and my armor—to find a more comfortable life? Give me that holy restlessness that cries to Thee for lost souls—that seeks a deeper walk with Thee. . . . The Lord is deal-ing faithfully with me—surely He will work deep if He digs deep. "Ye shall find" is the Word.

Exactly one year after her marriage to Vlado Fajfr, which had been a day of great hopes and expectations, Ruth had to admit that the Lord had to put her through a year's training to get her "back to Bethel."

OCTOBER 16, 1977: I live no longer—Christ liveth in me. Today I went back to Gilgal where I first was "circumcised" and put myself again under the knife. I declare again, no confidence in the flesh which I abhor above all things. I have written down my commitment that it might be definite. My soul is quiet. I see that the secret of the life of faith is moment by moment to be cast on God in spiritual bankruptcy. It is maintained, not by past victory (oh, no!) but present faith; not by experience of the past (I sure found that out fast!) or determination, but by faith in God—absolute dependence on God. It is, as it were, a "hand to mouth" existence.

A folded sheet of paper had been inserted in her diary on this day on which these words are written:

On this, the 16th Day of October, 1977, the first anniversary of my marriage to Vlado Fajfr, I take, by faith, Galatians 2:20 for my daily life. I am dead to all that would bind me. I am alive to my Lord alone. I claim and I have deliverance in the Name of Him who died and I will act upon it. My spirit is free, set free by His Spirit. I renounce the works of the flesh. I resist the devil—declare myself liberated through His blood. I have been and am now crucified. Yes! Christ lives in me. He shall have my supreme devotion, by His Grace. Amen. Ruth Fajfr.

A few days later she almost gasped as she realized how completely the Lord had given her a fresh outlook on her life with Vlado.

The Lord has opened my eyes at last! How have I been so blind so long—a whole year almost? The evening meal has always been, long before I came here, a time of sweet fellowship for the Fajfr family. And it must ever be so. They deserve it . I have wanted to share in this time, know what they are saying so that I could add my two cents, Now I am settled and happy on that score. I have accepted it. My 9 p.m. walk with Vlado fully satisfies me—when we can talk—in English. Praise God! I believe I really am set free at last!

OCTOBER 30: I have been thinking that if I never get the language, my being here gets prayer for this place. I may be brought down to a mere "point of contact" by His grace and wisdom, but I can receive the Lord's burden and pass it on to others who can and will pray for this place.

OCTOBER 31: Meditating while taking a walk today. Now I am beginning to realize the spiritual value of my being here—the prayer power from my friends around the world. GOD ANSWERS PRAYER—not only in my deliverance and care for the Fajfrs, but for our churches as well.

NOVEMBER 3: I was thinking this evening how blessed I am to live in a home where there is love and peace and quietness. How I praise God! I have been blind to all this blessing. O, Lord, forgive me.

NOVEMBER 11: What a day! Washed three loads of clothes, but the fog never lifted so had to hang them in the attic. In the afternoon I remembered a young couple was invited to "tea" to talk about the Lord with Daniel and Vlado. Baked an apple crisp, made open-faced sandwiches . . . I'm so happy to serve—even to serve refreshments and pray. Now, Holy Spirit, follow them until they are safe in the fold.

NOVEMBER 13: [Daniel Fajfr preached his first sermon.] He preached from Luke 5:17-26, "The Education of Faith." I was so filled with joy I could hardly keep from weeping. Vlado is so happy for what the Lord is doing in this family.

Ruth was learning to love this family, but the Lord was doing a deep work in her heart to prepare her for the years ahead. She quoted from Oswald Chambers:

The secret of the Christian life is not in serving Him much but in doing the will of God what ever that may be. . . . It is not so important HOW MUCH we do for the Lord, as HOW.

185

Ruth was coming to see that her greatest ministry was to be intercession. During a year when she could do little else but pray and seek the Lord for each day, she had been learning many precious truths.

In November she wrote:

Oswald Chambers says that we are sanctified, not to be fussy workers for God, but to be His servants and this is the work of His servants— vicarious intercession. "Let the weight of the burden for others crush the life out of you until gradually and patiently God lifts the life out of the mire. In the Ministry of the Interior all we have to do is simply take the matter before God and be made crushed grapes until the Holy Spirit produces such an atmosphere that the one who is in sin or in the wrong cannot endure it! That is God's method."

Ruth goes on to pray, "Lord, crush me for my loved ones, for revival in Usti and in Scotland, for these dear precious people here with such needs. And what of Poland's millions? All I can do in this place is intercede by the help of the Holy Spirit." And again, "O, God, so many unsaved here. I am the pastor's wife and can't say a word. But then, I can pray. Get hold of me, Lord, crush the life out of me for these people."

How the Lord heard her cry! Two years later, she wrote to Sharon:

Looking back over this letter, I realize that I have left out the most important thing in my life these days and which takes a lot of my time; it is our ministry of intercession and the blessedness of this unity in prayer and expectancy. When I was here in Usti, Easter Sunday three years ago, I had no conception of what joy and blessedness the Lord had in store for me when I would follow His leading (I only knew then that I was in love with Vlado Fajfr!). To me it was a "leap in the dark" but really it was not, because it was a step of faith and obedience, and our Lord never fails those who obey Him. I sure miss you and would love to walk in and have some fellowship with you. Love to your husband and Chad. Love Mom.

About the same time, she wrote Sheila:

Remember how I asked the question, "Can the Lord possibly bless by my presence in a meeting?" I believe He answered that question on Sunday when a lady said to me very hesitatingly, "Excuse my bad English, but I want to tell you, I loved you from the moment I saw you." How can this be unless she was saying she felt the presence of the Lord or was blessed some way by my presence. Do you think this is possible?"

And later she wrote:

I have never been more involved than I am right here with the goings-on. I am back into the swing of things and this time feel roots holding me steady. Also I have had already several opportunities to "share" and this melts me into the fellowship.

What she does not tell is that even before this, soon after she arrived in Czechoslovakia, the Lord put it on Vlado's heart to suggest that when they held a pastor's conference, the men should bring their wives. Because Christians in Czechoslovakia had to be so cautious when meeting together, they had never before considered such a thing.

Vlado's suggestion was accepted and the women came. What a joy they found in fellowship and prayer. During at least one session of each meeting, Ruth would speak to them, sharing things the Lord had taught her and asking the ladies to share their needs with her.

Like an adopted daughter, Noemi thrilled to be Ruth's interpreter. In these times she found her own life strengthened and deepened.

With these dear Christian women there seemed to be no language barrier to love, caring, and praying.

The Czech government was sensitive to world opinion and they liked to say that they permitted religious freedom in their country. In reality, the Communists made it very difficult for anyone with a strong faith in God. When this American asked permission for her husband to accompany her on her travels, the government could hardly deny the visa. So during the first ten years of Ruth and Vlado's marriage, he was able to travel with her to many places—America, Canada, Alaska, Mexico, the Bahamas, Japan, Singapore, India, Great Britain, and Scandinavia. Perhaps the most amazing miracle of all was permission to travel to Israel.

And in each country the Fajfrs visited, the Lord opened doors for Vlado to minister. When he returned with slides of all the countries, he received requests from many quarters asking him to give a slide-lecture. The Czechs had been cut off from the outside world for so long they were starved for knowledge of what other places were like. Through these slide presentations and in his own unique way, Vlado presented the gospel to people who otherwise would never have heard.

Let a man define to his own mind an object of prayer, and then let him be moved by desires for that object which impel him to pray, because he cannot otherwise satisfy the irrepressible longings of his soul; let him have such desires as will lead him to search out, and dwell upon, and treasure in his heart, and return to again, and appropriate to himself anew, the encouragement to prayer, till his Bible opens of itself at the right places—and think you that such a man will have occasion to go to his closet, and come from it, with the sickly cry, "Why oh! why is my intercourse with God so irksome to me?" Such a man must experience, at least, the joy of uttering hopefully emotions which become painful by repression. . . . Jeremy Taylor has said, "Easiness of desire is a great enemy to the success of a good man's prayer." [19]

— AUSTIN PHELPS

Chapter Nineteen
Harvest Time

On October 30, the Lord had opened Ruth's eyes to what He had in mind for her. She was to enter into His heart and His ministry. What was His on-going ministry? Intercession. "He ever liveth to make intercession for us." What was to be her ministry? Intercession. She was to be a small but very vital part in God's plan for Usti and North Bohemia.

Usti was a large industrial town of 85,000 people not far from the German border. Few people in the Communist world, much less from the West, had ever heard its name. Unlike Slovakia and small pockets throughout Czechoslovakia, Usti was not a religious place. Many had bowed without resistance to the invading force of socialism. Even the old people had long forgotten any faith of their youth and the young people knew nothing but the doctrines of atheism taught in the schools. In the eyes of men, Usti was an unlikely target for the arrows of God. In the eyes of the Lord, He knew that he had "much people in this city." (Acts 18:10).

Now that the Lord had shown Ruth what to do, she undauntedly set to work. Each day in her diary she wrote lists of names. Mostly the names were those of unsaved adult children or husbands of local church members. At first, Ruth loved these church people because they were Vlado's flock and she had heard him repeat their names in prayer day after day. But soon, as she went with Vlado to visit them and heard them pour out their troubles, Ruth entered into Vlado's compassion for them. She learned enough Czech phrases to ask the people about their families, their health, or their troubles. She found herself drawn to them and them to her. The more she loved them, the easier it was to carry their burdens to the Lord in prayer.

Personally, Ruth asked the Lord to teach her to reach a new level of intercession. She wrote a friend in the States:

> I could write pages about the things which are occupying our minds here—all of them His interest, but mine now. One thing comforts our hearts; "The Lord knoweth them that are His," and He will bring through those God has given to His Son in spite of all obstacles. But at the moment I am crying to Him for more power in prayer—power to bring forth to completion. I consider the words Hezekiah said in II Kings 19:3 and am wondering just what he meant by them. "This day is a day of trouble and of rebuke and blasphemy: for the children are come to the birth, and there is not strength to bring forth." To apply it to myself and to our church, we have by testimony and prayer brought a number of souls just so far and yet we seem not to have spiritual strength and power in prayer to give that last "push" which will deliver the new-born babe completely! God needs to do a new thing for me and for us all along this line. But He is working and we are rejoicing. I have such sweet fellowship in prayer with two of the sisters, young women, in our church each Thursday. One of them speaks English, which makes this possible.

Imperceptibly at first, the Lord began stirring other hearts, primarily to get down to prayer. But with prayer came hope and with hope the faith to believe God for revival. Daniel, who had now taken on the responsibility as pastor of the church to free up his father to travel and evangelize, had devoured James Stewart's books on revival. He began to preach about revival and other preachers who came by seemed to have the same message. The stumblingblock to faith was obvious: with a government imposing stringent restrictions upon believers and with a church harangued by an atheistic society, could they believe God for revival? They did believe God, and they laid hold of Him in prayer until they saw Him work.

Remembering the insight the Lord had given her the previous October, Ruth wrote to her prayer partners in America and other parts of the world, pressing them to pray.

> When I came to Usti, my husband had been here five years, though most of that time he was without permission to preach. Instead, he visited the sick, encouraged in a personal way the few believers, and cared for the church and grounds. At that time his first wife was very ill, becoming more and more an invalid, so he also cared for her and

his three children. Then, by the grace of God he was granted permission to preach again! The church was in a sad state because of conditions existing before he came, so that there were only a few elderly women, two or three older couples and one or two young families attending the church. When I came to live here as Mrs. Fajfr, things were a little better, but far from healthy.

We have taken to heart His word to us, and we believe that the foundation of any effort on our part is prayer—to humble ourselves and seek His face and pray. Already several prayer groups have been formed in homes; one for the young family men, one for women, and we trust soon as the weather warms up, one for the elderly women . Also in the youth meetings, in the mid-week and Sunday services—much time is spent waiting on the Lord in prayer. Then, we know you are praying for us too.

The young married men of the church began to desire to meet for Bible study.

Ruth wrote:

They come to this weekly Bible study with great interest. Several of these men have newly found the Lord and are "eating up" the Word as they read so many chapters a week for discussions when they come together. Others are seeking the Lord and are reading the Word eagerly. You see, they must first come to believe that "God is" and that the Bible is the Word of the God Who is! This is a great hurdle for them, since they have been drilled for years in the "no God" theory. We don't push or pull; we only give the Word and pray. But the men have a great influence on each other, as you know, and we praise God for what He is doing.

One evening after the Bible study, Daniel rushed into the room all excited over the blessed time they had had. "As we were praying, I was thinking. The women should have a time like this for prayer and Bible study. They need it, especially those whose husbands are unsaved. What do you think? Ruth, you could teach it."

But who would translate? They each looked at Jana. Her English was impeccable and Ruth was comfortable with her. Every Thursday thereafter the women would meet with Ruth and Jana and study the Bible and pray. As they prayed together, such openness developed among them that they began to share their troubles and bring questions about the

191

Christian life. This was the first time most of them had had a woman they could come to with their spiritual needs. Ruth was overjoyed to be once again in familiar territory, ministering woman to woman.

I must tell you about last night. A group of ladies met together with Jana and me. Their husbands kept the children at home. It was such a treat for them to get out and get together we almost had to send them home! We talked about John and he will be our chief interest in these coming weeks. Jana and I were no doubt blessed more than any, but everyone expressed joy at being able to come and seemed to greatly anticipate our fellowship together in the Word in the coming weeks. Oh, pray for me that I might be a blessing. [*Never knowing when her letters would be censored by the communists, Ruth often used unusual phraseology to convey her messages without arousing undue attention.*]

Jana Fajfr has written about those days.

It was hard for Ruth to learn Czech because it is a difficult language and because of her age. Still, she learned some words and sentences which she used when meeting people. In those days, not many people could speak English because we had little contact with the West. But Ruth could do a lot through an interpreter. She led our women's meeting held in our house and I was her interpreter. In this way she was able to minister to about twelve women, explaining the Bible and teaching them biblical principles. These meetings were so full of peace and love and a special understanding among the women that even after all these years the women love to remember her and that time. Also, a couple of the women who were not believers were saved. When the oppression which came to the church in the early 80's started, the meeting had to stop. But those women will never forget her though they are now in their 50s and 60s.

The Lord worked mightily among the young people and the few who were meeting together became earnest about their witness. One Friday evening, Jana C., a quiet girl in her middle teens, spoke up.

"Please, would you pray that I can give a witness at school. It is so hard for me."

All agreed they needed strength in this area. So they prayed together for courage and boldness.

Whether it was a suggestion from one of the others or a decision she made on her own, Jana C. resolved to carry her Bible to school on top of her books and in full view of all her classmates.

One of the girls in the class, who was as out-going as Jana C. was quiet, first called attention to the Bible.

"You carry that book with you all the time. I even see you reading it during lunch time. What's it about?"

Zuzana was full of questions. Jana C. explained it was the Bible and it told about God.

"Is that why you don't join the Young Communist Band?" Zuzana pressed.

Other classmates moved closer to hear Jana's reply. They had always wondered about this girl with the sweet face and a quiet disposition. Jana whispered a prayer for help and took the plunge. She explained that she was a believer, a person who believed that God is real and that He had sent His Son to die for man's sin. She confessed that she had trusted Jesus to save her.

Jana C. could see that her words were like a foreign language to the rest of the class, so she added, "Look, if you want to know more we have a youth group. You can come and learn all about it."

Zuzana continued to ply her with questions, as did many of her classmates. At the end of one class, a student jokingly wrote on the board that the SSM (Communist Youth Organization) would meet at— and he gave the address of the meeting hall and the date of the next youth meeting! When the day arrived, five boys showed up to mock and disrupt. They left sobered and impressed. Some classmates were saved and brought along family and friends. Others attended the meetings for a short while and drifted away.

However, when Zuzana took a stand for the Lord, everyone knew it! Soon, she and Jana brought along another friend, Hana.

Ruth wrote her friends:

There was quite a "blow up" at the school where Zuzana, Jana and Hana attend. These girls have been so active that finally their parents were ordered to come and talk with the principal. Zuzana's mother had already been, weepingly confessing that her daughter's "betrayal" was her fault since she had not taught her strongly enough in the doctrine of atheism at home. Hana's mother is a very strong communist. Only Jana's parents are believers. The other two girls are now housebound by their parents against the Friday night youth meeting in our home. But they turn up at every possible place where there is a Christian youth meeting or gathering of Christians of any kind. There are still several other young people who have not had courage to follow through with their desires to know more about "the way." Pray for these three girls who are the leaders in that school, but who graduate very soon. Pray that the persecution at home will only strengthen and purify them in their Christian faith.

And that was the beginning of a mighty work of God which caused the little meeting hall at 33 Zahradkach in Usti to burst at its seams. Many came to scoff but remained to pray! There were those who attended simply out of curiosity or fascination by this "religious sect." Some came seriously seeking the truth until they realized the cost and then they fell away. But many continued to come despite persecution from friends and families.

During this time, the Lord gave the whole church special days of refreshing. Easter, 1980, the church set aside three days for special meetings. Three preachers visiting the country were invited to take part. The men preached total abandonment to Christ as Lord as the only way to experience reality in the Christian life. It was just what the church needed.

Ruth wrote:

These past days have been full! But we have seen the Lord work in an unusual way—scenes I have not seen for years. On Saturday night we saw our people on their knees until 11 p.m. crying out to God for forgiveness and cleansing. Last night our little church hall was packed and the meeting went on from 6 til after 9:30. The main preacher was ill and walked upstairs ready to collapse when one of our young men who has been seeking, ran after him, fell on his knees and said, "Pray for me! I want to be truly saved!" He was trembling like a leaf. And the Lord touched him! . . . It is not only their message, but it is the power with which they preach that draws people. Daniel has been in Heaven these days. He brought his young people to sit at the feet of these godly men. Last night about fifteen people came from a town some 38 km away. I weep when I see the sincere hunger of the people. And what of the Authorities? We had informers in the meetings. If the Lord does not "shut the mouth of the lions" we've had it! But haven't we pleaded for this for years—that God the Holy Ghost would do a mighty work in our midst? So, we are in His hands to protect or to deliver us into their hands. What now? Prayer and more prayer!

In the early part of 1980, the State Secretary, who was in charge of keeping his eye on all the activities of churches in his area, was growing more and more concerned about the activities in Vlado's church. When Vlado went to him to ask permission to have a pastor's conference in Usti, the secretary refused. He also gave Vlado a stern warning.

"We know what is going on in your church. Too many young people are coming. You must not have so many meetings, or we will put a stop to it."

As Ruth later wrote:

> How do you stop a forest fire? You get it controlled in one place and it breaks out in four other places. All I know is that God is answering prayer and that's dangerous! Just cover us and ask others to remember us that His will may be done always. The Holy Spirit is like the wind that "bloweth where it listeth and thou . . . canst not tell whence it cometh and whither it goeth."

When the Holy Spirit kindles a fire and blows on it with the power of His enabling, it is out of the control of man. It was all they could do to keep up with what God was doing and leave the consequences with Him. Vlado, Daniel, Jana, and Ruth all found their hands full ministering to those who came to inquire. Mark, their younger son, had married and moved to the nearby town of Teplice. As the youth leader in the church there, he was experiencing similar success among the young people, mostly with young couples. So it was that other churches were being touched by what the Lord was doing in Usti.

> APRIL, 1982: I must admit that it is fantastic what the Lord is doing. It is true that one of our fine young men is the son of a high official with the police, and one girl who attends is daughter of a colonel in the Army! One girl after another finds the Lord Jesus as her Saviour and goes all out to bear testimony. Last Sunday a girl gave a most amazing testimony of how the Lord brought her into His saving grace and how her life was changed. For more than a year she has been attending our meetings—with no pressure from anyone. She just can't stay away! Another girl, a friend of hers, is the same. Sometimes her father locks the door to keep her from coming. But while she has been away from Usti for the summer, she has written a wonderful report of her salva-

tion—right there with her Bible and the Lord! No one is pressed or begged or enticed with worldly entertainment or anything; they simply come and they bring their friends. We picked up a hitch hiker just outside Usti and took him as far on the road to Prague as we were going. In conversation, Vlado gave him the gospel. Just after we dropped him off, this young man met Hana, one of our girls, and she encouraged him to come to the youth meeting. He came. Then he began to come to other meetings. He now brings his sister and his friend. He sits closer and closer to the speaker in the Bible Hour or Sunday evenings. Then there is another young lady who was brought by her brother. He quit coming, but she is a "live wire". She always brings someone new and she witnesses everywhere, even though she says she is still just seeking.

But it is not just among the young people that the Lord is working. When we name our young families, we see how each of these parents have been transformed by the Spirit in recent years. Last week at our family retreat at Rybniste, we had such a good time of fellowship with these young couples with their children around the Word of God. I taught the book of Ruth and Vlado taught Joshua. We work well together!

On the last Sunday of June, 1982, the Lord led Daniel to preach on Romans 8:33-39. The subject was, "Who shall separate us from the love of Christ? Persecution?" The following week, a husband and a wife from the church were told to appear separately before the Secret Police for interrogation. Then the Secret Police called for another couple and questioned them, then another, and still another.

"How many young people do you have attending? Give us their names. Who is their leader? How many are in your church? Do you have foreigners come to your church?" The interrogation went on and on. It was evident that the authorities already had a great deal of knowledge of what was going on in the church. Usually the believers could pick out an informer in their midst and they would be careful around that person. But now it was almost impossible to identify an informer because there were so many new people coming and showing an interest in the things of the Lord.

Finally, Daniel was called in.

He was asked about a visit of a couple of Americans two or three years ago. Also for the names of the young people who came on Friday nights. Vlado, who in his early years had been a lawyer, was fully prepared how he would answer when he was called in, but neither he nor Ruth were sent for. He was never given a chance to defend himself. The Fajfrs were amused to hear that the Secret Police had said to one of their members, 'Be careful. Do you know that Vlado Fajfr's wife is a famous American preacher? Look at all the people who have been baptized since she came here!'" Ruth remarked, "This credit I do not merit, I assure you. I have never mentioned baptism to any of our people!'"

Under the Communist authority, one official pastor in an area acted as overseer to the unofficial lay-pastors in the churches under him. This official pastor of the churches in North Bohemia went straight to their home after he had been called in by the State Secretary. The secretary had been extremely angry, ranting and raving until the pastor thought he would burst a blood vessel. The secretary informed the official pastor that the teen meetings, young people getting together on Friday nights, or teaching of little children would no longer be permitted. He expressed his opinion that the church had gone too far. Besides, what right did they have to meet in the basement of a house and not in a proper church building? He conveniently ignored the fact that the church did not have a building of its own and had been asking for permission to build for the past five years.

"From this day Vlado and Daniel Fajfr are forbidden to preach. I have revoked their permissions," the State Secretary said to the poor official pastor who had listened to the tirade.

Vlado thought that perhaps the State Secretary would cool down. He had always treated Vlado with the utmost courtesy, even when refusing to give him permission to do something! Vlado wondered if perhaps he should go and talk to him and reason him out of his decision. But as Vlado waited on the Lord, he was reminded that this was the Lord's business and that they were to "be still and know that I am God."

The State Secretary did not change his mind and finally the official word came that they were forbidden to preach. It was the third time Vlado had lost his permission to preach. Two times before he had been denied permission to preach because of his success among young people!

How did Daniel react? He told Ruth, "I am convinced that this is the pattern for our day. This is the normal Christian life, is it not? 'They that live godly shall suffer persecution.' The exception should be not to suffer persecution!"

Ruth wrote her friends:

You can believe that both of them are bursting to be back in the pulpit, but God has given them quietness and victory in this matter, even helping them to accept the decision of the Secretary. Of course, as ordinary members and elders in the church, my men can visit homes and hospitals and do many of the things they did previously in the Name of the Lord. And they can pray!—always the way is open upwards!

To another friend, she wrote:

The authorities do not know that they are promoting the work of the Lord in the best possible way! They have relieved these men from so many activities and responsibilities to give them more time for prayer and Bible study, visitation, etc., to "trim their lamps and sharpen their swords" as it were. I can't say that it is easy even now, but there is grace and quietness of spirit—and so many areas for which to pray.

First, everyone thought perhaps this was the sign that they were to move to another work. Then it came to Vlado that because of his reputation with the authorities, his son Daniel would have a far greater chance of getting his permission to preach back if Vlado was not part of the equation. The work in Usti still needed Daniel's presence and his ministry whether or not he could stand in the pulpit. So it was decided that Daniel and Jana should remain in Usti while the older Fajfrs moved to another place.

Vlado is convinced after much prayer and fasting and waiting on the Lord that our work in Usti and North Bohemia is finished and that the Lord is leading us to another area in our country. This is our request: that the Lord will reveal to us and to our central committee (Czech Brethren) where He wants us. Pray that in that place we shall eventually have Vlado's preaching status restored. There are several possibilities—which tests my motto of long-standing: "Dead to everything; ready for anything."

As Vlado prayed, the Lord impressed him with the needs of Slovakia. His maternal grandmother had been Slovak, and many of his childhood vacations had been spent with her. He could speak as fluently in Slovak as in Czech. Ruth tried to give her prayer partners some idea of how to pray.

You may know that Czechoslovakia is composed of three countries: Bohemia, Moravia and Slovakia. Bohemia and Moravia are considered Czech, though actually only the Bohemians are Czech. But Slovakia is an entirely different people group, language and culture. Bohemia touches the west, Slovakia is east bordering on the Soviet Union with Moravia in the middle. I am telling you this because we are considering moving to a town in Slovakia, maybe Zilina, in the western part of the country. I understand Zilina is a clean town about the size of Usti (85,000 population at this time) and has a university. There are some believers there but not yet an organized church. But still, we can lead a quiet life in our "old age" and seek to bring comfort to the brothers and sisters we find around there. We know there is plenty we can do and because you pray, He will accomplish His purpose in sending us there.

Our prayer now is that we shall not become too comfortable and slacken our pace. It is so easy for one as he grows older to be tempted to seek out the old arm chair for an easier life. But I have just read where Isobel Kuhn quotes Amy Carmichael who gives a good slogan for "seniors". "Climb or Die!" Mrs. Kuhn adds, "The Christian needs to press on continually, even if it seems unmerciful. Spiritual death begins to set in when a Christian slackens his pace and begins to look around for ease . . . prayerlessness means slow rot, deterioration!" And so I cry, "Lord let me burn out for Thee—don't let me rot."

— RUTH FAJFR AT AGE 80

Chapter Twenty
Zilina

Surely Ruth's vision of the coming years was typical of any seventy-three year old. It was time to slow down, take on less responsibility, and sort of slide into eternity! She was sure Vlado would be invited to speak in surrounding churches. He could witness to neighbors and to contacts made in the town. Of that, she was certain. They would stand with and encourage the little group of believers in Zilina. Ruth would pray, write letters and create a little *nest* in which they could comfortably live out their final years. "A quiet life in their old age," that's what she visualized.

Accommodations were extremely scarce. Ruth and Vlado thought to find a small apartment, or flat, in a group of flats. They had scarcely started looking before they learned that there was a house for sale only a couple of blocks from the town center. The house would give them plenty of room for themselves and could be used in many different ways for the ministry. When they went to see it, they admitted the Lord had designed it just for them! Downstairs were two extremely large rooms.

> Big house, big rooms! On the way to see the house, when I started to cry to the Lord that we not make a mistake, I couldn't; I had peace. At once I had a vision of the downstairs as a meeting place where precious souls would be saved. The other room could be our living quarters. Vlado was assured of its suitability because the owner seemed so anxious for us to have it. He lowered the price and agreed to give us the bed, a desk, and two chairs which he had previously wanted to sell us.

The kitchen was spacious enough for feeding a crowd. There was another apartment upstairs—a large room and bathroom with an entrance hall and a balcony outside. The garden front and back was small, but a lovely shady pear tree hung over the driveway and garage. The wiring needed to be replaced, a gas heater installed and the whole place painted, but they all agreed that it was a great buy!

Meanwhile, Ruth had to make an emergency trip to the States in April to help assess a situation with the Gospel Projects Board of which she was still part. While in the United States, she visited Sheila and Sharon and their families.

On returning to Zilina, she found the house still torn up. There were holes in the floor for the radiators, holes outside for the gas pipes, and a hole in the stairwell where it was to be widened. Noise of workmen in the bedroom, the kitchen, and the bathroom filled the house. She learned quickly that in Czechoslovakia, one had to feed the workmen as well as pay them. And the better you fed them, the better they worked!

Seeing the miraculous provision of the Lord kept them going. During the era of Communist rule, churches in Czechoslovakia helped each other construct buildings. Christians would take a couple of weeks off work, would bring whatever tools they had, and would work together to complete a job. Of course, they had to pray for permits to be granted and for building supplies to be provided. Time and again they saw God work miracles. Anyone who participated in the renovation of the church building in Bratislava in the 1970s would have to confess that God worked supernaturally. Some of the same men who helped re-model the church now came to Zilina and gave freely of their time and labor.

But building permits, materials, and equipment were in short supply. Ruth couldn't quite get over the kindly spirit and hard work of these men, especially one man who took six hours to drill a hole through a four-foot thick wall! Ruth cooked meals, cleaned up, made up beds, and helped keep the operation running as smoothly as possible. Vlado ran here and there coordinating the whole project.

Ruth gave a clear picture with entries in her diary.

AUGUST 5, 1983: This afternoon around 2:30 Dana and a friend, Galina, dropped by from the Tatras on their way home to C.B. We invited them to spend the night, seeing they had sleeping bags. Around 10:30 tonight the door bell rang again. Two boys from Hradec, sons of our plumber and electrician, wanted to come in out of the rain and spend the night. We had given the girls all the bedding, but Vlado rolled out the carpets we had taken up and fixed them a place in the living room. Seems to me this is literally going to be a "half-way house" and folks can't wait for us to get started! But we praise Him for all.

OCTOBER 18: The painter came again today, and his wife came to wait for him—came and sat down in our room. Also the lady from whom we bought bedroom furniture came and Vlado showed her all over the house. Makes me know there is no place or time when one can let down her hair!

From that time on, Ruth never knew what each day would bring.

Standa and Techy came to move radiators downstairs for painting. Tiler and his wife came to visit. Then the painter arrived with his helper. Zlata came to clean and wash doors and woodwork which was a great help to me for I tire so quickly. Then Vladimir, a new student from Olamouc, dropped by to see Vlado. This is Grand Central Station.

What had happened to peacefully settling into old age? Years before, Sharon, as a little girl, read to her Mom a poem she'd composed about old age.

> When my work on earth is through
> And I've seen, heard, smelt, and done,
> I'll sit right back in the rocking chair
> And wait for the Lord to come.

At the time, Ruth had laughed heartily, knowing that such a thing would never be her lot. She'd certainly had her share of "seen, smelt, and done", but there was no rocking chair in sight! Already the Lord was showing her a different pattern.

The group of believers in Zilina is quite new, having grown out of Bible-study meetings held in the home of a couple while they were students in the University here. When the man graduated, he got a job in the town, bought a house, and (with government permission!) converted one of the rooms into a meeting hall. Helping this couple is another couple with the same vision, who have settled in Zilina. Apart from these, most of those attending are students from other parts of the country who will move on after graduation. We shall be doing a pioneer work in our effort to reach Zilina and surrounding towns for

Christ and at the same time shepherd the sheep here. Thank you for your prayers on our behalf. On April 26th, Vlado will be 73 years of age . . . We have chosen for our future work the words of Caleb spoken at age 85—Joshua 14:12. " . . . Now, therefore, give me this mountain, whereof the Lord spake in that day; for thou heardest in that day how the Anakims were there, and that the cities were great and fenced: if so be the Lord will be with me, then I shall be able to drive them out, as the Lord said."

* * *

Before leaving Usti, Ruth commented:

This move to Slovakia will mean a lot to our family. The Fajfrs have been here in Usti more than ten years and have labored diligently to build up the church, and have seen the congregation grow from a few elderly people to a lively congregation of 80-90 on Sunday mornings. It will be a great wrench to the people here to see Vlado go. Also he has never been separated from his children in such a way before . . . Needless to say, Usti is the only home I have known here in this country and my life revolves around the family and church people here.

In 1976 at the age of 67, Ruth stepped into a new life—a new husband, a new country, a new language, a new ministry, and a new house. Six years later, she was doing it all over again—with the exception of a new husband! Truly, she would have followed Vlado Fajfr to the end of the world.

Once a friend in America, Ed Shoff, had asked her if she had any regrets.

"If I had known then what I know now about Vlado Fajfr, I would have followed him to—to Siberia!" she told him.

Instead, Ruth followed Vlado to Zilina.

The situation here is altogether different from our life in North Bohemia. Slovakia is strongly Roman Catholic and the Church has a great influence on the whole country. We never cease to marvel at the crowds that pack out the Catholic Church on the square each Sunday evening. Not only is the church filled to overflowing with people standing right to the doors, but a side hall is packed and jammed with over a hundred people standing and listening with rapt attention for over an hour— without even being able to see the face of the priest. Whenever my husband gives a witness to some of the local men who come to our house to work, they say, "Yes, we are Christian too." In Bohemia we were used to the response, "Oh, I don't believe in God." But these people are more blind to the true gospel than those who said they were atheists.

All over again, Ruth had to adjust to a new country and a new language. Just as she was beginning to understand what was going on in Czech, she had to exchange it for Slovak. Those who spoke Czech could understand Slovak and vice versa, but when it came to word endings, grammar and syntax, it was a totally different matter. She would practice again and again a few phrases she might use, but when the moment would come to use them, her mind would go blank—or else a conglomeration of Czech and Hungarian would come out! She found the going to be even tougher than she had thought. She was sure part of the problem was her age and the fact that she never seemed to have time for lessons. She had hoped to just "pick it up."

Ruth soon found, however, that since Zilina was a university town, some people spoke English. When students discovered that there was an American in town, they began coming to her door wanting to practice English with her! Some of the students were Christians, but many were not. Thrilled both with an opportunity to speak English and to have a witness, Ruth faithfully gave her testimony and shared the gospel with them. The Lord had sent people right to her doorstep! And they each wanted her to speak English!

Just over a year after they had purchased their home in Zilina, Ruth and Vlado found themselves settling comfortably into their new ministry. In March, Ruth wrote a letter to her prayer partners. She was full of all the Lord was doing in their midst and asked them to pray for the many contacts they had among the students. She proceeded to give a list of the names that they might pray specifically. A few weeks later she wrote her daughter.

I have been very, very foolish. Yes, I feel like a Judas. I can't tell you more, but we desperately need to be covered by the blood. Will you phone Marjorie and others to pray? My only comfort has been Daily Light yesterday (March 28), "The Lord is my Light and my salvation: whom shall I fear."

Later she was able to explain in a letter that was not sent through the postal system.

Recently we in our church here in Zilina went through a difficult time—a real attack of the devil on our minds and hearts. Several of our students, the best among the young converts, were called before the police, interrogated, their rooms searched and all Christian literature confiscated. Then they were raked over the coals for their activities in the university through their witnessing, inviting other students to the meetings and giving out literature. Vlado and I feared a repeat of our experience in Usti a couple of years ago and had prepared our hearts for—well, anything. But much prayer was made, both here and by you there, and the students were let off with a warning that next time they would not be let off so easily. They returned to us, much wiser, we trust, but with the prayer of Acts 4:29 on their lips. I had feared it was my letter which had been censored and had given the police the names of the students, though I did not give last names, but apparently, that was not where they got their information. As Vlado says, "We must be wise, but not afraid."

After this incident, when writing for prayer for their contacts, she gave them special names. There was *The Dancer* who was attracted to the things of the Lord, but who struggled to give up his dancing. Later, he became *The Ex-Dancer* who believed and was baptized! *The Hitchhiker* was another young man whom they had picked up on the highway and who wanted to be a writer and showed some interest in the things of the Lord. *The Violinist* came to practice her English and stayed to hear the good news. *The Gypsy*, *The Hippie*, *Mr. B.* and *Mrs. H.* all were names that became familiar to Ruth's prayer partners, and certainly they were easier to call before the Lord than the Czech and Slovak names.

By the end of the year, they saw such answers to prayer that they could only marvel.

Of course, you know that it is only the grace of God that Vlado has been allowed to travel with me to Germany. As a matter of fact, the Lord has worked wondrously in changing the whole attitude of the authorities in Zilina, both to ourselves and to the students. The situation in March was very serious. Then you prayed and we prayed and the Lord heard. The warning against propagating the gospel is as strong as ever, but the relationship between students and teachers has greatly improved even to the point of friendliness. The same is true concerning the Chief of Police. He has actually helped Vlado get his permission to travel in the West! Now we pray for him that he will be saved.

In 1986 another ministry opened up to them. The Communists were still in control and any activity such as Bible College training had to be done in secret. The Communists allowed one or two religious departments at their universities, but these were decidedly liberal. For evangelicals, other ways had to be found to train young, aspiring pastors. Some, like Daniel and Mark, took correspondence courses. Others found ways to meet in cell groups. One such group was held once a month in the Fajfrs' home. Even though neither of the two was a teacher, the Fajfrs left an indelible mark on the students who attended.

Tibor Mahrik, the current pastor of the church in Zilina, tells the story from his viewpoint.

> There are people who understand the beat of your heart despite your failure in communication, who know exactly how to approach you in the right time with the right words. It is to such people you feel that you can confidently open your mouth and your heart. Ruth was exactly this kind of personality—intelligent, extremely sensitive, observant and transparent. It didn't matter if you were a homeless person or a university professor, you had her attention.

> My first meeting with her was overwhelming. It was under the communist regime of 1986 and we used to have illegal Bible Education by extension on a regular basis when lecturers from Vienna traveled across the Iron Curtain to meet young, perspective church leaders. From the very beginning I had the opportunity to observe the Fajfrs in their home setting—their noble character, their modest, but generous hospitality, their simple faith coupled with a deep Bible knowledge.

> I like to tell this story. Once after Bible study, Vlado started to play the piano. Oh, he was excellent in filling the house with his music. He loved the old hymns. But he also liked to play jazz. Ruth was not such a lover of jazz; more she liked Beethoven. So after Vlado played a few bars of jazz, I saw Ruth enter into the room with a cup of tea for Vlado. I do not know what she said or indicated; we never knew. But after she left the room, Vlado slowly changed to a Beethoven sonata in such a marvelous way, even today, I wonder if there were any connection. However, another time, I asked Vlado to play some jazz for me, so he

did. In a moment, a cup of tea appeared on the piano brought in Ruth's hands, and you can guess what happened then. Yes, you are correct. The next thing we heard was a movement from *Apassionata* resounding from the keys! How I loved them both!

One time I had opportunity to spend the night. I offered to help Ruth clean up the mess we had left after eating. Ruth politely rejected my offer. "No, Tibor, this is my ministry. Your time will come and then you will minister to other people." What a lesson in servanthood!

After she had finished cleaning up, she sat down to a simple meal of yogurt. I couldn't stop the question in my mind. "Ruth, why don't you have some of the Coca Cola you have in your refrigerator?" You must know that during the communist regime, Cola was regarded as a luxury. Ruth looked at me for a moment and then answered. "What is in the refrigerator has not been bought for ourselves, but for our guests, like you," she said with a lovely smile.

In my mind Ruth is still speaking to our generation. Today, many young people have the mindset to escape from our country because of a "golden dream" they think will be fulfilled if they go to the West. When I meet such people, I want to tell them the story of one American lady, who, despite her age of over 60 years made such a decision to go to an eastern European country under communist regime . . . She left her life style and comfort zone in order to bring the Gospel behind the Iron Curtain. There is no reason for anybody to escape their homeland for a "golden dream." Such dreams can only be found in that very place where the Lord sends you. Otherwise it will not be true gold. Those, who like Ruth, are willing to go anywhere the Lord is calling them to go, will like Ruth, find golden streets in a golden city. There are only a few people who play an immense and irreplaceable role in your life. Ruth is one of those people.

One day in 1987, after reading the account of Amy Carmichael's fall and how she had spent the rest of her life as an invalid, Ruth cried to the Lord:

Lord, what about me? I, who am so susceptible to falling. Lord!!! Please don't let me fall—slip on the ice or make a misstep—or have my leg give way and cause a permanent injury! A dear friend fell recently, broke her hip and she died within a couple of weeks. Lord! Thou hast promised in Psalm 5 that you will be a shield around me. Hold thou me up! What a complicated affair if I had to go to hospital!

Two months later, what Ruth had feared most happened. She and Vlado had been in Bratislava for a special conference. She was walking down a steep set of steps at the railway station, carefully holding onto the rail, but at the very bottom she missed the last step and fell. She was taken to the hospital, operated on, and after a week transported to a hospital just twelve miles from Zilina.

The very day of her fall, the Lord had given Ruth the verse, "Ye shall be witnesses unto me. . . ." A couple of days later, in a letter sent to her family in America, she said, "Figure all that out and you conclude there are no accidents to the child of God! Don't worry about me or feel guilty because you are not here to help me. I am under the good care of the Lord and Vlado!"

Later she wrote:

"The steps of a good man are ordered by the Lord . . . though he fall he shall not be utterly cast down; for the Lord upholdeth him with His hand." We have discovered that not only the steps but the stops of God's children are ordered by the Lord. These past months I have experienced a "stop" such as I never knew before, but I . . . believe that even in this He delighteth in the outworkings of it. Certainly, it has given me much time to wait quietly before Him and enjoy sweet fellowship with Him.

After six weeks taking therapy in a hospital twelve miles from Zilina where Vlado visited her faithfully every day, Ruth was able to go home. As she followed the therapist's instructions, slowly but surely she began to get strength back into her limbs. In October she was still using one crutch, but she and Vlado felt it was time to celebrate.

I made a cake to celebrate our 11th anniversary and the fact my leg is healed. But the fire in the oven went out and the cake is half-done! Not to worry! We'll celebrate and that is the main thing. I guess it will take me a while to get back into a normal life again, but the main thing is that I'm healed! Vlado is beside himself with joy and relief. (We have heard so many tales of old folk who never "made it" when they broke a leg or hip.) God is Good!

Over the years, as Vlado daily walked up and down his street, he became acquainted with his neighbors, and the Lord put a special burden on his heart for their souls—for the officer in the military and his family across the street, for the railway man and his wife, for the grandmother with a handicapped son who lived in the opposite apartments, for Galina and her young daughter, and for the gypsy children often passing by the house. Every Thursday was given to prayer and fasting as they believed God for souls. God had put this desire in their hearts and they could believe Him for five precious souls living on Frana Mraza.

In light of this, the Fajfrs often held special meetings in their home, especially when Christian friends were visiting from America or when their sons came to visit. At such times Vlado would walk up and down the street, inviting neighbors to his home for a "talk." Many, inquisitive about what was going on at #12, would come and many heard the gospel for the first time. The Fajfrs now had more than just faces to pray for. These people became friends with names and needs, but who, most of all, needed to know the Saviour. Almost eighteen years after the Lord put this burden on Vlado's heart, he could look back and name at least three who had come to the Lord on their street. Undoubtedly, many more will meet Ruth and Vlado in Glory and say, "I first heard the gospel the day you stopped and spoke to me about Jesus Christ."

The Fajfrs' great burden was for the church. During holidays when the students returned to their homes, the church consisted of the Fajfrs, the two couples who had started the church, and a small handful of Plymouth Brethren who did not have a building of their own. Brother Stebel, their lay pastor, was an able and spiritual man. He agreed with Vlado that you cannot build a church with only students. In light of this, they began to pray specifically for three young families with children. Morning and evening in family prayers and during their own private devotions, they brought this one petition before the Lord. Within a year, a young Christian mother, Jana, with her son Ivan, began to attend. Very quietly but surely, the Lord began to work in the heart of Ivan, leading him to salvation. Still they prayed for young couples with children.

In June of 1987, Ruth wrote her prayer partners:

Shout hallelujah with us for the first of the three families for which we have been praying! They came to us of their own accord, led by the Lord alone. They live some fifteen kilometers outside Zilina and must come by train and walk from the station. They have two small children. Pray for the true salvation of both of them as we do not know yet where they stand with the Lord. Continue to pray for more families.

It was some years before this prayer was fully answered, but the Lord did not stop at three when He did answer. As usual, He answered abundantly above all they could ask or think.

"I see more than ever that my real ministry here is intercession," she wrote. Looking into her diaries for these days one sees under each daily entry a long list of names: Petra, Darina, Eva, Romata, Lidi, Stana, Marek, Roman. Day after day, month after month, year after year Ruth prayed for these people. And added to Czech and Slovak names were the Hunnycutts in Singapore, the Halls in Mexico, Imri in India, and Sylvia Sirag in the Bahamas. Always heavy on her heart were her own children and grandchildren in America. Their names are listed sometimes daily, but seldom less than once a week. Ruth also carried a burden for the children of friends in America. The list could go on and on. How did she carry this load? Intercession requires so much more than recitation of names and situations. The cries recorded in Ruth's diaries were cries of a heavy heart, agonizing, identifying with all that particular person was suffering. Without the Spirit's enabling, surely she would have broken under the heavy burdens she chose to bear.

But someone had to pay a price. Meditating on this, she wrote in her diary, March 13, 1988, a quote from Charles H. Spurgeon.

> We proclaim doctrinal or practical truth and, as Gehazi, we "lay the staff upon the face of the child," but we ourselves do not agonize for its soul. We try this doctrine and that truth . . . but so long as ever the truth which we deliver is a matter apart from ourselves, and unconnected with our innermost being, so long will it have no more effect upon a dead soul than Elisha's staff had upon the dead child.

Spurgeon was reaffirming the truth that prayer—*real prayer*—involves the whole being—the mind, the spirit, the will, and the affections. Such praying is labor. And Ruth could not lay it down.

Perhaps her secret was expressed in a prayer letter she mailed out in 1984:

> That old saint, Stockmeyer, said many years ago something which is

211

true even today: "Our own burden is lightened as we bear the burdens of others in our intercession. It is all wrong when people say, 'I have enough myself to bear; I cannot add to it by taking up the burdens of others.' Open wide the windows of thy heart, turn away from that which oppresses thee, bear the burden of another, and thou wilt see how it lightens thine own. Fresh air will rush into thine exhausted heart, and with it a new elasticity, a new breadth and endurance in bearing thine own burden. . . ."

As her years advanced Ruth felt the Lord taking her further and further along the path of intercession. At age 77, she wrote:

I want to thank Thee, Lord, for a special touch from Thee this year, enabling me to pray and minister the Word in the Spirit. But more than this—for a close relationship with Thyself and for a deeper burden for the lives of those around me. This is Thy doings! How long I have waited for this!! Yearned in my heart to know this intimacy and yet, never took time out to cultivate such fellowship alone with Thee.

Reading this makes one wonder at such a revelation. Here was a woman who had walked with her God since she was twelve years old, and even now in old age, she was discovering fresh vistas of His glory and beauty—and ever increasing joy in fellowship with her Lord.

Gradually, Ruth's life seemed to become one of continual prayer, not only in the time she spent on her knees, but all through the day as she sat in services or welcomed visitors in her home or joined with Vlado in visitation of the shut-ins. As she saw the Lord answer one prayer after another, she was compelled to trust the Lord for even greater things.

Of a visit to Usti she writes of how her heart was encouraged when she saw so many of their former prayers answered.

We arrived in time to attend the Christmas meeting of the young people here in Usti. As Vlado and I sat in a corner and looked out over the sea of faces—some 70 of them (!) I could not help thinking back to the first Christmas I shared with the young people—eight of them counting our three. I thought of Vlado's constant cry for "new faces" and my own weak faith as I wondered how we could expect "new faces" under the circumstances. Now, at this meeting I was amazed at the sight of so many new ones in the meeting—people I had never seen before. I considered the Gypsy Boxer who married into one of our families and who was saved and changed during a recent meeting. Also there was the Hippie who had come forward without really knowing what to expect. Now here he is saved, delivered from drugs, alcohol and tobacco and instead, drinking in every word. We heard testimonies of deliverance from sin and aimlessness—because someone cared enough to introduce them to the Savior. Then, I must not leave out those children from our own church families who have been saved and have the same serious spirit about the things of the Lord as their parents. But the thing that struck me the most was the spirit of prayer—when they all fell to their knees and cried fervently to the Lord that He shall continue to work in their midst. Another answer to prayer is that Daniel, after almost three years, now has his permission to preach and be a pastor and not only that, but, after ten years, permission to build a new church building!

Our other son, Mark, now serves as lay-pastor in the church in Teplice. He thus works closely with Daniel in the ministry. For some years Mark has been responsible for the work among the young people, during which time he has seen many souls saved and many young people from the world coming to the Saturday evening youth meetings. He has also been serving as a junior elder and spends much of his time visiting young families, for whom he has a special burden. Thus it is only a step for him to become a pastor. Meanwhile, his time is full with his secular job and the correspondence course of theology he is studying to prepare himself for the ministry. They expect their fourth child soon. Mark's wife, Jani, is a Sunday School teacher and also spends much time and energy entertaining guests in her home in the name of the Lord. So, I ask you to add Mark and Jani to your prayer list. You can imagine how thrilled we are to have all three of our Fajfr children serving the Lord, for our daughter Jana also is very active in the work of the church.

The Lord had answered so many prayers for Usti and Teplice in such an astounding way, surely He could do, would do, the same for Zilina.

* * *

There is no letter or diary entry that reveals that Ruth or Vlado or anyone else ever prayed, or even hoped for the unthinkable—the fall of the Iron Curtain. They were so sure that the Lord could and would work despite all the hindrances of Communism that it never dawned on them that the fall of Communism was part of His plan.

In November of 1989, however, American newspapers screamed with blaring headlines: "Czech Hard-Liners Forced From Power."
And they reported:

> More than half a million demonstrators Saturday scoffed at a Communist Party shake-up and cheered Dubcek as he urged leaders to resign and make way for democratic reforms . . . The beleaguered government bowed to some of the protesters' demands . . . declaring a willingness to give non-Communists greater power. Also Saturday, the entire Communist Party leadership of Prague resigned under increasing pressure for reform . . .

Five other East bloc countries had yielded to pressures for democratic reform, but none did so as tidily as Czechoslovakia; therefore, those 44 days of almost bloodless revolt became known as *The Velvet Revolution*. In towns and cities across the country, people went to the streets, demanding reform and freedom. In Prague, there were continual chants of "We want democracy. We want democracy."

On the day workers in Usti nad Labem called for a strike, a great demonstration was held in the town square. The weather was bitterly cold, but hundreds of citizens gathered to express their solidarity with protesters in Prague who were crying for freedom.

The Communist leaders first stood to explain their side of the story. The people listened in silence.

Then those opposing Communism stepped to the platform and everyone cheered. Daniel Fajfr, in a loud, clear voice asked the crowd, "Who said 'Love Truth, Speak Truth, Live for the Truth, Fight for the Truth?' With one voice the people cried, "Jan Hus!" Then there arose a chant, "We Want Truth. We Want Truth."

Having gotten the people's attention, Daniel shouted, "You will find the Truth which Jan Hus proclaimed in the Bible, God's Word. May it please God that very soon in that bookstore," and he pointed to a store on the other side of the square, "you will be able to buy Bibles and other books filled with Truth."

In Teplice, Mark, too, seized the opportunity to take a leadership role in the new spirit sweeping the country. With the gift of a "smuggled in" machine, he began to print and widely distribute leaflets about the need for change. Because of the initiative of the two Fajfr sons, fresh opportunities arose for them to present the gospel, giving them "a wide and effectual door."

Transformation followed the revolution. As the call for freedom gave way to reality, the entire face of the country changed. To an outsider, it was incredible. Town folk, who previously turned their heads when passing by, now stopped to chat. Busloads and trainloads of people that formerly had been as silent as tombs, now resounded with laughter and loud voices of people calling one to the other. The town square filled with courting couples, little children splashing in the fountains, and groups of teenagers clustered together, chatting and joking.

As the rest of the country celebrated and rebuilt their nation, the Fajfrs' lives continued the same as before, only with new opportunities to present Christ to the people of Zilina. Soon afterwards, they found themselves living in a newly-formed country, an independent Republic of Slovakia.

One of the most delicious fruits Christians produce in old age is a calm, quiet confidence in God.

— CHARLES H. SPURGEON

* * *

The vows of God are upon me. I may not stay to play with shadows or pluck earthly flowers till I my work have done and have rendered up my account.

— AMY CARMICHAEL

Chapter Twenty-One
Fruit that Remains

I always wanted to be a missionary—a conventional missionary, settling in one place, learning a language, building a solid work for His glory. In Budapest, I dreamed of holding the children of my first class of girls on my knee years from then, and telling them about the first year of the Women's Training School in Budapest. "My trunk is in the attic," I used to declare. "I'm here to stay!" Then came James Stewart; then came Hitler and the War. . . . and Scotland, and U.S.A. and "journeyings oft." Emptied from vessel to vessel (Jeremiah 48:11), I was never allowed to settle on my leas, never allowed to relax into complacency because of the continual "gnawing" of the Spirit of God on my "inner man" as He worked for true sanctification in my heart and life.

—Ruth Stewart Fajfr

Commenting on Jeremiah 48:11, Ruth expanded her thoughts on why the Lord had worked with her as He had.

Moab was like wine which had not been poured off the dregs,—his "taste" therefore was strong and bitter and had a bad smell rather than the sweet smell pure wine has. But "behold" says the Lord, "I will send those who will not only empty him, but will break the bottles!" Oh, Lord, thank you that you did not allow me to settle as long as I needed emptying to get rid of the dregs! Thank you that you never took your eye nor your mind off me in my desperate need—as you sought to "sweeten me"!

Ruth accepted those years of moving from one place to another, never being able to stay in one place long enough to put her roots down and to see a ministry grow, as the Lord emptying her and ridding her of the *dregs* in her life—those things which were not Christ-like.

"Delight thyself in the Lord, and He shall give thee the desires of thy heart." That she had done. First in Usti, and then particularly in Zilina,

217

the Lord was giving her the desires of her heart.

> My life here is an answer to a dream. All my life, I have wanted to settle down, and watch a church grow, and families grow. I've wanted to be in one place long enough to see the process—young people being saved, marrying, and having children. Then seeing those children saved. And that is what is happening here. Isn't it wonderful!

The Lord promised in Matthew 19:29 that anyone giving up houses and land, brothers and sisters, or wives and children for His sake, would receive again a hundredfold in this life. This promise was fulfilled in Ruth's life. Her greatest sacrifice was to give up her children! Now, the Lord was giving her a hundredfold. Spiritual children! Ruth delighted in being there for these young people, sharing in their struggles and problems, and watching them grow in the things of the Lord.

One of her first spiritual *sons* was Joseph.

> We have another son who came to live with us in May after his father put him out of the house for turning his back on the Roman Catholic Church. Joseph is a real son in the faith . . . He drinks in the Word every chance he gets whether at family devotions here in the home or in every meeting he can get to. He overflows with joy and thanksgiving over his new-found Lord and is such a joy to us!

Joseph, or Jozko as he was affectionately called, also treasured those times spent with the Fajfrs.

> I will never forget one time when Vlado was away to a meeting and there was only Ruth and I in the kitchen. As we cleared the table, I was telling her my problems I had on my mind. Suddenly she stopped, "Let's sit down and pray. I can clean the table later." We called on the Lord about my problems and when we were finished, she smiled and said, "He understands!" That is the way she was. I miss her. She was my spiritual Mom. I can still hear the special way she used to say, "Jozko!"

She wrote to one of her daughters:

> "I have another son, "Mike," who is really good in electronics. He is a lot different from Jozko who is out-going. Mike is an introvert, thoughtful and very clever. He comes to talk to me and we pray about his

future."

Mike wrote recently, remembering Ruth's input in his life.

"When I moved to Zilina, I had a difficult problem in my life, a situation with my grandfather . . . The Fajfrs immediately organized irregular prayer meetings in their house where we could fight the problem on our knees and the Lord answered our prayers . . . Ruth also urged other people around the globe to pray for us and so many people asked the Lord for my future wife in several continents on this planet. Others at home were saying, "At your age you need to hurry up and get married." But Ruth calmed me down saying, "Don't rush, you have enough time. The Lord will send you the right one in His best time for you." She was right and I would not have so wonderful a wife if I had forced my own will before the will of the Lord.

Another one of her *boys*, Jan, can never forget the impression she left on his life.

When I met her she was already 70 years old and she was a real lady! I recognized two very special things about her character. When anyone brought a problem to her, she would say, "We will see. First we must pray about it." In everything she had an endless trust in God and knew how to pray. It is a lesson for us.

Jan became an elder in the church in Zilina. Ruth lived to see him married to a beautiful Christian girl—one of her *girls*, actually—and be blessed with two little girls of their own.

Peter was one of her sons she met through English classes. As a leader in Intervarsity Fellowship in Slovakia, he recently wrote to tell of the impact those days made on his life.

One story we experienced with Sister Ruth, I will remember forever. My fiancee, Eva and I graduated from university. We made the decision to marry soon and start our family. But there was the problem of where we would live. Under socialism we could get a flat, easily for free or for cheap, but now, in the early days after the velvet revolution, everything had changed. The prices increased so rapidly that people were buying almost everything they could before they got any higher. The price for a flat increased four times its previous value. We were in shock. With sorrow we explained the situation to Sister Ruth. Do you know what she did? She got up, rubbed her hands together, and with a mysterious smile and a twinkle in her eyes she said, "The Lord has His plan and He will provide!" Then she added, "I am looking forward to seeing how the Lord is going to solve your situation." Then she prayed. I thought, "Well, she is from America and how can she really understand our situation? She probably could easily buy one of these flats. But, we are only able to save a few crowns a month."

My view had to change! Sister Ruth was right! The Lord provided. We were able to buy a flat under miraculous circumstances. And the Lord continues with His care. We have learned some good lessons from Sister Ruth. We have made a commitment to open our home, to share the truth of the Scriptures with our neighbors and friends, to serve people, and to trust Him in everything. He has a plan and He will provide!

Ruth had spiritual daughters, too. She especially looked forward to the visits of Eva, who could speak English with her. Eva had just left her home to marry Ľubo and to live in Zilina with her husband's family. As she said:

It was not an ideal situation for a new wife. I had a lot of questions and apprehensions about my new job and my new marriage. And I was lonely. Almost every day I would visit the Fajfrs to get help. They never turned me away, but would answer my questions and pray with me. Later, I mostly observed her in the church. I will never forget Ruth's ever-ready smile—full of hope, joy, and a little amusement when she was speaking with my children. To see her, you would think she was a lady, coming to spend the fall of her life relaxing in the beautiful mountains of Slovakia. But, no, she worked hard to the very end, even when her legs didn't obey her. She prayed, she invited people to her house, she counseled, she gave her Bible studies at the church. One time I was at her home when a group of Americans came and she prepared dinner for them. She couldn't walk very well, so I was ready to help her. I'm not sure how, but suddenly everything was ready even without my help and she served without any nervousness or fuss. She was an extraordinary lady!

Vera was another, a student at the university who spent a lot of time in the Fajfr home. Ruth's diary is full of prayers for this daughter. Vlado who had led her to the Lord, had spoken at her wedding feast, and prayed the prayer of dedication for her first child! In 1991, she wrote a letter full of praise.

> I will never forget your prophetic words to me, "You will have a husband and the Lord has a great plan for your life." It is true! I have to thank you and Vlado for your many prayers. Our God has begun to work out His plan in our lives. We are now in . . . , a town full of sinners, but our Lord is able. Several people have been saved and are coming to our church and I know others will. I am happy that my husband and I can be God's instruments. I thank my God and you for your prayers, Vera.

Ivana was a teenager who lived on Frana Mraza. Though Ivana remembers being aware of the presence of the Fajfrs on her street, she had little contact with them until Vlado visited their home to invite her uncle to the Monday night Bible study in the Fajfr home. On the way out he met Ivana coming from school and invited her to practice English conversation with his wife.

> I was curious, attracted by the chance to speak with a real American. I went for the first time and then I kept going. I was attracted to this 85 year-old woman though I was only 18. Now I know it was God who connected us. Vlado gave me a Bible and I started reading it. Often Ruth and I would discuss the things I had questions about. Later, I went to an English Bible camp where I had more of my questions answered. After eight months of prayer by Ruth and Vlado, I came to know the Lord. Now, I realize that this would not have normally happened. It was God who caused me to love her and connect with her so closely.

Perhaps young people were drawn to Ruth because she was so *alive*. They had never met anyone quite like her. Indeed, Ruth was saintly, but when these young people came to her for words of wisdom, they found her very human. She never acted as though she had *arrived* in her spiritual life. In fact, she seemed so sympathetic to every problem, that most of the young people thought she had gone through the same experience. This *saint* had fought the same temptations they were fighting. Now she could take them to those Scriptures that had spoken to her under similar circumstances.

These same young people probably would have been shocked reading her diaries and seeing that she still looked on herself as nothing more than a sinner saved by grace. In 1991, the last year that she kept a consistent diary and at 82 years old, Ruth day by day evidenced the cries of a soul hungry for the true and living God.

> Use me, Lord, whether it be in the kitchen or in front of an audience, or wherever. I am so backward about going forward to proclaim Christ.

Other entries echo the same strain:

> I have that "dark brown" feeling today, depression-like, as though everything is out of sorts. O My Father, don't let me grow sour in my old age. Forgive me, cleanse me, sweeten me by Thy Spirit. I give myself—I pour myself out before Thee and breathe in Thy Spirit.

> Lord, teach me to pray—really pray—to touch the Throne by myself, for my family and friends, for the lost in Zilina and around the world.

> Lord, thank you for these words, "He will baptize you with the Holy Spirit and with fire." Baptize me, Lord, with the Spirit. Burn in me for purity and power to make my life count. Give me power in prayer. Give a passion for lost souls.

Such are the cries of all true saints until they reach Home.

In 1993 Ruth's book, *Letters From Ruth,* was translated into Czech. Previously, editors of the Czech Brethren magazine placed a translated letter in each issue, and the response had been so great that they decided the whole book should be translated into and published in Czech. Under Communism, the denomination was able to print one book a year other than its denominational paper. Christian books were few and far between unless you could read German or English. Even in the early days of Czech freedom, few Christian books were published, and absolutely nothing that addressed the needs of Christian women.

Jana Fajfr wrote about this.

> It is important to emphasize Ruth's influence through her book. Vera Javoruicka translated this book and in the autumn of 1993 in Prague, Ruth made a presentation and signed many copies. Women from all over our country read the book and were encouraged because in it Ruth perfectly described their problems, no matter their age or situa-

tion. It was as though she could enter into the lives of women who were young and successful, but equally into those who were betrayed, lonely, helpless and in despair. Christians and non-Christians alike loved her, many without having even met her, because of this. I still hear women talk about this book in various parts of my country, so the blessing goes on.

The daughter of a friend wrote to Vlado.

My niece who lives in Bratislava brought us a very precious book of your wife, *Letters from Ruth.* In every letter we found much profit for us because these letters were written by a faithful follower of Jesus Christ who shared with us her own personal life experiences. She showed us the way to live a victorious life which is the sure way to joy and peace. I thank the Lord for this extraordinary book.

Before going to Czechoslovakia, Ruth had prayed, "O, God, make the time I live so full of Thee that the influence will go on and on." The Lord was answering her prayer, though she seemed totally unaware of the impact she was making

After a visit in the fall of 1995, Sheila told her mother's friends at a meeting:

When I am in America, I often think, if only I could bring Mom back with me and wait on her—make her life a little easier in her last days. Then I visit her. I see young people seek her out to talk over their problems with her and get her to pray. I sit during devotions, morning and evening and hear her call out one name after another. She comes to me with a smile on her face. "See how busy I am? It is like this all the time—always so much to do!" I see how in love she is with Vlado-Dad and he with her. These people are her people. She is happier here, in this place at this time than she has ever been.

Silently I sense she is praying, as David prayed, " . . . I have declared thy wondrous works. Now also when I am old and grayheaded, O God, forsake me not; until I have shewed thy strength unto this generation, and thy power to every one that is to come."

What do godly Christians do when they get old? I can tell you. They carry on with what they have been doing all their lives. Studying, praying, teaching, witnessing, trusting the Lord and obeying Him—all these things are as natural to them as breathing. My sister said the other day,

"Dad and Mom have simplified life down to two things—Trust and Obey!" It's true.

Every time I visit, I see her gradually fading away—a little more stooped, a little more difficulty in getting around, more apt to forget who's coming or what she was going to prepare for dinner. But she has no thought of quitting. One more Bible study (which takes her all week to prepare for she must stay closely with her notes or she will forget!). One more meal to prepare for visitors. One more afternoon spent counseling one of her dear "children." One more letter to encourage a lonely missionary on a foreign field. "There's no time to quit!" she says. "Guess I'll rest when I get to Heaven. Or maybe when I have new legs I won't have to!"

Americans used to sing a song that went like this:

> Old soldiers never die;
> They just fade away.

I never quite understood that song until now. I think I can say, "Old missionaries never die; they just fade away—'til finally one day, they take one more step and find it Heaven!"

> Oh, matchless honor, all unsought,
> High privilege surpassing thought,
> That Thou shouldst call me, O, Lord, to be
> Linked in such a work, O God, with Thee!
>
> To carry out Thy wondrous plan
> To bear Thy message unto man;
> To trust with Christ's own word of Grace,
> To every soul of the human race.
>
> Let the victors when they come,
> When the forts of folly fall,
> Find the body by the wall.
>
> Let me die working,
> Still tackling plans unfinished, tasks undone
> Clean to its end, swift may my race be run.
> No laggard steps, no faltering, no shirking;
> Let me die, working![20]

Gone they tell me is youth;
Gone is the strength of my life;
Nothing remains but decline,
Nothing but age and decay.

Not so! I'm God's little child.
Coming the days of my prime!
Coming the strength of my life!
Coming the vision of God!
Coming my bloom and my power!

* * *

E'en down to old age all my people shall prove,
My sovereign, eternal, unchangeable love
And when hoary hairs shall their temple adorn,
Like lambs they shall still in my bosom be borne.
Like lambs they shall still in my bosom be borne.

Chapter Twenty-Two
Transplanted to Glory

In September 13, 1996, in the last letter Ruth wrote to one of her daughters before her fall, she said:

> As for myself, I am the same—praising the Lord for his loving care and that I am mentally, physically, and spiritually in normal condition and in the perfect care of my husband!!

On September 23, ten days later, Ruth tripped over a scatter rug in her kitchen, fell, and shortly afterward was taken to a hospital. For the first week, the doctors contemplated whether or not to operate. Belatedly, they operated and replaced Ruth's hip. The mind-set in the medical community was a carryover from fifty years of Communism—"Give the limited care and medicine to the young and let the old die. They are little use to society." So when the hip replacement on Ruth was performed, an old fixture was implanted instead of a modern one. The doctors and nurses were pleasant and kind. Vlado spent every free moment by Ruth's side because no one around her could speak English. Each day, Ruth's friends from the church dropped by, bringing sunny smiles and flowers. When Ruth developed an infection, the elders came to pray. A slight improvement in her condition made everyone hopeful that she would recover.

Sheila had planned a visit for October 23, but upon hearing of her mother's fall, she wrote Vlado, "Please let me know if I should come sooner or later, whatever time I am needed most to help you. I only need a 24-hour warning."

She and Vlado agreed that it would be best to come when Ruth first came home from the hospital. And she was there when her mother was discharged. It was a bitter-sweet visit. Mother and daughter rejoiced in being together and had precious fellowship speaking of family and friends back home and the continued progress of the ministry in Zilina. But when Sheila tried to lift her mother into a chair beside the bed, Ruth would cry out in pain. The nurse had left a walker that Ruth was to use a little each day. She found this exercise very painful. In a foreign country and not able to speak the language, Sheila found herself frustrated. She didn't know how to go about getting help. A doctor came by the Fajfr home once and a nurse came a couple of times for therapy sessions, but something was still wrong with Ruth and no one was saying what.

Sheila's mind and spirit were in a turmoil when she said good-bye to her mother. Her family, duties, and ministry were all waiting for her at home in America. Yet how could she leave with her mother in this condition? It was evident that without help Vlado would not be able to take care of Ruth. To take Ruth back to America was not an option.

On the train ride to Prague, Sheila cried out to the Lord, "Lord, what are we to do? There seems to be no answer. Have you forgotten to be gracious? What of Mom's testimony—'God is faithful'? In despair, she opened her Bible to Isaiah 32:18, "And my people shall dwell in a peaceable habitation and in quiet resting places." In awe she read the verse again with a mingling of joy and peace flooding her heart. She leaned back in the carriage with a sigh of relief. The Lord was going to tend to it, just like her mother had always said.

And he did! Though Jana Fajfr was on her way to Zilina to assess the situation, Ruth's American family never imagined that she would sacrifice her job, friends, church life, and comfortable apartment to go live the next four years with her father and step-mother. But that was God's answer. And Jana came to look on it as her special calling from the Lord.

Leaving her job, Jana moved to Zilina to help Ruth and Vlado. Armed with a medical book, common sense, and a fierce love for Ruth, she hounded doctors and nurses to get the treatment for Ruth she needed. It did not take her long to realize that the first surgery had been botched, leaving Ruth with an open wound, chronic infection and extreme pain. She also realized that if Ruth went back to the nursing home she would die within a few weeks due to the lack of attention and the poor sanitary conditions.

Jana resolved that she could give Ruth better treatment at home just by keeping her clean and comfortable. Through a friend in the Czech Republic, Jana was able to get some topical antibiotics for the wound and through Sheila, oral antibiotics. At times when the medicine was low, and Jana wondered how she would get more medicine, the Lord always provided.

Jana described those days.

I came to Zilina to take care of Ruth in the autumn of 1996. She was in a very bad state, especially physically. The doctors did not tell the whole truth about her illness. In fact, I found that out some months later after my personal investigations (taking the x-rays to a doctor friend in Usti to read because I was sure that, contrary to what the doctors in Zilina were saying, she was really suffering and that there was something substantially wrong with her leg). After three months in the hospital in Zilina, she was accepted at the Martin University Hospital. There she underwent another operation. Her condition improved but because of her initial treatment, she suffered the rest of her life with chronic osteomyelitis. The hospital was a dreadful experience for her because few people could speak English, so father and I took turns staying with her. By the grace of God and our special care, she was able to leave the hospital.

Father and I were convinced that the Lord would show us how to help her live a life without pain and infection. We tried very hard, and with the help of friends in Usti and our family in America she received good medicine which helped her to live better and even happily. The pain we could alleviate most of the time, but not the infection, I am sorry to say. Also, she was never able to walk again.

Jana determined to create the highest level of living for Ruth that someone could have in her condition. A regimen was established and followed faithfully. Three times a day she prepared nutritious meals, coaxing Ruth to eat when often she had no appetite. Three times a day, she bathed Ruth and dressed her hip wound. Every afternoon, unless it rained, she would dress up Ruth, always adding a colorful scarf or jaunty hat to make her look her best. Then off Vlado and Ruth would go! Usually they would go out for a couple of hours, walk up Frana Mraza, greet the neighbors, stroll through the town and down into the square where they often treated themselves to ice cream, and return through the park and home. Along the way, Vlado would stop to hand out gospel leaflets to people sitting in the square or in the park. Ruth loved to watch the children playing in the sunshine or young couples relaxing in the sun. Both benefited—Vlado got his exercise and Ruth got plenty of fresh air.

At the end of June, 1997, she wrote for the last time to Sheila:

> I am not doing well these days but hope for a fresh touch from the Lord. Thank you for your prayers. We celebrated my birthday June 24th. [*She was 88.*] Daniel was here. Jana baked a chocolate cake with a rose on the top! How good is the Lord to give me these special occasions. How good He is too to send our Jana here to take over. She more than just helps me, I praise the Lord for her. Apart from my condition, all goes well here. Jana cooks such good meals. I am able to get around about the house and go out each day, but only in the wheel chair.

Ruth's daughters began visiting her twice a year instead of once, always thinking it might be the last time to see her. Their visits also allowed Vlado and Jana to get away for a few days to rest. Sheila and Sharon loved the town of Zilina and the church there. The times with their mother were moments to always treasure in their minds and hearts. But one thing bothered them. Their mother said so little. She did repeat Scripture verses when they had devotions and sang along with them, too. And she was always ready to pray, but her mind would wander after a couple of sentences, and she would stop.

"I wonder if she really senses the presence of the Lord. Does she experience the comfort of the Holy Ghost those hours we see her lying in bed looking out the window?" they asked one another.

One evening during devotions, Sharon sat on one side of her mother and Sheila on the other. Sheila described this precious moment.

> The reading was from Matthew 5, "Blessed are the poor in spirit . . . blessed are they that hunger and thirst . . ." As soon as we started to pray, we could tell it was different this night. Suddenly Mom burst into praying—it's the only way I can describe it. "Blessed, blessed when the Holy Spirit sends down hunger into our souls. Oh, thank you that when I wake up and open my eyes, there is quietness and your presence and—-and freedom! We just praise you, dear Lord and thank you!" Sharon started singing, "No, Never Alone," and Mom joined in with such fervor we stopped singing and let her finish. Then she started praying again, this time asking that the Lord would keep her beloved safe and bring him home to her. I began to sing, "My Jesus, I love

Thee, I know Thou art mine." Suddenly with a loud clear voice, Mom joined in, initiating the second verse herself. As the hymn finished, she burst out into prayer again, "Yes, Lord, I thank you that Thou art mine and that You love me. I thank you that your sweet Holy Spirit is with us this very minute."

By this time, tears were streaming down Sheila and Sharon's cheeks. What a precious, holy time. Yes, the Lord's presence was real to her. The Holy Spirit was still ministering to her heart. He had been there all along, strengthening, comforting, sustaining. Why had they ever doubted?

While caring for Ruth, Jana had many occasions to experience the sweet presence of the Lord.

During this time, especially during the last year, I felt very strongly united with her and for me it was the desire of my heart to serve her till her end. This I can say nearly two years after her death and will say it always. I even felt sometimes that my life after this service is not so important for me, somehow I was very dedicated and committed to this service. She was a real friend to me, stronger was the fellowship than ever before. It was mostly in those last months of her life here on earth, that I felt, even when her mind did not work as it should, she had that strong contact with her sweet Saviour. I remember sometimes in the summer of 2000, we prayed together on Wednesday evenings when Father was at the Bible study. I felt the Lord's presence was so strong that I did not even want to leave her it was so exceptional. Though being sick and not capable of doing anything for herself, she gave me such a strong testimony of a living Christ, such as a healthy person could never give. It was a testimony of complete faith and love.

It was said of Anne Lindburgh by her daughter, "Although my mother is more than 90 years old, often confused in her mind, and in fragile health, we are still redeemed, gentled and sustained by her." Lindburgh's words describe perfectly how Ruth's family and friends felt during Ruth's final four years. People came in just to greet her or pray with her. Some she remembered, others she did not. But each visitor seemed blessed just by her smile and her presence. Ruth's life was speaking louder than her words had ever spoken.

Ivana often dropped in when she was home from university.

As I watched Ruth's mind working slower and slower each month . . .

it came time for me to serve Ruth. I visited her regularly and I knew she was always glad to see me and always recognized me and smiled. To the very end she kept her sense of humor, for we had always had our own special good-bye. I would say, "See you later, alligator" and she would reply, "After while, crocodile." Right up to the last day before she died, she returned our special farewell with a smile and a wave of her hand. Yes, you are right, she was a testimony to me right up to the end—her eyes filled with peace and love, her face always smiling, and her prayers filled with thankfulness and absolute trust in the Lord.

Sharon, too, observed that as her mother's mind slipped away, two characteristics remained evident—her thankfulness and her sense of humor. Despite her condition, she was constantly thanking those who cared for her, whether it was someone in the family or just a visitor who dropped by. Once while she was thanking the Lord for the food, her mind went blank—"and help us to know how to eat it!" she finished.

"We always called on her to pray because her conversations with her God were so much sharper than her conversations with us. What struck us was that at this stage in her life she no longer had room for requests. Praise and worship, the two things that will occupy her in Glory, had replaced intercession. Was it because she was already closer to heaven than she was to earth?" Sheila noted.

What tickled Ruth's daughters were her continued witticisms. At times she reverted to the slang and expressions of her youth, which sent everyone into gales of laughter. Or she would suddenly startle them by breaking out with a popular song from her teenage years, often at a most inopportune time!

On other occasions, she would be sitting quietly watching the activity round her and then come out with something so witty, they would be speechless.

Many years earlier Ruth had prayed that just her presence alone would be a fragrance of the Lord Jesus Christ. As never before, the Lord was answering her prayers. One of her neighbors, Katerina, for whom Ruth had prayed so long, came often to take her for a stroll in her wheelchair. When the family tried to thank her, Katerina would simply say, "I love her! I want to be with her."

Vlado and Jana had always prayed that Ruth would live to the end without pain and agitation. Their prayer was answered. Ruth Mahan Stewart Fajfr died quietly at noon on October 2, 2000. Her two loving caregivers were by her side. Both had given around-the-clock care to their loved one for years and could now let her go with no regrets.

When Sheila and Sharon were trying to thank Jana for her faithful care of Ruth, she replied, "Yes, in one sense I do this in your place because you cannot be here. But mostly I do it for Ruth. She came to our country when no one would dare do such a thing. She gave up her life for us. This is the least I can do to pay her back."

Amazingly, close friends Paul and Carolyn Reno of Hagerstown, Maryland, happened to be in London when word arrived that Ruth had been called Home. Ruth considered Paul her pastor for he had made several trips into Slovakia just to minister to her. He and his wife were able to take the next plane out of London, arriving in Zilina in time to take part in the funeral.

Ruth's son, Jim Stewart, having suffered from a brain tumor and having died in September after a three-month illness, had gone on ahead of his mother by a few weeks. But, Sheila and Sharon, still grieving over their brother's death, traveled immediately to their mother's funeral. The Fajfr family came down from North Bohemia.

The funeral service was conducted in Slovak, but the Americans present were able to sing along to the hymn, *In the Sweet Bye and Bye*. Paul Reno spoke, representing those family and friends blessed by Ruth's ministry in the States. Pastor Tibor Marhek spoke for those who had known and loved this dear saint in the past twenty-four years in Slovakia and the Czech Republic.

Was the sacrifice worth it? Sheila and Sharon had asked each other the question over and over as they flew to Prague and traveled the eight hours by train to Zilina. They had given up their Mom all their lives. And she had given them up. Now, those snatched times together were over, never to be reclaimed.

"We never really had Mom for any period of time like these people did. Now we never will," Sharon expressed to Sheila as they grieved together. "These folk could come see Mom and talk to her and pray with her anytime they wanted to. We never really had that—at least, not in person. I can't help feeling jealous."

Though long ago, Sheila and Sharon had placed their mother on the altar, in their grief the question still plagued their minds.

At the funeral, they looked around them. They looked into the face of their stepfather, Vlado, and saw the strength and endurance of his life's journey, made joyful by Ruth's presence. They counted the Fajfr children and grandchildren whose lives and ministry had been touched by this praying *Maminka*. They knew that Jana, sitting beside them, would never be the same after the years spent with Ruth. They were aware of the filled hall, neighbors, acquaintances, students, church family, visiting pastors and wives from other parts of the country—all somehow affected by the life of one woman.

Smiling through their tears, they exchanged a *knowing nod*. It was worth it! Well worth it! They even dared to hope that their sacrifice had also been one of those seeds that, dying, brings forth much fruit.

A message was sent to loved friends and family in America:

How can we do anything but praise our blessed Lord for His goodness! On October 2, 2000, Ruth Stewart Fajfr arrived safely Home straight into her dear Savior's arms after a lengthy sojourn of 91 years . . . Her faith is now sight! . . . Sharon and I were able to attend the funeral held in Zilina, Slovakia, where she and her husband, Dr. Vlado Fajfr, spent the last 18 years of their ministry. Over 120 people were in attendance and the funeral was a testimony to the many lives she had touched in her later years, despite her age and her difficulty with the language. Young and old alike told us of the impact she had made on their lives through her sacrificial living, her rejoicing spirit and her prayers.

> Dead?
> She that is breathless with wonder
> Understanding at last His grace
> Feasting her eyes on the matchless
> Loveliness of His face.
> Dead?
> Can we call it dying
> That life is filled to the brim
> Dead?
> In the light of His presence
> She is living—forever—with Him.

Epilogue

The story goes on. Ruth Stewart Fajfr has been transplanted into the Lord's Garden, but her *root* is still here. I read these verses from Job, chapter fourteen which centuries ago gave great hope to Job and still give hope today. "For there is hope of a tree, if it be cut down, that it will sprout again, and that the tender branch thereof will not cease. Though the root thereof wax old in the earth and the stock thereof die in the ground; yet through the scent of water it will bud, and bring forth boughs like a plant . . . If a man die, shall he live again?"

I see more in this passage than the resurrection. The stock dies, but the root remains, bringing forth new sprouts, and "boughs like a plant." And the "scent of water"? Would this not be that heritage of the Word and the Spirit which bears fruit in the next generation and the next? This was Ruth's burden and desire—that not only the children of her womb, but her spiritual children, birthed by her prayers, would pass on to their progeny this story of God's faithfulness. Why else would she painstakingly record the story of her life? For fame? Never. "Just an ordinary person" she so often called herself, but one who had discovered what extraordinary things God does with the ordinary.

"If a man die, shall he live again?" The answer resounds in the hearts of those who knew this woman, and many, who never having met her, will read her story and experience a life change, "Yes, Ruth lives on in the lives of her children, and their children, and their children's children!"

Sharon had the same thought when she wrote these words:

> *Stripped of summer's leafy coat,*
> *the weathered old apple tree*
> *leans against a bare November day.*
> *Along each wizened, crooked arm,*
> *apples, ruby and ready,*
> *hang like lustrous ornaments.*
> *Beneath a heavy sky*
> *before the coming of the snow,*
> *the tree stands exposed and bent,*
> *and yet the fruit remains.*[21]

— Sharon Stewart Wilkerson

Reflections on a Life
Spent for Christ

Reflections
by the Publisher

The Cross was the central focus of Ruth Stewart Fafjr's life. She found cleansing, then the secret to victory over sin and self at that blessed place called Calvary. Over the years, she learned to make her abiding place beneath the Cross. All she possessed, she owed to the Cross.

Ruth often prayed a prayer that she filed in her diary on July 11, 1976: "Lord, I surrender life and all it entails to thy will—to Thy plans and purposes."

The story of her life is a testimony to the fact that she lived in submission to the Lord of Glory.

History is replete with examples of self-sacrificing surrender to the cause of Christ and to the proclamation of the Gospel of the grace of God to sinners.

As he labored for the Lord in Africa, David Livingston faced daily companions of hunger, disease, loneliness, failure, and disappointment. The trial that laid heaviest on his heart, however, proved to be the many years of separation from his wife and children.

Every step of Jonathan Goforth's progress in reaching the Chinese for Christ was marked by a small grave!

Hudson Taylor buried a wife and a precious daughter in China.

For five long years Isobel Kuhn lived under communist-forced separation from her daughter.

Each of these missionaries had one consuming goal—to make known to the world the glories of a gracious God who loves sinners so much that He would send His Son to die for them.

Ruth was no different. The cross she bore was just as heavy. Only her place of service was different. She was not sent with the Gospel of our Lord Jesus Christ to China, nor to Africa, nor to Cambodia. Her mission field was at the side of an untiring, Spirit-filled evangelist whose heart beat was for Europe.

Europe—civilized, cultured, religious. Europe with a glorious past of Reformation victories and of storied spiritual giants such as Luther, Zwingli, Calvin, and Hus. The Europe of historical spiritual renown had become a mission field.

European Enlightenment blinded philosophers; higher criticism seduced theologians.

Once thriving and evangelical churches of the Reformation sank in a spiritual quagmire. Eastern Europe suffered in bondage to the Orthodox Church and Western Europe lay strangled by liberalism.

When God thrust James Stewart into the ministry as an evangelist, spiritual needs in Europe were as great as in any mission field in the world.

At first, James tried to work and support native pastors, evangelists, and workers. Soon he saw that the Gospel work would require a more intense effort. Europe needed missionaries.

The Lord used James Stewart to open up Europe to modern-day missionary work. But it cost James and Ruth dearly.

The itinerant mission responsibilities God gave to James required him and his wife to be separated for long periods of time from their children.

Little is found in Ruth's letters or diaries that reveals the great conflict she as a mother must have felt during those periods of separation. Her letters do reveal a great love for her children. Though sometimes separated by an ocean from her children, Ruth expressed a daily concern about what each child was going through on a particular day or week. In most cases, the only way she could bear the burden of separation was through prayer. She would ask her Heavenly Father to do for her child that which she could not do. Then, and only then, she would write a letter, pouring out her mother's heart.

> I get so lonely for the three of you sometimes that I want to cry. . . . I dream of you day and night these days and long to see you. I am just plain homesick for you and Jimmy and Sharon and all we knew this time last year. But for the sake of the blessed Saviour and the peoples of Europe who have never heard the Glad Tidings, we must be sepa-

rated for yet a little longer. . . . The hardest thing I have ever had to do is leave my chldren in the care of someone else. I have to daily put my natural affections on the altar. It has been especially hard to leave Sharon. She seems to need me more than the other two. But if I were to stay home and be out of the will of God, Sharon would miss what the Lord has for her and so will I.

In one of her Bible studies about the woman who prepared a room for the prophet, Elisha, Ruth bares her heart concerning her own children.

You know, we are determined on the salvation of our children, aren't we? And salvation is not the end; it is only the beginning of our prayers. If you think that the moment your children get saved, you've got it made, well, we who have children who are older know that it is only the beginning of heart-ache and the need for desperate, agonizing prayer. Sometimes I take down my old diaries and I glance over them and see my heart cry, first for this one, then for that one. There is that constant hammering at the door of Heaven for my children, and I refuse to take anything except God's best for them. I am still there, and I will be there as long as I live. Only through the Lord Jesus Christ can we see our children saved and growing in the Lord. Oh, this is a wonderful mother—a mother who refused to let go as long as there was any need in her child!"

In the following pages Sheila Stewart Doom and Sharon Stewart Wilkerson offer open and frank thoughts about those periods of separation from their mother and how it effected their lives.

Then a special page is dedicated to Ruth's love for her son, Jimmy, and his family. In the good providence of God, Jimmy was called to his Heavenly Home less than a month before his mother entered into glory.

Finally, space is given to Ruth Stewart Fajfr's abiding love for the grandchildren she was never able to be around for any length of time.

Our Lord Jesus Christ said, "And every one that hath forsaken houses, or brethren, or sisters, or father, or mother, or wife, or children, or lands, for my name's sake, shall receive an hundredfold, and shall inherit everlasting life." (Matthew 19:29).

In following the Lord, Ruth had to make such sacrifices. But she and her children found the Lord's promises to be wonderfully sure.

Reflections of a Daughter
by Sheila Stewart Doom

I have before me my legacy from Mother—a cardboard box of letters. Why are they so precious to me? Even today, I can pick up one, read it, and Mother is with me again—prodding, encouraging, rebuking, and always helping me to see my life in the light of what the Lord is doing in me. Only in snatches here and there did my mother and I share a home or a meal together, so it was through letter writing that we had a mother-daughter relationship. In these letters Mother shared her life with me in intimate detail and I with her. Every week we were apart, she wrote a letter— nearly fifty letters a year since I was in my teens. I didn't have the wisdom to keep them all in those early years, but over the past thirty years I have hoarded them as precious treasures. Starting with the time that she was restricted in her movements because of Dad's illness, Mother has written long, long letters, often three or four, single-spaced, typewritten pages, sharing with me not only what was going on in her life, but her prayers and desires for me and my family, what the Lord was teaching her from the Word at that moment, and her prayer requests for all those people dear to her heart.

In November of 1955, when I was 16 and in boarding school, Mom wrote:

> God bless you, my dear and help you in your studies, your devotional life, your social life and all phases of your life. It is not easy to be a chosen vessel for the Lord, through whom the Lord wants to do a mighty work in the world. It makes you have a conscience so you can't do carelessly the things others do with joy. The Spirit is so close to you, poking you, reminding you, shaping you, making you conscious every day that you are His and not your own. It has been that way with me always. "Others may. You cannot," He says to me. "You

are a chosen vessel unto me, sanctified, and while not fit, you are being made fit for the Master's use. It is a wonderful calling to know the Lord has His hand on you; that nothing happens by surprise or accidentally in your life, for all things are planned for your shaping and your growth. Even the lives you rub shoulders with and the little disappointments and grievances—all are known to Him and used by Him for your "making". One day, when you are prepared, He will fill you so completely with Himself that all your life will be energized by His personality and His power and His love.

On a more practical note she wrote:

JANUARY, 1955: I live with you through every experience of which you write me. I know how you enjoy being one of the girls and yet your sense of loyalty and respect for those who have the rule over you. This is right. Don't let clamor and backbiting and gossip make you cynical or cheap or belittling. Stay above it all by being true to your quiet time and your Lord and your calling.

OCTOBER, 1957: Your friend, D. is so happily in love, and she looks forward to settling down to live a normal life. This would be the easy way for you too, as it would have been for me, had I not seen the vision and heard the call and answered and followed. I am afraid, my dear girl, that in this way you are like your old mother—you will ever be drawn upward and onward, discovering new joys, new possibilities and avenues for serving, adoring and pleasing the Lord you love.

Later when I married and started having a family, I began to do the same to her, pouring out my troubles, my failures along with the joys and progress of our particular ministry at that time. Through these long missives, we could pray together. We could laugh together over my children's antics. We discussed what the Lord was teaching us at that particular time. But for the most part I was on the receiving end.

One thing I know, Sheila. When the Lord gives quietness, who can make trouble? Dig deep and rest deep down in the wounds of our Lord till these calamities be overpassed. God is not done with you yet, so don't let the devil put you out of action before your time.

Now I want to thank you for your Mother's Day card. As I look back and see all the weaknesses and faults—flaws in the way you children were brought up, I wonder—marvel—that you turned out so well. And if you really feel as you wrote, it is grace—all of grace—that it is so. I know how you feel when you look at the way you so often "muddle through" with your children, especially the boys. But perhaps one day they will send you such a card and say the same things you have said to me . . . It is a marvel to me, especially, that Sharon is not rebellious, pointing a finger at me for the life she had to live—from pillar to post. And yet—it was a good life, if she but realizes it. And she does. I have always taken heart at the claim of the English that "It is winning the last battle that wins the war." Take heart, Honey, when things all seem to be for nothing. The last battle is yet to be fought, and you shall see . . . I hope you will be here to see, as the Lord has allowed me to be here until now.

As I said to you in my letter that I have such a conviction God has heard our prayers for you and your need that somehow I can't agonize over it any more. I have no imagination how He will answer, but that is His business. Now you have recognized traits in your self which you abhor and cry out against, leave them at the foot of the Cross for our Lord to deal with. Don't keep taking inventory; let Him lift these things from you and believe He has done it! Remember it is His love you are crying for and it is His love which is shed abroad in our hearts by the Holy Ghost. By faith I can see it already done in your life and now you can get down to business helping others who are still in the struggle.

Sheila, about your message on Job to the ladies. I lived through it all. I marvel at the things the Lord is teaching you and that you are able to pass these things on to others. You may never know how far this message will go, for you may be one of those grains that will fall into the ground—hidden—to die to self that there may be much fruit! But you can take it by faith that our Lord is working. You have been "pressed beyond measure" for twelve months (as you have been) in order to squeeze out three messages to those few women.

One time, after receiving a Mother's Day card in which I had thanked her for teaching me how to live for the Lord, Mother replied, "When did I ever teach you? That's the problem—I feel you missed out on so much because I was not there to teach you."

"But, don't you realize that all these years your letters have been my textbook. And your life. All I have to think is, 'How would Mom react in a situation like this?' and I know what to do," I replied. "And Sharon testifies to the same thing."

Reflections of a Daughter
by Sharon Stewart Wilkerson

The most beautiful sight in the world was the sight of my mother emerging from a vehicle, an airport terminal, or in her latter years waiting for my arrival, sitting in a wheel chair pretty and soft in her pink dressing gown. As a child, the anticipation of my parents' arrival always threw me into such excitement that I was often in a worked up state by the time they actually arrived! After the initial hugs and kisses, Daddy would capture the attention of any children in the families I lived with. He always had gifts for us or games for us to play. Meanwhile, Mom would visit with the adults. Once, after my cousins and I had been pre-occupied with finding money Daddy had hidden, Mom commented on the fact that I had hardly paid her any attention. I blurted out, "Daddy's funny and he's got money!"

But once the burst of excitement was over, I would be ready to snuggle up next to Mom. That's when I would study her face. Her face fascinated me. Her skin was soft and I loved the way her eyes crinkled when she smiled. Love and kindness seemed etched in every line and crease. When she would leave again, I drew great comfort from the memory of her face.

Though Mom and Dad provided love through their prayers, letters, visits and financial provisions, they were seldom there with me in the day to day run of things. Someone had to get me out of bed, make sure I was dressed, fed, and sent off to school. Someone had to cook, clean and pick up after me. Someone had to comfort me and put bandages in the shape of a kiss on my scratches and bruises. Someone had to discipline me, make me do my homework, teach me how to iron, set the table and fold diapers. Someone had to help me celebrate my birthday, tell me Bible stories, and tell me how to live for the Lord.

In my case, that "someone" was duplicated many times. Only Heaven will reveal the many saints who opened their hearts to me, sending me an Easter outfit, subscribing me to a Christian magazine, driving a distance to be at my high school graduation when my parents could not be there. Others invited me into their homes for two months or two years. One time it was with two dear sisters in the city of Copenhagen, Denmark, another time with the Wittenborgs, a missionary couple in Germany. Omri and Dorothy Jenkins took me into their home twice, once in Barry, Wales, and another time in London. In the States I lived for two and a half years with my Aunt Mildred and her family, the Schweigerts, on an 180-acre farm in Alabama. My cousins became like brothers and sisters to me.Then when Mom and Dad were in meetings making Asheville their base, I was welcomed into the homes of "Uncle Ralph and Aunt Jacque" Sexton, Pastor Bob Griffith and Hazel, Pastor Leslie and Elizabeth Ditchfield. These dear friends not only opened their homes to me, but gave me the love and attention I so needed.

I like to tell this story because it shows how the Lord really cared about me and provided in an amazing way. My brother and sister were attending the boarding school for missionary children that was connected to the Swansea Bible College founded by Rees Howells. In 1953, during their Bible Conference, my parents were speaking of their missionary work and mentioned that they were on their way to Greece to minister in a camp. They added that they were praying about someone to care for me during that time.

Former students of the college and regular attenders of the Bible Conference, Norman and Nolly Brend began to pray about this. The Lord gave them the Scripture from Exodus 2:9, "Take this child and nurse it for me." It was arranged that I would spend a day with them in their home to see how I fit in with their family of three small children who were very near my age. I shall never forget the day I arrived at Leigh-on-Sea on the east coast of England. At first I clung to Mom, but when we sat down to a meal, "Aunty" Nolly was so warm and gave me a special little utensil to rake my food onto my fork. Later, "Uncle" Norman took me out to the side of his garage where he had prepared four little garden plots that he had made for his three children, Peter, Mary, Elizabeth—and me! I was so excited with my little garden with its beautiful pansies that when mother came to say goodbye, I looked up briefly and waved goodbye. Usually, I wailed and clung to her, "Please don't leave me off." Poor Mom, though relieved, was crestfallen, not realizing that I thought it was goodbye for just a few days. What I did not know was this was to be my home for the next few years.

The thoughtfulness and love the Brends showed me as a little girl was again poured out on me when they moved their family to Swansea to be parents to a long list of missionary children who came and went. Following in my brother and sister's steps, I too attended this boarding school and found the Brends once again my second parents. From that time to this I am included in the Brend family. They phone me on my birthday and send anniversary cake through the mail. Uncle Norman is entering his ninetieth year and Aunty Nolly is close behind. This precious couple have had a share in all that the Lord did through my parents, along with all those other dear ones who "parented" and "spoiled" me, and I can never thank them enough for their love and sacrifice. Now that I am a mother and have my own children, I see two things. First, the cost it was to Mom to give us up to the care of others, and the Lord's blessed provision in giving me many mothers and fathers.

Despite all our absences, I never doubted my parents' love. Daddy sent me postcards and other items from all over the world. One time I received a gingerbread house from Germany that was reduced to small pieces by the time I got it! Mom's contribution is still with me today in the form of letters. She told me of her missionary endeavors, poured out her mother's heart in yearnings to be with me, and gave advice and comfort in response to long forgotten traumas about which I had written her! (Letters were forwarded on from place to place until they caught up with them.) I was always aware that I was a part of their ministry, my part being to adjust to whatever environment and situation I was in at the time.

Reflections of a Mother's love

Jimmy Stewart

If only Jim were here, he would love to say a word about his Mom. At this writing he is with the Lord, and with her in Glory. He, as her only son, held a special place in her heart. No matter what the circumstances, she kept the communication lines open and treasured each letter she received from him, reading it over and over again, and then laying it before the Lord with its many requests for prayer.

FEBRUARY 11,1963: I am praying much for and about Jimmy. Our Lord has a plan and He will guide—Only Lord, prepare him for all that you are preparing for him, for Thy Glory!

JAN. 1, 1964: I here record the outstanding answers to prayer for the Old Year . . . Jim's entry into Birmingham Bible Institute (in England) and the marked change in him . . . Looking back I would broadcast, "What hath God wrought!"

Nov. 19, 1964: The Lord is faithful—I could record on every page— got another wonderful letter from Jim showing spiritual growth. Praise His Name!

DECEMBER 20, 1966: Two years ago tonight Jim came with Jennifer to Berwick. Now they have Nicola who is 4 months. Dear Lord, how I thank Thee for Thy miraculous guidance of these dear ones and Thy provision for them.

DECEMBER 12, 1967: Letter from Jim which gladdens our hearts for he is happy in having been with his co-worker in all-out evangelism. How I praise God for this experience with other mature men! And for Jim's love for lost souls! . . . For this we thank God and pray our Jim will continue to grow and mature.

Reflections of a Grandmother's Love

As she saw her own children going on with the Lord, her great burden became the grandchildren. As soon as her first, Susan Heather, came along, she became aware of the godly heritage she had to pass on to them. She wrote in her diary in July of 1964, "All the way home I have been thinking of writing a private auto-biography for my grandchild. I know my life would not be of public interest, but somehow, I feel I am so ordinary, my grandchildren might take courage when they see how our Lord has led me personally all the way—Oh, so patiently and gently. Truly, that He should give me to live and work with James Stewart is a miracle in itself!"

Again she said to her daughter, "I have been filling out the book you gave me, 'A Legacy for my Loved Ones.' It has made me realize I have nothing to brag about—of honors or prizes, in any field. I cannot think of anything in which I excelled as a school girl! Not much challenge and inspiration for my grandchildren, nor for a biography. As a matter of fact, I can't think of a reason for publishing my story *unless it would be to encourage other children and young people who are as I was, the last one to be voted 'Most likely to Succeed*!' I am sure that in the high school senior class, Ruth Mahan never crossed the mind of any one of those voting for the 'most' categories.

Though she never got around to writing this "private" auto-biography, she left them a legacy of love, letters, and her prayers. To her granddaughter, Jana, she wrote, "My dear, I am so happy to have your letter. Your letters always gladden my heart because you talk about the Lord. We are of one spirit and one desire, you and me. How I long to see you face to face. And I shall one day, here, or there or in the air! . . . Praise God for His faithfulness. Together we will hold up your friend before the Lord, until he deals with her in answer to our prayers . . . I am so glad you can pray and have fellowship with your mother. Oh, what blessed fellowship we two had in the Lord, and now she has got you. Isn't God good! Just know I am praying for you and love you even though we cannot be together. Trust Him fully! Grandma."

And to her grandchildren in New York, she wrote, "Noemi, write me again—a nice newsy letter like the last one. I gaze at your photo and marvel at the way you have grown. And Jesse, thank you for your letter. I look forward to every bit of news from the Wilkersons. And Chad, take care in the car this winter if you are driving. Oh, I cry to God to protect you." And to Sharon, "Oh, you don't know how much I enjoy your letters telling about each of the children. I gaze at their photos and try to imagine them in their daily life. How I praise the Lord for each of your three!"

The grandchildren missed out on the kind of grandma who lived nearby, ready to baby-sit, or have them over for a week in the summer, the kind who baked pies and kept the cookie-jar full. In a sense it was a real loss because only the older ones really felt they knew her. Every few years she would come and stay a week. While visiting Sharon for a few days in 1987, she related to Sheila their good times. "We are having a ball! I love the children. Grandpa loves the privacy of his room, the cold weather, the lovely countryside as well as our walks with Jesse and Noemi to the post office and back. Then you should see Grandpa playing ball with Jesse! Jesse is a real boy with a real temper and a charm that kills! So the time passes quietly and pleasantly. I enjoy just being with Sharon and talking. We are having a good visit together these days."

Admittedly, it simply was not enough time to make a strong connection with them. But what they lost in her presence, they gained in her prayers. Day after day in her diaries she recorded her prayers for them. For a grandson, "Oh, Lord! Open his eyes to see your claim on his life. Deal with him until he is utterly surrendered—all on the altar and ready to do Thy will alone! For Thy glory!"

In a letter from her son, Jim, he told her about their time at a Christian holiday camp, Spring Harvest, and what a blessing they were receiving. "Dan went to 'Whiz Kids.' Most of it was about the Holy Spirit and the kingdom of God. He absorbed it all and came back full of questions . . . Nic and Dave had to work so were unable to go. We pray every day for their salvation and that the Lord will touch their lives!" Jen wrote a few days later, "We had a great time at Spring Harvest and Daniel learned so much . . . I'm still praying hard for our children each day."

Letters like this sent their grandmother to her knees, "Thinking and praying much for my grandchildren—Noemi, Chad, Jesse, for Sheila's children. Answer Jim and Jen's prayers—and mine—for Nicola, David, and Dan. Save Robert, Katka, and Tomas and little Mark too—soon." This prayer was repeated over and over again at least once a week, and those times she was burdened for a particular one of them, repeatedly every day of the week. This went on from the birth of each child until her call Home. No grandmother could have loved and prayed more had she lived next door! She sincerely believed the Lord had left her here on earth to "pray them through." And oh, how she rejoiced when she heard that one of them had been saved!

Often she turned Psalm 71:17-18 into a prayer:

O God, thou hast taught me from my youth: and hitherto have I declared thy wondrous works. Now also when I am old and grayheaded, O God, forsake me not; until I have shewed thy strength unto this generation, and thy power to every one that is to come.

End Notes

[1] *Golden Bells Hymnbook*, (London:Sunday School Mission, 1925) p. 185.

[2] Mrs. Charles Cowman, *Charles E. Cowman* (Los Angeles, California: Oriental Missionary Society, 1928) p. 331.

[3] Frank Houghton, *Amy Carmichael of Dohnavur* (London: SPCK, 1953) p. 49.

[4] Baker J. Cauthen and Frank K. Means, *Advance to Bold Mission Thrust* (Foreign Mission Board, Southern Baptist Convention, 1981) pp. 194,195.

[5] Eva Stuart Watt, *Dynamite in Europe* (Philadelphia, Pennsylvania: Revival Literature, 1956) pp. 100, 101.

[6] Alice Miller, *The White Cliffs of Dover* (London: Muethen and Co., 1941) p. 3.

[7] Gregory Mantel, *Beyond Humiliation* (Minneapolis, Minnesota: Bethany Fellowship, 1975) p. 129.

[8] Ibid., p. 19.

[9] Ibid., p. 216.

[10] Isabel Kuhn, *In thhe Arena* (Chicago: Moody Press, 1958) p. 124.

[11] Mrs. Charles Cowman, *Charles E. Cowman* (Los Angeles, California: Oriental Missionary Societ, 1928) p. 214.

[12] Amy Carmichael, *Toward Jerusalem* (Fort Washington, Pennsylvania, Christian Literature Crusade, 1996) p. 2.

[13] Ibid., p. 104.

[14] Ibid., p. 28.

[15] Taken from *Loneliness* (Yanceyville, North Carolina: Harvey and Tait, 1984) p. 55.

[16] Ibid., p. 55.

[17] John Piper, *The Hidden Smile of God* (Wheaton, Illinois: Crossway, 2001) p. 14.

[18] J. Danson Smith, *Best Loved Poems* (Edinburgh, Scotland: B. McCall Barbour, ND) p. 49.

[19] Austin Phelps, *The Still Hour* (Carlisle, Pennsylvania: Banner of Truth, 1984) p. 38.

[20] Mrs. Charles Cowman, *Charles E. Cowman* (Los Angeles, Califormia: Oriental Missionary Society, 1928) p. 331.

[21] First Published in "Ancient Paths," Issue 6, Spring, 2000) p. 5.

Books by Ruth Stewart Fajfr

Better Than Wine
Meditations in the Song of Solomon

Evangelism in Print
The Story of Revival Literature

From the Land of Moab to the Line of the Messiah
Studies in Ruth

I Will Fear No Evil
The Biography of Vlado Fajfr

James Stewart: Missionary

Letters From Ruth

Our Heavenly Inheritance
Studies in Joshua

The Prototype Church
Studies in I Thessalonians

Published by
Revival Literature
Box 6068 • Asheville, NC 28816
1-800-252-8896

revivallit@juno.com